# Contents

W9-AHG-290

# Using this guide

This Nicholson guide has been specially designed to enable both the Londoner and the visitor to get the best out of London by using public transport. The introduction deals practically with all aspects of transport in the capital, including an easy-to-use listing of the principal bus routes servicing Central London.

The A–Z gazetteer features more than 500 places, sights and attractions clearly presented in alphabetical order. Wherever possible, gazetteer entries are map referenced to the Central London maps at the back of the book (e.g. **Houses of Parliament 3P4**). At the end of every entry, the nearest Underground station is given, as well as the numbers of the buses which stop at or near the place described. In some cases, British Rail stations and Green Line coach numbers are supplied where these services provide an alternative or better means of arriving at a particular destination. Stations on the Docklands Light Railway are also given where applicable.

The final section of the guide is devoted to 10 sightseeing days in London. Each day has its own theme (e.g. Royal London) with an itinerary which can be followed in its entirety or dipped into for suggestions on how to spend a few hours or more. All the places included in the days out section are fully described with transport details in the gazetteer.

With comprehensive information, street and transport maps, this guide can genuinely claim to get you there. But, London is a fast-paced city. Its services and facilities can often change at short notice. So to avoid disappointment, it is always recommended to telephone in advance before embarking on a special journey and to check all travel details with London Transport's 24-hour information service on 01-222 1234.

Symbols and abbreviations used in the guide:

| | | | |
|---|---|---|---|
| ⊖ | Nearest Underground station | *L* | Lunch |
| ▥ | Buses stopping at or nearby | *D* | Dinner |
| ⇌ | Nearest British Rail station | | |

The word *Charge* denotes an entrance fee.

# THE GUIDE TO
# LONDON
## BY
# BUS & TUBE

*Judy Allen*

ROBERT NICHOLSON PUBLICATIONS
in association with
London Transport

A Nicholson Guide

First published 1987
Reprinted 1987
Second edition 1989

Published by Robert Nicholson Publications
16 Golden Square London W1R 4BN in association with
London Regional Transport 55 Broadway SW1H 0BD

Design by Bob Vickers
Line drawings by Matthew Doyle

The author would like to thank the editor, Jacqueline Krendel, for her
encouragement and assistance during the compilation of the first edition of this
guide. Thanks are also due to London Transport's Travel Information Service for the
prompt and invaluable supply of information on all aspects of travelling in London.

Typeset by Rowland Phototypesetting Ltd,
Bury St Edmunds, Suffolk
Printed in Great Britain by Scotprint Ltd,
Musselburgh, Scotland

ISBN 0 948576 41 3

87/2/325

# How to use London Transport

The public transport system in and around London is very extensive. For some journeys, bus is best – and certainly it is preferable for those who want to enjoy the view. For some journeys the Underground is best – and certainly it is faster. In South London, where the Underground system is more limited, British Rail Network SouthEast fills the gaps. For long journeys, a combination of two, or even of all three, modes of transport may be necessary. London Transport (LT) is ready to advise on any and all possible journeys within the whole Greater London area.

If the timing of a journey is crucial, it is wise to bear in mind that the advertised departure and arrival times, in particular of buses, are ideals which cannot always be achieved. Wet roads, rush hour traffic jams, and road works all conspire to delay overland transport.

LT has come a long way since the days of horse-drawn buses – a visit to the London Transport Museum in Covent Garden shows just how far. This fascinating and extensive collection of buses, trams, trolleybuses and tube trains appeals to all ages, especially as visitors are encouraged to try out some of the controls themselves.

## London Transport Information

### Twenty-four hour information

For any information on travel in Greater London – routes, fares, times – telephone 01-222 1234 at any time of the day or night. In addition Travelcheck, a tape-recorded message service which is frequently updated, provides information about how bus and Underground services are running – telephone 01-222 1200 at any time.

### Travel Information Centres

These Centres give detailed information on any aspect of travelling in and around London; offer free bus and Underground maps and other travel literature; sell special tickets; and take bookings for guided tours on which special discounts are often available. They are at:

**Euston Station** *Open Mon–Thur & Sat 07.15–18.00; Fri 07.15–19.30; Sun 08.15–18.00.*

**King's Cross Station** *Open Mon–Thur, Sat & Sun 08.15– 18.00; Fri 08.15–19.30.*
**Oxford Circus Station** *Open Mon–Sat 08.15–18.00; closed Sun.*
**Piccadilly Circus Station** *Open Mon–Sun 08.15–18.00.*
**Victoria Station** *Open Mon–Sun 08.15–21.30.*
**Heathrow Terminals 1, 2, 3, Station** *Open Mon–Sat 07.15– 18.30; Sun 08.15–18.30.*
**Heathrow Terminal 1, Arrivals** *Open Mon–Fri 07.15–22.15; Sat 07.15–21.00; Sun 08.15–22.00.*
**Heathrow Terminal 2, Arrivals** *Open Mon–Sat 07.15–21.00; Sun 08.15–22.00.*
**Heathrow Terminal 3, Arrivals** *Open Mon–Sat 07.15–14.00; Sun 08.15–15.00.*
**Heathrow Terminal 4, Arrivals** *Open Mon–Sat 06.30–18.30; Sun 08.15–18.30.*
**West Croydon Bus Station** *Open Mon 07.00–19.00; Tue–Fri 07.30–18.30; Sat 08.00–18.00; closed Sun.*

**Underground Stations**
Underground stations in Central London also carry a stock of free bus and Underground maps.

# London Buses

The first London omnibus, drawn by three horses, travelled from the Yorkshire Stingo pub in Paddington to The Bank of England on 4th July 1829. Today there are approximately 5,000 motor-driven buses, organised into 350 routes, covering 1,700 miles of road.

The red double-decker London bus is a well-known feature of the London scene, although there are a few red single-deckers too. Buses of different colours may be found on some LT routes – look for the familiar bar and circle symbol on the front of the bus to tell you if your LT ticket is valid.

## Routes

An extensive network of routes covers London and outlying areas and links with British Rail stations and the London Underground system to ensure that any part of Greater London is accessible from any other part.

## Bus stops

There are two different types of bus stop, each with its own symbol; the compulsory stop 🚏 at which every bus will stop, and the request stop ◉ at which the bus will only stop if you hold out your hand in good time; if the bus is full it won't stop at all. If you are on the bus and wish to get off at a request stop, you must ring the bell, again, in good time.

Most bus stops in Central London are named. The name is written on the bus stop sign and in some cases on the shelter as well.

All bus stops in Central London, and many in outlying areas, carry information on routes and on planned times of buses, including last buses. Many also carry a map of the immediate vicinity. If you are in a one-way traffic system, this map will clearly show where you may pick up the bus on its return trip.

## Queueing

It is customary to queue (better known to Americans as making a line) at bus stops – and a lot of bad feeling can be generated by anyone who slips on to a bus ahead of the queue!

## Paying

On one-person operated buses, the driver will take the fare as you enter. These buses are entered from the front.

On buses which have both driver and conductor, the conductor will come to you to take the fare. These buses are usually entered from the back.

## Smoking

There is no smoking at all on single-decker buses, on the lower deck of double-decker buses, or at the front of the top deck. Smoking is permitted on the rear seats of the top deck only.

## Luggage

Luggage is taken on board at the discretion of the driver or conductor – and the same applies to dogs.

## Night buses

Night buses – which have the prefix N added to their route numbers on bus maps and time-tables – serve all major points in Central London and very many outlying areas too. They take over where last daytime buses leave off between *23.00* and *24.00*, continue until first buses start out, and tend to be speedier than day buses because there is so little traffic. All major night bus routes pass through Trafalgar Square.

Note that it is wise to hold out your hand for a night bus, even at a compulsory stop, in case the driver doesn't see you in the dark.

## Red Arrows

The one-person operated single-decker Red Arrow buses are principally railway station links, shopper and commuter buses. There are nine of them:

the 501 links Waterloo, Holborn and London Bridge and operates *Mon–Fri, but not evenings*;

the 502 links Waterloo, St Paul's and Liverpool Street and operates *Mon–Fri, but not evenings*;

the 503 links Russell Square, Oxford Street and South Kensington and operates *Mon–Sat, shopping hours only*;

the 505 links Waterloo, Old Street and London Bridge and operates *Mon–Fri, but not evenings*;

the 506 links Victoria and Paddington and operates *Mon–Fri, but not evenings*;

the 507 links Victoria and Waterloo and operates *Mon–Sun, including evenings*;

the 509 links Liverpool Street and Oxford Circus and operates *Mon–Fri, shopping hours only*;

the 510 links Victoria, Tower Gateway (first station on the Docklands Light Railway) and Aldgate and operates *Mon–Sun, but not late evenings or early Sun morning*;

the 513 links Waterloo, Fleet Street and London Bridge and operates *Mon–Fri, rush hours only*.

## Minibuses

London Transport also operate some Minibus routes using small, single-decker buses running at frequent intervals. The following routes in Central London are Minibus operated: C1, C2, 28, 31. There are also many more in the suburbs.

# London Underground

The London Underground system, the first in the world, was opened in 1863 with the Metropolitan Line, which then consisted of seven stations between Paddington and Farringdon. It now serves 248 Underground stations, as well as a further 20 or so British Rail stations.

London Underground stations can be easily recognised by the distinctive symbol ⊖. The Underground, often called 'the tube' by Londoners, is the fastest method of getting from A to B in London because it avoids the traffic.

# Routes

An extensive network of routes travels under Central London and on to the outlying areas. The system also links with British Rail stations. A complete Underground map, on which the different routes are colour-coded, is prominently displayed in every Underground station. See p. 176 of this guide.

# Paying

There is a ticket office in every station. In many there are also automatic ticket machines which can give change. It is essential to have a ticket before boarding the train.

# Ticket gates

At most stations you pass through an automatic ticket gate in order to reach the trains. Feed the ticket in to the ticket gate, pass through, and remember to pick up the ticket the other side. You will also need to feed your ticket into a similar machine on the way out at most stations. The machine will retain your ticket if your journey is complete, or return it to you if it is still valid for travel.

# Escalators

Stand on the right; keep moving on the left. Dogs and small children must be carried.

# Smoking

No smoking is allowed on Underground trains at any time, nor is smoking permitted at any Underground station.

# Luggage

There is no restriction on reasonably-sized luggage, and dogs travel free.

# Weekends and evenings

The following central area Underground stations are closed at weekends or in the evenings due to lack of demand:
Aldwych *open Mon–Fri peak hours only; closed evenings and Sat & Sun.*
Cannon Street *closed evenings and Sat & Sun.*
Chancery Lane *closed Sun.*
Kensington Olympia *closed Sun.*
Mornington Crescent *closed Sat & Sun.*

Shoreditch *open Mon–Fri peak hours only and Sun mornings; closed all Sat and evenings.*
Temple *closed Sun.*
West Brompton *closed Sat & Sun.*

## Last Underground trains

Last trains leave Central London between *24.00 & 24.30 Mon–Sat* and between *23.30 & 24.30 Sun.*

# Airport Connections

## Heathrow

### Airbuses

There are two Airbuses, each with plenty of luggage space, which connect the individual terminals at Heathrow with Central London. They can also accommodate wheelchairs. Travelcards are not valid on airbuses.

The **A1** travels between Victoria Station and Heathrow, calling at Hyde Park Corner, Cromwell Road (Forum Hotel) and Cromwell Road (junction with Earl's Court Road). The A1 *operates every day from early morning to mid evening* at approximately 20-minute or 30-minute intervals. Total journey time is 50–75 minutes.

The **A2** travels between Russell Square and Heathrow, calling at Euston Station, Great Portland Street, Baker Street, Marble Arch, Bayswater Road (Albion Street, Lancaster Gate and Queensway), Notting Hill Gate and Holland Park (Kensington Hilton). The A2 *operates every day from early morning to mid evening* at approximately 20-minute or 30-minute intervals. Total journey time is 65–80 minutes.

Night bus **N97** provides an all-night link between Central London and Heathrow *every night.*

### Underground link

There is an Underground link between Central London and Heathrow on the Piccadilly Line, with a train running every 5–10 minutes. You can travel direct from the following stations: Baron's Court, Covent Garden, Earl's Court, Gloucester Road, Green Park, Hammersmith, Holborn, Hyde Park Corner, King's Cross, Knightsbridge, Leicester Square, Piccadilly Circus, Russell Square and South Kensington. The journey from Central London takes approximately 45 minutes. The Piccadilly Line links up with other lines on the London Underground system. It is possible to get to Heathrow from any station on the Piccadilly Line but there might not always be a through train, so you may have to change at Hammersmith or Acton Town.

# Gatwick

British Rail runs the Gatwick Express from Victoria Station. There are *four trains an hour from 06.00 to 24.00*, and *one train an hour from 24.00 to 06.00*. Buy a through ticket, via Victoria, from any Underground station. Journey time from Victoria is 30 minutes.

# Zones

To ensure that fares are fair, London has been divided into zones. There are four bus zones. The Central Zone covers the West End and the City. Its boundaries are Kensington to the west, Shoreditch to the east, Elephant and Castle to the south, and Baker Street and King's Cross to the north. The Inner Zone is a ring about three miles wide which encircles the Central Zone. There are also Outer Zones 3 and 4/5 covering the suburbs. Underground zones are the same, but Zones 4 and 5 which are separate Underground zones are treated as one for bus routes.

# Special Tickets

LT issues certain special tickets, which can save both time and money.

## Travelcards

These may be purchased to cover one or any combination of two or more zones for a week or longer. They are valid on bus (with the exception of Airbus routes to and from Heathrow), Underground and British Rail within the London area. You need a small passport-sized photograph. There is also a one-day Off-Peak Travelcard which *cannot be used before 09.30 Mon–Fri,* but can be used at *any time on Sat & Sun*. No photograph is required for the one-day ticket.

## Weekly, Monthly and Annual Bus Passes

These can be purchased to cover one, two, three or four zones. You need a small passport-sized photograph. There are also Daily Bus Passes available for use in the suburbs for which no photograph is needed.

## Child Bus Passes and Travelcards

These offer the same facilities as the adult passes, but a passport-sized photograph and proof of age must be presented to a London Post Office or Travel Information Centre which will issue a Child-Rate Photocard, which in turn must be presented when buying the Child Bus Pass or Travelcard.

## Where to buy Special Tickets

The Travelcard passes are available from the LT Travel Information Centres and railway stations. Other special tickets and passes are also available from Underground stations and some passes may also be bought from selected newsagents or from bus garages.

# Sightseeing Bus Tours

The Original London Transport Sightseeing Tour is the only one to use traditional red London buses with the open platform at the back. All tours are accompanied by a qualified guide.

## Boarding points

Board the bus in the Haymarket, or at Speaker's Corner (Hyde Park), at Baker Street Station or at Victoria Underground Station. *Tours run daily*, at roughly hourly intervals, *between 10.00 and 17.00*, and take about 1½ hours.

## Paying

Pay as you board the tour, or book in advance at one of the LT Travel Information Centres where you get a discount and can ask for a special discount ticket which allows entry to London Zoo or to Madame Tussaud's ahead of the queues.

## Sights to see

The tours take in all the main sights of London, including Piccadilly Circus, the National Gallery, Nelson's Column, Horse Guards, the Houses of Parliament, Lambeth Palace, St Clement Danes, the Mansion House, HMS Belfast, the Tower of London, St Paul's Cathedral, Westminster Abbey, Buckingham Palace, the Royal Albert Hall and Marble Arch.

# *Sightseeing Coach Tours*

*Day and half-day tours run all year*, although there are fewer in the winter months than during the summer season. Each coach carries a well-informed tour guide. Lunch is usually included, and the price is always inclusive of any admission charges. A few tours combine bus and river boat for best effect.

## Boarding point

All coaches depart from Wilton Road Coach Station in Victoria. Courtesy coaches are provided from the main hotel areas of London to connect with the tours which start in Wilton Road.

## Booking

Booking in advance is wise. Go to any of the LT Travel Information Centres; to Wilton Road Coach Station or any National Express agent; to any major London hotel; to the London Tourist Board Information Centre at Victoria Station; to Selfridges or Harrods. Or book by post from Travel Information London Transport, 55 Broadway, London SW1H 0BD. Any of the above will supply free leaflets with full details of available tours. For further information telephone 01-877 1722.

## Sights to see

There are various London tours from full-day tours to speciality tours, including 'London and the River by Night', and 'Royal Greenwich River Cruise'. There are also many tours and excursions going further afield including tours to Richmond and Hampton Court; Royal Windsor; Leeds Castle; Stratford-upon-Avon and Warwick Castle; Stonehenge and Bath. Ask for details at any LT Travel Information Centre.

# *Lost Property*

With luck and honesty, anything left on a bus or Underground train should turn up at the Lost Property Office, 200 Baker Street, NW1; *open 09.30–14.00 Mon–Fri*. Personal callers and postal enquiries only. There is also a 24-hour recorded information service on 01-486 2496.

# Docklands Light Railway

This light railway, which opened in summer 1987, serves the Docklands area with its rapidly expanding new business, leisure and accommodation developments. Panoramic views are offered to travellers for much of the route. The railway is currently being extended to Bank, in the City, and in connection with this and other expansion work, the railway service is replaced by buses at certain times, particularly at weekends. For information on any aspect of the DLR telephone 01-222 1234.

# Green Line Coaches

The Green Line coaches are not run by LT but provide useful links with points outside Greater London. Information about these services can be obtained by telephoning 01-668 7261.

# British Rail

British Rail is best known for the Inter-City trains which link major towns and cities all over the country. However, it also runs many suburban lines under the Network SouthEast banner. In South London, the Network SouthEast suburban trains provide a useful alternative and, indeed, a vital supplement to bus and Underground travel – especially as the London Underground has a limited service south of the River Thames.

---

**London Transport 24-hour information service**
For any information on travel in Greater London – routes, fares, times – telephone 01-222 1234 at any time of the day or night.

# Guide to Central London Bus Routes

Below is a guide to the principal Central London bus routes included in this book, showing the main places they serve.

All routes operate in both directions so you can use the information here to tell you in which direction the bus should be travelling to get you where you want to go. For example, if you are at Aldwych and want to take bus 6 to Little Venice, you know you want to get on one travelling towards Kensal Rise. The names printed in capital letters (eg BAKER STREET) are terminal points.

Details of other buses not included in this list (and rush hour variations) are given on the bus stops they serve or you can call in at any LT Travel Information Centre or telephone 01-222 1234.

**1**
Mon–Sun
TRAFALGAR SQUARE, Strand, Aldwych, Waterloo, Surrey Docks, Greenwich, BROMLEY COMMON.

**2A/2B**
Mon–Sun
BAKER STREET STATION, Oxford St, Marble Arch, Park Lane, Hyde Park Corner, Victoria, Vauxhall, Brixton, CRYSTAL PALACE.

**3**
Mon–Sun
OXFORD CIRCUS, Regent St, Piccadilly Circus, Trafalgar Sq, Whitehall, Westminster, Lambeth Bridge, Brixton, CRYSTAL PALACE.

**4**
Mon–Sat
WATERLOO, Aldwych, Fleet St, St Paul's, Barbican, Islington, Finsbury Park, ARCHWAY.

**6**
Mon–Sun
KENSAL RISE, Little Venice, Edgware Rd, Marble Arch, Oxford St, Piccadilly Circus, Trafalgar Sq, Strand, Aldwych, Fleet St, St Paul's, Bank, Liverpool St, HACKNEY WICK.

**7**
Mon–Sun
BLOOMSBURY (Mon–Sat only), OXFORD CIRCUS, Oxford St, Marble Arch, Paddington, Ladbroke Grove, EAST ACTON (and to Kew and RICHMOND on Sun).

**8**
Mon–Sun
WILLESDEN, Kilburn, Marble Arch, Oxford Circus, Holborn, Bank, Liverpool St, Shoreditch, Old Ford, BOW (and to Stratford and PLAISTOW on Sun).

**9**
Mon–Sun
LIVERPOOL STREET STATION*, Bank*, St Paul's*, Fleet St,* ALDWYCH, Strand, Trafalgar

Sq, Piccadilly, Hyde Park Corner, Knightsbridge, Kensington, Hammersmith, MORTLAKE. (*Mon–Fri rush hours only.)

**10**
Mon–Sun
HAMMERSMITH, Kensington High St, Knightsbridge, Hyde Park Corner, Marble Arch, Oxford St, Tottenham Court Rd/Gower St, Euston, KING'S CROSS.

**11**
Mon–Sun
LIVERPOOL STREET STATION, Bank, St Paul's, Fleet St, Aldwych, Strand, Trafalgar Sq, Whitehall, Westminster, Victoria, Sloane Sq, Chelsea, Fulham, HAMMERSMITH (and to SHEPHERD'S BUSH Mon–Sat except evenings).

**12**
Mon–Sun
EAST ACTON, Shepherd's Bush, Notting Hill Gate, Bayswater Rd, Marble Arch, Oxford St, Regent St, Piccadilly Circus, Trafalgar Sq, Whitehall, Westminster, Elephant & Castle, Camberwell, Peckham, DULWICH.

**13**
Mon–Sun
ALDWYCH*, Strand*, Trafalgar Sq*, Piccadilly Circus*, Regent St*, OXFORD CIRCUS, Oxford St, Marylebone/Baker St, St John's Wood, Swiss Cottage, Golders Green, NORTH FINCHLEY. (*No service to these points on Sun.)

**14**
Mon–Sun
PUTNEY HEATH, Fulham, South Kensington, Knightsbridge, Hyde Park Corner, Piccadilly, Shaftesbury Av, TOTTENHAM COURT ROAD. (Runs on to/from Euston in rush hours, Sat shopping hours and Sun, and to/from King's Cross and CROUCH END on Sun.)

**14A**
Mon–Sat
TOTTENHAM COURT ROAD STATION, Euston, King's Cross, Holloway, CROUCH END.

**15**
Mon–Sun
LADBROKE GROVE, Paddington, Edgware Rd, Marble Arch, Oxford Circus, Regent St, Piccadilly Circus, Trafalgar Sq, Strand, Aldwych, Fleet St, St Paul's, Monument, Tower, Aldgate, Stepney, Poplar, EAST HAM.

**15B**
Mon–Fri
OXFORD CIRCUS, Regent St, Piccadilly Circus, Trafalgar Sq, Strand, Aldwych, Fleet St, St Paul's, Bank, Aldgate, Stepney, Poplar, EAST HAM (not evenings).

**16**
Mon–Sun
VICTORIA, Hyde Park Corner, Park Lane, Marble Arch, Edgware Rd, Maida Vale, Kilburn, Cricklewood, NEASDEN.

**16A**
Mon–Sat

OXFORD CIRCUS, Oxford St, Marble Arch, Edgware Rd, Maida Vale, Kilburn, Cricklewood, BRENT CROSS (not evenings).

**17**
Mon–Sat

LONDON BRIDGE*, Southwark Bridge*, St Paul's*, FARRINGDON STREET, Holborn, Gray's Inn Rd, King's Cross, Holloway, Archway, NORTH FINCHLEY. (*No service to these points evenings or Sat.)

**18**
Mon–Sun

KING'S CROSS*, Euston*, BAKER STREET, Marylebone Rd, Paddington, Kensal Green, Harlesden, Wembley, SUDBURY. (*No service to these points evenings; no service at King's Cross on Sun.)

**19**
Mon–Sun

TUFNELL PARK, Holloway (Sun only), FINSBURY PARK, Islington, Bloomsbury, Shaftesbury Av, Piccadilly, Hyde Park Corner, Knightsbridge, Sloane Sq, Chelsea, Battersea, CLAPHAM JUNCTION (and to TOOTING BEC on Sun).

**22**
Mon–Sun

HOMERTON, Liverpool St, Bank, St Paul's, Holborn (Sun only), BLOOMSBURY, Shaftesbury Av, Piccadilly, Hyde Park Corner, Knightsbridge, Sloane Sq, Chelsea, Parsons Green, PUTNEY COMMON.

**22B**
Mon–Sat

TRAFALGAR SQUARE, Piccadilly Circus, Shaftesbury Av, Charing Cross Rd, Holborn, St Paul's, Bank, Liverpool St, Hackney, HOMERTON.

**24**
Mon–Sun

PIMLICO, Victoria, Westminster, Whitehall, Trafalgar Sq, Leicester Sq, Charing Cross Rd, Tottenham Court Rd/Gower St, Camden Town, HAMPSTEAD HEATH.

**25**
Mon–Sun

VICTORIA, Hyde Park Corner, Green Park*, Bond St*, Oxford St, Bloomsbury, Holborn, St Paul's, Bank**, Leadenhall St**, Aldgate, Whitechapel, Mile End, Stratford, ILFORD/BECONTREE HEATH. (*Eastbound service runs instead via Park Lane and Marble Arch after 20.30 Mon–Sun. **Runs via Tower Sat and Sun.)

**27**
Mon–Sun

ARCHWAY, Camden Town, Marylebone Rd, Baker St Station, Paddington, Notting Hill, Kensington, Hammersmith, Chiswick, Kew, RICHMOND.

**28**
Mon–Sun

GOLDERS GREEN, West Hampstead, Kilburn, Notting Hill, Kensington, Fulham, WANDSWORTH.

**29**
Mon–Sun
VICTORIA, Westminster, Whitehall, Trafalgar Sq, Leicester Sq, Charing Cross Rd, Tottenham Court Rd/Gower St, Camden Town, Holloway, Finsbury Park, WOOD GREEN/ENFIELD.

**30**
Mon–Sun
HACKNEY WICK, Islington, King's Cross, Euston, Marylebone Rd, Baker St, Oxford St, Marble Arch, Park Lane, Hyde Park Corner, Knightsbridge, South Kensington, Earl's Court, WEST BROMPTON.

**31**
Mon–Sun
CHELSEA, Earl's Court, Kensington, Notting Hill, Kilburn, Swiss Cottage, CAMDEN TOWN.

**35**
Mon–Sun
HOMERTON, Shoreditch, Liverpool St, Gracechurch St, Monument, London Bridge, Elephant & Castle, Camberwell, Brixton, CLAPHAM JUNCTION.

**36**
Mon–Sun
QUEEN'S PARK, Paddington, Edgware Rd, Marble Arch, Park Lane, Hyde Park Corner, Victoria, Vauxhall, Peckham, Lewisham, HITHER GREEN.

**38**
Mon–Sun
VICTORIA, Hyde Park Corner, Piccadilly, Shaftesbury Av, Bloomsbury, Holborn, Islington, LEYTON.

**39**
Mon–Sat
VICTORIA*, Cheyne Walk*, BATTERSEA, Clapham Junction, PUTNEY. (*No service on Sun.)

**43**
Mon–Sat
LONDON BRIDGE, Bank, Moorgate, Islington, Holloway, Archway, MUSWELL HILL.

**44**
Mon–Sun
LONDON BRIDGE*, St George's Circus, Lambeth Palace, Vauxhall, Battersea Park, Wandsworth, Tooting, MITCHAM*. (*Runs on to/from ALDGATE on Sun mornings and SUTTON all day Sun.)

**45**
Mon–Sun
SOUTH KENSINGTON, Chelsea, Battersea, Clapham, Stockwell, Brixton, Camberwell, ELEPHANT & CASTLE. Extended to Blackfriars every day except Mon–Sat evenings, to FARRINGDON STREET Mon–Fri (but not evenings) & Sun, and to KING'S CROSS, Holloway and ARCHWAY on Sun.

**47**
Mon–Sun
SHOREDITCH, Liverpool St, London Bridge, Deptford, Lewisham, CATFORD.

**49**
SHEPHERD'S BUSH, Kensington High St, South

| | |
|---|---|
| Mon–Sun | Kensington, Battersea, Clapham Junction, Streatham, CRYSTAL PALACE. |
| **52**<br>Mon–Sun | VICTORIA, Hyde Park Corner, Knightsbridge, Kensington, Notting Hill, Ladbroke Grove, Willesden, MILL HILL. |
| **52A**<br>Mon–Sat | VICTORIA*, Hyde Park Corner*, Knightsbridge*, NOTTING HILL GATE, Ladbroke Grove, East Acton, ACTON. (*Sat only.) |
| **53**<br>Mon–Sun | OXFORD CIRCUS, Regent St, Piccadilly Circus, Trafalgar Sq, Whitehall, Westminster, Elephant & Castle, New Cross, Blackheath, Woolwich, PLUMSTEAD. |
| **55**<br>Mon–Sun | TOTTENHAM COURT ROAD STATION, Bloomsbury, Old Street, Shoreditch, Hackney, Leyton, WHIPPS CROSS. |
| **63**<br>Mon–Sun | KING'S CROSS, Farringdon, Ludgate Circus, Blackfriars, Elephant & Castle, Peckham, Honor Oak, CRYSTAL PALACE. |
| **68**<br>Mon–Sun | EUSTON*, Russell Sq, Holborn, Kingsway, Aldwych, Waterloo, Elephant & Castle, Camberwell, Norwood, CROYDON. (*Runs on to Camden Town and Chalk Farm on Sun.) |
| **73**<br>Mon–Sun | VICTORIA, Marble Arch, Oxford Circus, Tottenham Court Rd, Euston, King's Cross, Islington, STOKE NEWINGTON. (Some journeys continue to Tottenham.) |
| **74**<br>Mon–Sun | CAMDEN TOWN, The Zoo, Regent's Park, Baker St/Marylebone Rd, Oxford St, Marble Arch, Park Lane, Hyde Park Corner, Knightsbridge, South Kensington, Cromwell Rd, Earl's Court, West Brompton, Fulham, Putney, ROEHAMPTON. |
| **76**<br>Mon–Sat | VICTORIA, Lambeth Bridge (Mon–Fri rush hours), WATERLOO, Blackfriars, St Paul's, Bank, Moorgate, Hoxton, Stoke Newington, Tottenham, NORTHUMBERLAND PARK. |
| **77/77A**<br>Mon–Sun | KING'S CROSS, Euston, Russell Sq, Holborn, Kingsway, Aldwych, Strand, Trafalgar Sq, Whitehall, Westminster Bridge/Millbank, Vauxhall, Clapham Junction, WANDSWORTH/TOOTING. |

**78**
Mon–Sun
SHOREDITCH, Liverpool St, Aldgate, Tower Bridge, Bermondsey, Peckham, Dulwich, FOREST HILL.

**82**
Mon–Sun
VICTORIA, Marble Arch, Baker St, Swiss Cottage, GOLDERS GREEN. (Runs on to North Finchley, BARNET on Sun.)

**88**
Mon–Sun
TURNHAM GREEN, Acton Green, Shepherd's Bush, Notting Hill Gate, Bayswater, Marble Arch, Oxford Circus, Piccadilly Circus, Westminster, Tate Gallery, Stockwell, Clapham, TOOTING. (Runs on to Mitcham, MERTON on Sun.)

**113**
Mon–Sun
OXFORD CIRCUS, Oxford St, Marylebone/Baker St, St John's Wood, Swiss Cottage, Hendon, Mill Hill, EDGWARE.

**135**
Mon–Sat
MARBLE ARCH, Oxford St, Great Portland St, Camden Town, ARCHWAY (not evenings).

**137**
Mon–Sun
OXFORD CIRCUS, Marble Arch, Hyde Park Corner, Knightsbridge, Sloane Sq, Chelsea Bridge, Clapham, Streatham, CRYSTAL PALACE.

**141**
Mon–Sun
WOOD GREEN, Haringey, Hoxton, Moorgate, St Paul's, FARRINGDON STREET, Elephant & Castle*, Old Kent Rd*, Brockley*, Catford*, GROVE PARK**. (*No service on Sun. **No service on Sat or Sun.)

**159**
Mon–Sun
WEST HAMPSTEAD, Abbey Rd, St John's Wood, Baker St/Marylebone, Oxford St, Regent St, Piccadilly Circus, Trafalgar Sq, Whitehall, Westminster, Lambeth Bridge, Kennington, Brixton, STREATHAM/THORNTON HEATH.

**168**
Mon–Sat
WATERLOO, Aldwych, Kingsway, Holborn, Russell Sq, Euston, Camden Town, Chalk Farm, HAMPSTEAD HEATH.

**170**
Mon–Fri
ALDWYCH, Strand, Trafalgar Sq, Whitehall, Westminster, Vauxhall, Battersea Park, Wandsworth, ROEHAMPTON.

**171**
Mon–Sun
ISLINGTON*, Rosebery Av*, Holborn*, Kingsway*, ALDWYCH, Waterloo, Elephant & Castle, Camberwell, Peckham, New Cross,

FOREST HILL. (*No service to these places Sat or Sun – see **171A**.)

**171A**
Mon–Sun
TOTTENHAM, Islington, Rosebery Av, Gray's Inn Rd, High Holborn, Fetter Lane, Fleet St, Aldwych, WATERLOO.

**177**
Mon–Sun
ELEPHANT & CASTLE, New Cross, Greenwich, Woolwich, PLUMSTEAD/ABBEY WOOD. (Runs near to Thames Barrier between Greenwich and Woolwich.)

**188**
Mon–Sun
EUSTON, Russell Sq, Holborn, Kingsway, Aldwych, Waterloo, Tower Bridge (southside), Surrey Docks, GREENWICH.

**400**
Mon–Sun
VICTORIA, Trafalgar Sq, Aldwych, Tower Hill, GREENWICH. (Runs 10.00–16.00 May–Sep only. Travelcards are NOT accepted on this service.)

**501**
Mon–Fri
WATERLOO, Kingsway, Holborn, St Paul's, Bank, LONDON BRIDGE. (Red Arrow service – not evenings.)

**502**
Mon–Fri
WATERLOO, Aldwych, Fleet St, St Paul's, London Wall (returning via Bank), LIVERPOOL STREET. (Red Arrow service – not evenings.)

**503**
Mon–Sat
SOUTH KENSINGTON, Knightsbridge, Hyde Park Corner, Marble Arch, Oxford St, British Museum, RUSSELL SQUARE. (Red Arrow service – shopping hours only.)

**505**
Mon–Fri
LONDON BRIDGE STATION, Monument, Liverpool St, Shoreditch, Old Street, Bloomsbury, Kingsway, Aldwych, WATERLOO. (Red Arrow service – not evenings.)

**506**
Mon–Fri
VICTORIA, Park Lane, Marble Arch, Edgware Rd, Lancaster Gate, PADDINGTON STATION. (Red Arrow service – 07.00–18.00 only.)

**507**
Mon–Sun
VICTORIA, Lambeth Bridge, WATERLOO. (Red Arrow service – runs evenings.)

**509**
Mon–Fri
LIVERPOOL STREET STATION, Barbican, St Paul's, Aldwych, Trafalgar Sq, Piccadilly Circus, OXFORD CIRCUS. (Red Arrow service – shopping hours only.)

**510**
Mon–Sun

VICTORIA, Lambeth Bridge, Elephant & Castle, London Bridge, Monument, Tower (returning via Aldgate), TOWER GATEWAY. (Red Arrow service – not late evenings or early Sun.)

**C1**
Mon–Sat

WATERLOO, Westminster Bridge, Parliament Sq, Victoria, Belgravia, Sloane Sq, Knightsbridge, South Kensington, KENSINGTON HIGH STREET. (Minibus service.)

**C2**
Mon–Sun

REGENT STREET, Oxford Circus, Portland Place, Regent's Park (for Zoo), Camden Town, PARLIAMENT HILL FIELDS. (Minibus service.)

**Z1**
Mon–Sun

MARBLE ARCH, Baker St, LONDON ZOO, CAMDEN TOWN. (Runs summer only. Travelcards are NOT accepted on this service.)

**CARELINK**  Inter-Station link for disabled passengers between Waterloo, Victoria, Paddington, Euston, King's Cross/St Pancras and Liverpool Street Stations. (Runs 09.00–18.00 Mon–Sun.) (Travelcards are NOT accepted on this service.)

---

**London Transport 24-hour information service**
For any information on travel in Greater London – routes, fares, times – telephone 01-222 1234 at any time of the day or night.

# A

## Abbey Road Studios
3 Abbey Rd NW8. 01-286 1161. The studios where the Beatles recorded their earliest LPs are not open to the public, but anyone may use the zebra crossing made famous on the sleeve of the 'Abbey Road' album.
⊖ St John's Wood (then walk via Grove End Rd)
🚌 46, 159

## Achilles Statue 3Q1
Hyde Park Corner W2. Set up in honour of the Duke of Wellington on 18 June 1822 – the seventh anniversary of the Battle of Waterloo. The 'women of England' who commissioned it were disconcerted to discover they had funded England's first public nude. Made by Sir Richard Westmacott out of 33 tons of bronze guns captured from the French.
⊖ Hyde Park Corner
🚌 2A, 2B, 9, 10, 14, 16, 19, 22, 25, 30, 36, 38, 52, 52A, 73, 74, 82, 137, 503, 506

## Adelphi Theatre 3N5
The Strand WC2. 01-836 7611. The fourth theatre on the site, this building went up in 1930 and can seat 1,500.
⊖ Charing Cross, Embankment
🚌 1, 6, 9, 11, 13, 15, 15B, 77, 77A, 170, 176, 509

## Admiralty Arch 3N4
The Mall SW1. Sir Aston Webb's massive triple arch of 1910 – a memorial to Queen Victoria – bestrides the eastern end of the Mall.
⊖ Charing Cross
🚌 1, 3, 6, 9, 11, 12, 13, 15, 15B, 22B, 24, 29, 53, 77, 77A, 88, 109, 159, 170, 176, 184, 509

## Albany 3N3
Piccadilly W1. Privately owned apartments, with several famous residents often of a literary or political persuasion. A patrician Georgian mansion built by Sir William Chambers in 1770.
⊖ Piccadilly Circus
🚌 3, 6, 9, 12, 13, 14, 15, 15B, 19, 22, 22B, 38, 53, 88, 159, 509

## The Albert 3P4
52 Victoria St SW1. 01-222 5577. Grand, imposing Victorian pub with original gas lights and engraved glass windows. Bar snacks. Excellent restaurant serving traditional English roasts and full English breakfasts too, *at 08.00*. New Scotland Yard's local, and popular with MPs (there's a division bell in the restaurant). *Pub open normal licensing hours Mon–Sun. Restaurant open 12.00–21.30 Mon–Sun.*
⊖ St James's Park
🚌 11, 24, 29, 76, 507, 510, C1

## Albert Bridge 51Y
SW3. Fairytale cantilever and suspension bridge built by R. W. Ordish in 1873 with a hut at each end where tolls were collected until 1879. Signs ask troops to break step when crossing to reduce the strain. Still threatened by the weight of modern traffic despite the addition of a central support.
⊖ Sloane Square (then bus 19, 22, then walk), South Kensington (then bus 45, 49, 219)
🚌 39 (direct), or 11, 22 to King's Road then walk, or 19, 45, 49, 219 to Cheyne Walk

## Albert Memorial 2H4
Kensington Gardens SW7. The ultimate mid-Victorian memorial, built in lavishly Gothic style by Sir George Gilbert Scott in 1863–72. The figure of the Prince, cast in bronze by Joseph Durham, is shown studying the catalogue to the Great Exhibition. The steps and podium seethe with the works of various sculptors, representing the continents, the arts and industry.
⊖ South Kensington, High Street Kensington
🚌 9, 10, 33, 49, 52, 52A, C1

## Albery Theatre 3N4
St Martins La WC2. 01-836 3878. Formerly the New Theatre. Architecturally appealing and once the home of the Old Vic Company, this is one of the Wyndham theatres (others are Criterion, Don-

mar Warehouse, Piccadilly and Wyndham's) and theatre tours are available.
∈ Leicester Square
🚌 24, 29, 176

## Aldwych Theatre 3M5
Aldwych WC2. 01-836 6404. The home of the Aldwych farces of the 20s and 30s and later of the Royal Shakespeare Company which is now at the Barbican. Presents varied productions to a potential audience of 1,004.
∈ Covent Garden
🚌 1, 4, 6, 9, 11, 13, 15, 15B, 68, 77, 77A, 168, 170, 171, 171A, 176, 188, 501, 502, 505, 509, 513

## Alexandra Park & Palace
N22. 01-883 0809. Two hundred sloping, tree-planted acres, with a boating lake, miniature golf, a garden centre, dry ski run, nature conservancy area and children's zoo. There are regular outdoor band concerts on summer weekends and itinerant fairs. The Palace has two halls – The Great Hall and The West Hall – offering exhibitions, spectator sporting events and concerts. In the Palm Court Area you will find a coffee-shop-cum-restaurant and The Phoenix, a real ale pub. Park open *24 hrs*; Halls *open for exhibitions and events*; Restaurant & Pub *open 11.00–23.00 Mon–Sat; 12.00–22.30 Sun.*
∈ Finsbury Park (then bus W3)
🚌 W3
⇤ Alexandra Palace (then bus W3)

## Alfred the Great
Trinity Church Sq SE1. The origin of this famous statue is unknown but it possibly came from Westminster

Hall, in which case it dates from 1395 and is by far the oldest statue in London.
∈ Borough
🚌 21, 35, 40, 95, 133, 510, P3

## All Hallows by the Tower 4
Byward St EC3. 01-481 2928. Founded in 675, rebuilt during the 11th, 13th and 15th centuries and restored after Second World War bomb damage. Has London's best collection of memorial brasses, an upstairs refectory which serves light lunches on week days, and a Roman mosaic floor, cAD122, in the crypt. *Open Mon–Sun. Crypt museum open daily by arrangement with verger.* Charge.
∈ Tower Hill
🚌 15, 42, 78, 510, Sat & Sun 25

## All Hallows by the Wall 4S5
83 London Wall EC2. 01-588 3388. 13thC church on and beside the medieval City wall, rebuilt 1765–7 by the younger Dance. The huge pulpit is reached by way of the vestry, itself just over the wall and, strictly speaking, outside the City. *Open Mon–Sun.* Free.
∈ Liverpool Street
🚌 9, 11, 21, 43, 76, 133, 141, 502, Sun only 279A

## All Soul's Church 3L3
Langham Pl W1. 01-580 4357. Built by John Nash in 1822–4 when he designed Regent Street which sweeps away to the south. The parish church of the BBC from which Morning Service is broadcast live most *Tue, Wed & Fri.*
∈ Oxford Circus
🚌 3, 6, 7, 8, 10, 12, 13, 15, 15B, 16A, 25, 53, 73, 88, 113, 135, 137, 159, 176, 503, 509, C2

## Almeida Theatre Wine Bar
1a Almeida St N1. 01-226 0931. Innovative touring productions and an annual contemporary music festival. Wine bar can be enjoyed as well as, or instead of, the theatre. *Open 11.00–15.00 & 17.30–23.00 Mon–Sat; 19.00–22.30 on performance Suns.*
∈ Angel, Highbury & Islington
🚌 4, 19, 30, 43, 263A, 279, 279A

## Ambassadors Theatre 3M4
West St WC2. 01-836 1171. Cosy,

intimate theatre where 'The Mousetrap', now at its partner theatre, the St Martin's, began its phenomenally long run.
θ Leicester Square
🚌 14, 19, 22, 22B, 24, 29, 38, 176

### Anchor 4T3
Bankside SE1. 01-407 1577. The original pub on this site, whose clientele was a hideous mix of smugglers, press gangs and warders from The Clink prison, was destroyed in the Fire of London. This building is 18thC with exposed beams, open fires, rough walls, five small bars and three restaurants. The antique bric-a-brac includes a first edition of Dr Johnson's 'Dictionary'. *Open Mon–Sun. Restaurant closed L Sat.*
θ Mansion House (then cross Southwark Bridge), London Bridge (then walk via Cathedral and Clink St)
🚌 17, 21, 35, 40, 43, 44, 47, 48, 95, 133, 149, 501, 505, 510, 513, P3, P11

### Annabel's 3N2
44 Berkeley Sq W1. 01-629 2350. Exclusive and expensive nightclub, richly furnished with Royalty, aristocrats and stars. Short but distinguished menu; rarely short of asparagus or truffles. Very hard to join although a member may find it easier to arrange temporary membership for an overseas friend than full membership for a resident.
θ Green Park
🚌 9, 14, 19, 22, 25, 38 to Green Park Station

### Antiquarius Antique Market 5X1
135–141 King's Rd SW3. 01-351 5353. Covered complex of small purpose-built stalls where it is a pleasure to get lost amongst the fine and applied arts, silver, jewellery, Edwardian silk blouses, Victorian dolls' houses, furniture and bric-a-brac. *Open 10.00–18.00 Mon–Sat.*
θ Sloane Square (then bus)
🚌 11, 19, 22, 49, 219

### Anything Left-Handed Ltd 3M3
65 Beak St W1. 01-437 3910. For those with sinister bent – more than 100 tools and gadgets for

south-paws. *Open 10.30–17.00 Mon–Fri; 10.00–14.00 Sat.*
θ Oxford Circus, Piccadilly Circus
🚌 3, 6, 12, 13, 15, 15B, 53, 88, 159, 509

### Apollo Theatre 3M4
Shaftesbury Av W1. 01-437 2663. Turn-of-the-century theatre which began by staging musicals and now offers straight plays and light comedies.
θ Piccadilly Circus
🚌 3, 6, 9, 12, 13, 14, 15, 15B, 19, 22, 22B, 38, 53, 88, 159, 509

### Apollo Victoria 3P3
17 Wilton Rd SW1. 01-828 8665. Once an enormous cinema, the auditorium has been transformed to allow the hit musical, 'Starlight Express', to skate around the audience.
θ Victoria
🚌 2, 2A, 2B, 11, 16, 24, 25, 29, 36, 36A, 36B, 38, 39, 52, 52A, 73, 76, 82, 185, 506, 507, 510, C1

### Apsley House 3O2
149 Piccadilly W1. 01-499 5676. An Adam house, altered in the early 19thC by Wyatt (who added the portico and the Bath stone facing), which was known as No 1 London when it was the home of the first Duke of Wellington. Now administered by the Victoria and Albert Museum and a perfect setting for the Iron Duke's silver, plate, porcelain and priceless paintings – including works by Velasquez, Rubens and Murillo. *Open 11.00–16.50 Tue–*

*Sat; 14.30–18.00 Sun. Closed Mon, Fri & Nat Hols. Charge.*
θ Hyde Park Corner
🚌 2A, 2B, 9, 10, 14, 16, 19, 22, 25, 30, 36, 38, 52, 52A, 73, 74, 82, 137, 503, 506

**Aquascutum**                    **3N3**
100 Regent St W1. 01-734 6090. Established in 1851, this smart department store on three floors has a large selection of quality men's and women's clothes and accessories. Noted for its own-label high fashions and fashion classics – rainwear, knitwear, tweeds, coats, suits, jackets, town and country casuals. By appointment to HM The Queen Mother who purchases her weatherproof coats here. *Open 09.00–17.30 Mon–Wed, Fri & Sat; 09.00–19.00 Thur. Closed Sun.*
θ Piccadilly Circus
🚌 3, 6, 9, 12, 13, 14, 15, 15B, 19, 22, 22B, 38, 53, 88, 159, 509

**Army & Navy Stores**          **3P3**
105 Victoria St SW1. 01-834 1234. Suppliers to the services in the 1890s. Now a generously stocked

department store with self-service restaurants on the 1st and 2nd floors and a coffee and croissant bar on the ground floor. *Open 09.00 (09.30 Tue)–18.00 Mon–Sat.*
θ St James's Park
🚌 11, 24, 29, 76, 507, 510, C1

**Arsenal Stadium**
Avenell Rd N5. 01-226 0304. HQ and pitch of the famous red and white football club, founded by workers at the Royal Armaments Factory at Woolwich – hence the name.
θ Arsenal
🚌 4, 19, 236

**Artillery Museum**
The Rotunda, Repository Rd, Woolwich Common SE18. 01-854 2242. The Rotunda is a Nash-designed architectural 'tent', which originally stood in the grounds of Carlton House. The guns and muskets contained within it date from the 14thC to the present day. *Open 12.00–17.00 Mon–Fri; 13.00–17.00 Sat & Sun. Closes 16.00 Nov–Mar. Free.*
🚌 53, 54, 75
⇌ Woolwich Arsenal

**Arts Theatre Club**            **3M4**
6 Gt Newport St WC2. 01-836 2132. Opened in 1927 as a club theatre to circumvent the Lord Chamberlain's censorious restrictions. Nowadays the Arts Club itself is separate from the two theatres, one small and one a studio, which offer a variety of plays in the evenings. In the afternoons the Unicorn Theatre puts on children's plays for schools with public matinees on Saturday and Sunday. Restaurant and bar open before performances.
θ Leicester Square
🚌 24, 29, 176

**Asprey's**                      **3N2**
165 New Bond St W1. 01-493 6767. A family firm whose name has come to be associated with quality and high prices. Offers luxury gifts, up-market luggage, elegant jewellery, gold and silverware, some of it made by their own craftsmen. *Open 09.00–17.30 Mon–Fri; 09.00–13.00 Sat.*
θ Green Park
🚌 25

**Baden-Powell House**    **2J4**
Queens Gate SW7. 01-584 7030.
The headquarters of the Scout
movement, guarded by Donald Potter's granite statue of its founder,
General Lord Baden-Powell. Inside
is a permanent exhibition on the
history of the movement and on the
life of B-P himself. Also serves as a
hostel for members of the Scout
and Guide movements. *Open
07.00–23.00 Mon–Sun. Closed
Xmas.*
⊖ South Kensington, Gloucester
Road
🚌 49, 74, C1

**Ball Court**    **4T5**
Next to 39 Cornhill EC3. Straight
out of Dickens. Within the Court
the 18thC Simpson's Chophouse
opens on weekday lunchtimes to
serve olde English food – including
their speciality of stewed cheese.
⊖ Bank
🚌 15B, 25

**Bank of England**    **4S4**
Threadneedle St EC2. 01-601 4444.
The old lady of Threadneedle Street
is the guardian of the nation's gold.
Security naturally precludes casual
visitors, but the messengers and
doormen – in their pink coats, red
waistcoats and top hats – are often
colourfully visible. The outer walls
are still the ones designed by Sir

John Soane, the Bank's architect
from 1788–1833. Visits, by appointment only, must be booked well in
advance.
⊖ Bank
🚌 6, 8, 9, 11, 15B, 21, 22, 22B,
25, 43, 76, 133, 149, 501

**Bankside**    **4T3**
Southwark   SE1.   Southwark's
waterfront, notorious in the 16thC
for its taverns and whorehouses,
bear-baiting rings and playhouses,
has been rebuilt and landscaped
into an attractive riverside walkway, dominated by Sir Giles C.
Scott's monumental electric power
station. Here are: the Bankside
Gallery with its changing exhibitions of the work of contemporary
British painters; the Shakespeare
Globe Museum which echoes the
area in its Elizabethan hey-day;
Rose Alley where the Rose Theatre
stood; and a reconstruction of
Shakespeare's Globe Theatre is
currently underway and due to
open in 1992. There are fine views
across the river to the City and St
Paul's – Wren is said to have lodged
in 49 Park Street and from his windows he could watch the Cathedral
rise.
⊖ Blackfriars
🚌 45, 59, 63, 76, 141, 149, P11

**Banqueting House**    **3O4**
Whitehall   SW1.   01-930  4179.
Splendid survivor of the royal
Palace of Whitehall, principal
London residence of the Court dur-
ing the reign of Henry VIII. The pres-
ent hall, built in 1625 by Inigo
Jones, was the first Palladian build-
ing to be completed in England.
Inside, the ceilings were painted for
Charles I by Peter Paul Rubens.
Outside a tablet marks the window
through which the King stepped to
his execution. *Open 10.00–17.00
Tue–Sat; 14.00–17.00 Sun. Closed
Mon and when in use for Govern-
ment functions.* Charge.
⊖ Charing Cross
🚌 3, 11, 12, 24, 29, 53, 77, 77A,
88, 109, 159, 170, 184

## Barbican Arts Centre          4R4

Barbican EC2. Admin: 01-638 4141. Telephone bookings (inc. credit card bookings): 01-628 8795/01-638 8891. This walled city within the City, notorious for the size and complexity of its design, is the country's largest arts centre, with a wealth of facilities. The Barbican Theatre, reached from levels 3–6, is the home of The Royal Shakespeare Company who also use the small studio theatre, The Pit, on level 1. The Barbican Hall on levels 3 and 6 is the home of the London Symphony Orchestra, and also offers a wide range of musical experiences from guest performers. There is an art gallery and an open-air sculpture court reached from level 8; a cinema on level 1 (and two more on level 9 – one of which is used only for conferences or lectures and the other for films and conferences); a library on level 7, its collection biased towards the arts; The Cut Above restaurant on level 7; the Waterside Café beside an artificial lake with real ducks on level 5; a wine bar called Wine on Six on level 6; and bars and snack bars on levels 1, 3, 5 and 6. The extensive Conservatory, on level 8, is open at weekends only; the large book, stationery and gift shop on level 7, and its smaller counterpart on level 4, are open daily. Also within the complex are the City Business School, The Guildhall School of Music and Drama, St Giles Cripplegate church where Cromwell was married and Milton

is buried. In addition, there are Exhibition Halls reached via a walkway on level 8, and numerous residential apartments. Centre *open 09.00–23.00 Mon–Sat; 12.00–23.00 Sun & Nat Hols.*
⊖ Barbican, Moorgate
🚌 4, 9, 11, 21, 43, 76, 133, 141, 214, 271, 502, 509, 279A

## Bar Crêperie          3M4

21 South Hall, The Market, Covent Garden WC2. 01-836 2137. Captures the busy alfresco flavour of the market perfectly. Eat savoury or sweet crêpes, salads or pastries, at a table with a good view of the varied buskers. Plenty of room inside if it rains. Wine or coffee to drink and a flourishing take-away service. *Open 13.00–24.00 Mon–Sun.*
⊖ Covent Garden
🚌 1, 6, 9, 11, 13, 15, 15B, 77, 77A, 170, 176 (all go to the Strand)

## Barnum's Carnival Novelties          2J1

67 Hammersmith Rd W14. 01-602 1211. A cornucopia of plastic creepy-crawlies, party hats, monster masks, and all the equipment for expressing intemperate joy – hooters, bleepers, rattles and streamers. *Open 09.00–17.30 Mon–Fri; 10.00–16.00 Sat.*
⊖ Kensington Olympia
🚌 9, 10, 27, 28, 33, 91

## Baron of Beef          4S4

Gutter La, off Gresham St EC2. 01-606 6961. Very traditional, vastly popular City restaurant with an all-English ambience. Chief speciality is the roast beef and Yorkshire pudding from the trolley. Lobster, sole, salmon and roast duck are also tempting. Delicious summer pudding served all year round. A fine wine list catering for the connoisseur and everyman. Essential to reserve for lunch. *Open LD Mon–Fri to 21.00. Party bookings evenings & Sat.*
⊖ St Paul's
🚌 4, 8, 22, 22B, 25, 141, 501, 502

## Battersea Arts Centre

Old Town Hall, Lavender Hill SW11. Admin: 01-223 6557. Box office: 01-223 2223. The recently refurbished theatre hosts visiting fringe drama productions, with performances from Wednesday to Sunday evenings. There are occasional arts festivals, weekend arts workshops for adults, and a children's day on Saturday with classes, workshops and suitable live shows. Interesting bookshop and licensed café and bar, too. *Open 10.00–18.00 Mon & Tue; 10.00–23.00 Wed–Sun.*

Ө Vauxhall (then bus 44, 77, 77A, 170), South Kensington (then bus 45, 49, 219)

🚌 19, 35, 37, 39, 44, 45, 49, 77, 77A, 170

### Battersea Park 5Y2

SW11. 01-228 2798. The marshy area, known as Battersea Fields, where the Duke of Wellington and the Earl of Winchelsea once fought a duel, has been stabilised with earth displaced by the building of Victoria Docks. It is now a most attractive 200-acre park with a curvaceous boating lake where waterfowl live, a deer enclosure, a small children's zoo (01-228 9957) with penguins, pygmy goats and pony rides, playing fields, a running track and tennis courts. Sculpture by Henry Moore. Brass and jazz bands play here on summer Sunday afternoons, and the three best known of the many lively events held within it are the Easter Parade, the Historic Vehicles Rally in May, and the South London Carnival in August. *Open dawn–dusk.* Free.

Ө Sloane Square (then bus 137)

🚌 19, 39, 44, 45, 49, 137, 170, 219

🚆 Battersea Park

### Beckton Alps

Corner Alpine Way & Whitings Way E6. 01-511 0351/2. Dry ski slope, with wide views from the top. Tuition and ski hire available, with special rates and hours for members. Après ski refinements include bar, restaurant, shop, sunbeds and fitness room. *Open Apr–Aug 09.00–22.30 Mon–Sun; Sep–Mar 09.00–24.00 Mon–Sun.*

Ө East Ham (then bus 101)

🚌 101, 173

### Beefeater by the Tower of London 4T6

Ivory House, St Katharine's Way

E1. 01-408 1001. Essential to book for the five-course medieval banquets which are served nightly. Jugglers entertain, Henry VIII in full costume proposes the toasts, there are wenches, much roistering and some audience participation. *Open 20.00–23.30 Mon–Sun (unless there's a private function).*

Ө Tower Hill

Docklands Light Railway: Tower Gateway

🚌 15, 42, 78, 510, Sat & Sun 25

### Belfast, HMS 4U5

Symons Wharf, Vine La SE1. 01-407 6434. The largest cruiser ever built for the Royal Navy is most suitably reached by ferry from Tower Pier, or else by gangway from Symons Wharf on the South Bank. She is now a permanent museum and her bridge, engine rooms, gun turrets, decks, galley and sick bay may all be explored. *Open 11.00–17.50 Mon–Sun. Closes 16.30 in winter.* Charge.

Ө London Bridge, Tower Hill (then ferry)

🚌 15, 42, 47, 78, 100, 188, 510, P11, Sat & Sun 25

### Belgravia 3P1

Thomas Cubitt converted a swamp almost level with the Thames and intersected by mud banks into the posh village of Belgravia. Draining the site, he filled the swampy land with gravel from St Katharine's Dock. In 1827 he started on streets, mansions and houses from designs by George Baseri, Disraeli's uncle. Cubitt died in 1856, but his firm then completed Cubitt Town in

Poplar, one of the great industrial parishes on the Thames. Take a stroll around Belgrave Square with its magnificent terraced buildings, or pay a visit to The Grenadier pub in Wilton Row. Once used as a mess by the Duke of Wellington and his officers, it is now a popular place to sit outside in summer beneath the vine.

θ Knightsbridge

🚍 2A, 2B, 9, 10, 14, 16, 19, 22, 25, 30, 36, 38, 52, 52A, 73, 74, 82, 137, 503, 506, C1

### Bendicks                    3P1

195 Sloane St SW1. 01-235 4749. The perfect spot for breakfast, morning coffee, lunch and cream tea with all the trimmings. *Open 08.30–19.00 (to 19.30 Wed) Mon–Sat; 10.30–18.30 Sun.*

θ Knightsbridge

🚍 19, 22, 137, C1

### Bermondsey Antiques Market

Bermondsey Sq SE1. Properly called New Caledonian Market. Deals in antiques and bric-a-brac for the trade, though individuals are welcome. The earlier you arrive the more likely you are to find a bargain. *Open 04.30–13.00 Fri only.*

θ Borough, London Bridge

🚍 1, 42, 78, 188

### Berwick Street Market         3M3

Soho W1. Very lively general market in the heart of Soho. The fruit and vegetables are particularly good quality, and prices reasonable, especially at the southern end of the street. *Open 09.00–18.00 Mon–Sat.*

θ Piccadilly Circus

🚍 3, 6, 7, 8, 9, 10, 14, 15, 15B, 19, 22, 25, 38, 73, 159, 503, 509

### Bethnal Green Museum of Childhood

Cambridge Heath Rd E2. 01-980 2415. An appealing outpost of the Victoria and Albert Museum with much material for those interested in the social history of childhood. Also fascinating for those eager to peer into dozens of minutely equipped dolls' houses, to compare the facial expressions of Victorian with modern Teddy bears, and to marvel at miniature trains, mechanical toys, puppets, theatres and kaleidoscopes. Regular workshops and activities are arranged for young visitors. *Open 10.00–18.00 Mon–Thur & Sat; 14.30–18.00 Sun. Closed Fri. Free.*

θ Bethnal Green

🚍 8, 106, 253

⇌ Cambridge Heath

### Billingsgate                  4T5

Lower Thames St EC3. The famous fish market moved to a new site in the West India docks in 1982, leaving Horace Jones' building of 1875 deserted and in the grip of permafrost from all the ice used over the years to keep the fish scales gleaming. The problem has now been resolved and a new development of offices, shops and restaurants is under construction.

θ Monument

🚍 15, 21, 35, 40, 43, 44, 47, 48, 133, 501, 505, 510, 513

### Billingsgate Wholesale Fish Market

North Quay, West India Docks Rd, Isle of Dogs. 01-987 1118. London's principal fish market, moved from its age-old location in the City, flourishes as ever. Can be wet underfoot and pungent of aroma. *Open from 05.30 Tue–Sat. Closed Sun & Mon.*

θ Mile End (then bus D4)

Docklands Light Railway: Poplar

🚍 D4

### The Blackfriar               4T3

174 Queen Victoria St EC4. 01-236 5650. Wedge-shaped building in the shadows of Blackfriars railway

bridge, with arguably one of the richest and strangest pub interiors in London. The main bar is an Art Nouveau temple of marble with bronze bas-reliefs of friars. The inner bar has an arched mosaic ceiling, red marble columns and more friars, accompanied by demons, fairies and alabaster animals. *Open Mon–Fri. Closes by 22.00 & all Sat & Sun.*

⊖ Blackfriars

🚌 45, 59, 63, 76, 141

### Blackheath
SE3. 01-858 1692. 275 acres of open grassland, used for general recreation and adjoining the attractive Blackheath Village with its old pubs and good bookshop. Ideal for kite-flying and watching the sunset. Good views in all directions, especially from Point Hill in the northwest. Occasionally welcomes a circus or funfair. *Open 24 hours.*

🚌 53, 54, 75, 89, 108

⇌ Blackheath, Maze Hill

### Blooms Restaurant 4S6
90 Whitechapel High St E1. 01-247 6001/377 1120. Bustling Kosher Jewish restaurant dishing up immensely generous portions of kreplech (dumpling) soup, salt beef, gefilte fish and lockshen pudding. Or, try a take-away salt beef sandwich from the counter inside the door. Licensed. *Open LD Sun–Thur, L only Fri. Closed D Fri, all Sat & Jewish Hols.*

⊖ Aldgate East

🚌 5, 15, 15B, 25, 40, 67, 253

### Bloomsbury 3L4
WC1. An area of 18thC terraces and calm leafy squares whose title still conjures up a literary and elegantly Bohemian flavour. Between the wars Virginia Woolf, Vanessa Bell, Duncan Grant and Lytton Strachey amongst others formed 'the Bloomsbury set' in the shadow of the British Museum with, at its heart, the domed reading room where so many influential writers have researched and written – and still do. The Russells, Dukes of Bedford, once owned the area and their various names, including Tavistock and Woburn, still seem to claim it.

⊖ Holborn, Russell Square, Tottenham Court Road

🚌 7, 8, 10, 14, 14A, 19, 22, 22B, 24, 25, 29, 38, 55, 68, 73, 77, 77A, 134, 168, 171, 176, 188, 501, 503, 505

### Boadicea 3O5
Westminster Bridge SW1. Designed by Thornycroft in 1902, this statue shows the ancient British Queen with her daughters in a war chariot.

⊖ Westminster

🚌 12, 53, 77, 109, 170, 184, C1

### The Body Shop 3M3
32 Gt Marlborough St W1. 01-437 5137. Principal shop in a chain of distinctive green shops selling natural skin products, soaps, bath oils and pot pourris. Very environmentfriendly. Inside everything smells as good as it looks. Many branches, some selling pop jewellery, simple toys, gift baskets filled with ownbrand toiletries and all kinds of knick-knacks. *Open 10.00–18.00 Mon–Sat, to 19.00 Thur. Closed Sun.*

⊖ Oxford Circus

🚌 3, 6, 7, 8, 10, 12, 13, 15, 15B, 25, 53, 73, 88, 159, 503, 509, C2

**Bombay Brasserie**　　　**2J4**
140 Gloucester Rd SW7. 01-370
4040. Large, fashionable Indian restaurant, with plants, fans and
wicker chairs. Dishes from several
regions include Bombay thali,
chicken dhansak, Goan fish curry.
Cobra coffee flambé to finish. Reserve table. *Open to 24.00.*
⊖ Gloucester Road
🚌 49, 74

**Bond Street, Old & New**　　**3M2**
W1. The 17thC financier, Thomas
Bond, built Old – New was added
as a continuation around 1721.
Fashionable and expensive shop-
ping street for good clothes, furs,
Persian rugs, jewellery, pictures
and prints. On the second floor of
the Time-Life building at 153 is a
little-noticed frieze by Henry Moore
– Time-Life Screen.
⊖ Green Park (for Old Bond
Street)
🚌 9, 14, 19, 22, 25, 38 (for Old
Bond Street)
⊖ Bond Street (for New Bond
Street)
🚌 6, 7, 8, 10, 12, 13, 15, 16A, 25,
73, 88, 113, 135, 137, 159, 503
(for New Bond Street)

**W. & F. C. Bonham &**　　**2H6**
**Sons**
Montpelier Galleries, Montpelier St
SW7. 01-584 9161. Fine art auctioneers dealing in oils and water-
colours, prints, books, clocks,
silver, porcelain, furniture, jewellery, carved frames and decorative
arts. Enquire about the occasional
evening 'theme' auctions – marine
pictures to coincide with the Boat
Show and Cowes Week, for example – and about the sales of veteran and vintage cars and auto-
mobilia out at Syon Park in
Brentford. *Open　08.45–20.00
Mon;　08.45–18.00　Tue–Fri;
14.30–17.00 Sun. Closed Sat.*
⊖ Knightsbridge
🚌 9, 10, 14, 19, 22, 30, 52, 52A,
74, 137, 503, C1

**Bonham's Chelsea Galleries**
65–69 Lots Rd SW10. 01-352
0466. Sales of antique reproduction
and contemporary furniture, carpets and rugs, toys, mechanical
music, and the middle price ranges
of prints, ceramics and books. Enquire for sale times and also for

times of the regular Beginners Collectors Sales. *Open　08.45–19.00
Mon;　08.45–17.00　Tue–Fri;
10.30–13.00 Sat. Closed Sun.*
⊖ Sloane Square (then bus 11, 22)
🚌 11, 22

**Boosey & Hawkes**　　**3M2**
295 Regent St W1. 01-580 2060.
Music publishers with a well-
stocked shop at the end of a
corridor behind an unassuming
frontage. Books, teach-yourself
manuals, sheet music – even gift-
wrap with a musical motif. Advice
available for professional musicians. Useful stock of leaflets on
current musical events in the front
hall. *Open　09.00–17.00 Mon–Fri;
09.00–13.00 Sat.*
⊖ Oxford Circus
🚌 3, 6, 7, 8, 10, 12, 13, 15, 15B,
16A, 25, 53, 73, 88, 113, 135, 137,
159, 176, 503, 509, C2

**Brass Rubbing Centre**　　**3N3**
St Martin-in-the-Fields, Trafalgar Sq
W1. 01-437 6023. Here are replicas
of 70 British and European brasses,
instructions on how to take a rubbing and the necessary materials. A
small monumental animal comes
cheaper than a large crusading
knight. *Open　10.00–18.00 Mon–
Sat; 12.00–18.00 Sun. Charge.*
⊖ Charing Cross
🚌 1, 3, 6, 9, 11, 12, 13, 15, 15B,
22B, 24, 29, 53, 77, 77A, 88, 109,
159, 170, 176, 184, 509

**Brent Cross Shopping Centre**
Brent Cross NW4. 01-202 8092.
Large and successful shopping
centre with well-stocked branches
of numerous reliable High Street
shops – among them John Lewis,
Mothercare, C & A, Fenwicks,
Waitrose, Our Price. Also several
cafés, restaurants and a wine bar.
*Open　10.00–20.00　Mon–Fri;
10.00–18.00 Sat.*
⊖ Brent Cross
🚌 16A, 26, 112, 113, 142, 143,
172, 182, 186, 226, C11

**Britannia Leisure Centre**
40 Hyde Rd N1. 01-729 4485. Large
indoor sports centre. Squash, badminton, weight-training, table
tennis, basketball, volleyball, martial
arts, swimming pool with wave
machine and waterfall, sauna, sunbed, spa bath. Also tennis courts

(some grass), and five-a-side pitches, all floodlit. Tuition in most activities, over-50s classes, activities for the disabled, clubs for children and adults. No membership requirement.
θ Old Street
🚌 76, 141, 271

**British Film Institute**  *3L3*
21 Stephen St W1. 01-255 1444. The national archive, an extensive collection of over 20,000 films, 750,000 original stills, 19,000 books and scripts. *Open 10.00–17.00 Mon–Fri.* Membership necessary.
θ Tottenham Court Road
🚌 7, 8, 10, 14, 14A, 19, 22, 22B, 24, 25, 29, 38, 55, 73, 134, 176, 503

**British Museum**  *3L4*
Gt Russell St WC1. 01-636 1555. The imposing building by Sir Robert Smirke, which went up in 1823–47, houses one of the largest and greatest collections in the world. Its treasures are so rich and varied that no one should even attempt to see them all in a single visit. Here are Babylonian, Greek, Etruscan, Roman, British, Oriental and Asian antiquities – prehistoric, medieval and later. Here are prints, drawings, maps, coins, medals, sarcophagi, papyri, jewellery, vases, domestic utensils and royal accoutrements. Among the most dramatic and famous of the many priceless exhibits are the Elgin marbles, the Egyptian mummies, the mighty Assyrian bulls and lions, the Rosetta Stone, Magna Carta and the Sutton Hoo Ship Burial. There are tours of the circular domed reading room on the hour from 11.00–16.00 and regular lectures, film shows, gallery talks and special exhibitions. Good cafeteria, too. *Open 10.00–17.00 Mon–Sat; 14.30–18.00 Sun. Free.*
θ Tottenham Court Road, Russell Square
🚌 7, 8, 10, 14, 14A, 19, 22, 22B, 24, 25, 29, 38, 55, 68, 73, 77, 77A, 134, 168, 171, 176, 188, 501, 503, 505

**British Piano & Musical Museum**
368 High St, Brentford, Middx. 01-560 8108. The finest collection of reproducing piano systems and reproducing pipe organs in Europe, all under one roof in a 100-year-old church. Also orchestrions, orchestrelles, player pianos, music boxes and a giant Wurlitzer. The 90-minute guided tour includes performances by most of them. There are evening concerts, too, send s.a.e. for details. *Open Apr–Oct 14.00–17.00 Sat & Sun. Closed weekdays, Nat Hols & winter.* Donation welcome.
θ South Ealing (then bus 65), Gunnersbury (then bus 237, 267)
🚌 65, 237, 267
🚆 Kew Bridge

**British Rail Collector's Corner**  *1C5*
Cobourg St NW1. 01-922 6436. If driven by an urge to possess an obsolete British Railways name plate, a hand lamp, signal, station clock or railman's hat, this is the place to go. It's a little hard to find but the enthusiasts manage. *Open 09.00–17.00 Mon–Fri; 09.00–16.30 Sat. Closed Sun & lunchtimes. (Times subject to alteration without notice.)*
θ Euston
🚌 10, 14, 14A, 18, 30, 68, 73, 77, 77A, 168, 188

**British Telecom Tower**  *3L3*
Howland St W1. Built by the Ministry of Public Building & Works in 1966, the Tower (formerly known as the Post Office Tower) is a dramatic landmark. It is 580ft (176.9m) high and houses telecommunications equipment and offices. The revolving restaurant used to pro-

vide a spectacular panorama of London but is now closed.
θ Goode Street, Warren Street
🚌 10, 14, 14A, 18, 24, 27, 29, 30, 73, 134, 135, 253

### British Travel Centre   3N3
Rex House, 4–12 Lower Regent St SW1. 01-730 3400. New home of the British Tourist Authority Information Centre, incorporating the American Express Travel Service Office, British Rail ticket office and a bureau de change. Details on where to go throughout the UK. Book a room, coach trip or theatre ticket, buy plane or train tickets, hire cars – all under one roof. Also exhibitions, videos, travel bookshop and gifts. *Open 09.00–18.30 Mon–Sat; 10.00–16.00 Sun.*
θ Piccadilly Circus
🚌 3, 6, 9, 12, 13, 14, 15, 15B, 19, 22, 22B, 38, 53, 88, 159, 509

### Brixton Market
Brixton Station Rd SW9, and all around. Large and exuberant general market with a strong West Indian flavour, further enlivened by loud reggae music. *Open 08.00–18.00 Mon–Sat. Closed Wed afternoon & Sun.*
θ Brixton
🚌 2, 2A, 2B, 3, 3A, 35, 37, 45, 59, 60, 95, 109, 133, 159, 196, 250, P4

### Brixton Windmill
Blenheim Gdns, Brixton Hill SW9. 01-673 5398. An early 19thC tower mill which was in use until 1934. It was closed for some years, but has now been refurbished in order to grind corn once more, though using a 40-year-old motor rather than its sails. *Open 09.30–2 hrs before dusk Mon–Sun. Free.*
θ Brixton (then bus)
🚌 59, 60, 95, 109, 133, 159, 250

### Broadcasting House   3L2
Langham Pl W1. 01-580 4468. The HQ of BBC radio, compared by some to a beached ocean liner. Much drama is now based at the Maida Vale Studios because the vibrations from the Bakerloo line, which pass underneath here, threaten to get in on the act.
θ Oxford Circus
🚌 3, 6, 7, 8, 10, 12, 13, 15, 15B, 16A, 25, 53, 73, 88, 113, 135, 137, 159, 176, 503, 509, C2

### Brompton Cemetery   2K3
Old Brompton Rd or Fulham Rd SW6. Spreading Victorian necropolis crowded with ornate tombs and ranks of tall gravestones. The stands of Chelsea football ground loom over the wall in a nice juxtaposition of the quick and the dead. The domed chapel is no longer open but its flanking WCs are. Gates close at dusk – and just as well. *Open 08.00–dusk Mon–Sun. Free.*
θ West Brompton (Mon–Fri), Earl's Court (Sat & Sun)
🚌 30, 31, 74, C3

### Brompton Hospital   2J5
Fulham Rd SW3. 01-352 8121. Founded in 1842 to care for the victims of consumption and still specialising in diseases of the chest and heart.
θ South Kensington
🚌 14, 45

### Brompton Oratory   2H6
Brompton Rd SW7. Actually 'the church of the London Oratory'; the Oratorians are a community of priests who follow the teachings of the Florentine St Philip Neri and were introduced to Britain by Frederick William Faber and by Cardinal Newman whose marble statue stands outside the priests' house next door. The church is Italianate Roman Catholic, with a baroque marbled interior, designed by Herbert Cribble in 1878. Some of the fine statues come from the Cathedral of Siena. *Open daylight hours – please respect services.* Donation welcome.
θ South Kensington
🚌 14, 30, 74, 503, C1

### Brown's
Albemarle St W1. 01-493 6020. Take tea in this sumptuous hotel in a very English, country house setting. They serve sandwiches, cakes and tarts from *15.00–18.00 Mon–Sun.*
θ Green Park
🚌 9, 14, 19, 22, 38

### Buckingham Palace   3O3
SW1. The Sovereign's London residence. Built in 1705 as the Duke of Buckingham's house, remodelled into a palace by Nash in 1830, refaced by Sir Aston Webb in 1913.

Its 40 acres of grounds are the setting for prestigious summer garden parties – by invitation only. The military pomp and pageantry of the changing of the guard starts daily at *11.30* (alternate days in winter). The Royal Standard flies to proclaim the royal presence.
θ Green Park, Victoria, Hyde Park Corner
🚌 2, 2A, 2B, 9, 10, 11, 14, 16, 19, 22, 24, 25, 29, 30, 36, 36A, 36B, 38, 39, 52, 52A, 73, 74, 76, 82, 137, 185, 503, 506, 507, 510, C1

**Bull's Head Pub**
373 Lonsdale Rd SW13. 01-876 5241. Large Victorian building overlooking the Thames where top international jazz musicians play nightly and Sunday lunchtimes. Carvery and snack bar in the pub itself, and the Stable Restaurant offers traditional English food in the evenings and Sunday lunchtimes. Pub *open L & D Mon–Sun;* Restaurant *open D Mon–Sat & L Sun.*
θ Hammersmith (then bus 9)
🚌 9
🚉 Barnes Bridge

**Bunhill Fields Burial      4R4
Ground**
City Rd EC1. Originally Bonehill Fields, by the 17thC it was known

as The Dissenters' Burial Ground. Among those interred here are John Bunyan and Daniel Defoe
*Open 09.00–16.00 Mon–Sun.*
θ Old Street
🚌 43, 76, 141, 214, 271

**Burberrys      3N4**
18 Haymarket SW1. 01-930 3343. Shop famous for classic raincoats, cut in English style, for men and women. Also stocks suits and accessories such as hats and scarves. *Open 09.00–17.30 Mon–Sat; until 19.00 Thur.*
θ Piccadilly Circus
🚌 3, 6, 9, 12, 13, 14, 15, 15B, 19, 22, 22B, 38, 53, 88, 159, 509

**Burberrys      3M3**
165 Regent St W1. 01-734 4060. Classic clothes and accessories. *Open 09.00–17.30 Mon–Sat; until 19.00 Thur.*
θ Oxford Circus
🚌 3, 6, 12, 13, 15, 15B, 53, 88, 159, 509, C2

**Burlington Arcade      3N3**
Off Piccadilly W1. Charming and elegant Regency shopping arcade, with original windows, mostly full of jewellery and cashmere. You may not run, sing or whistle here, and there is a uniformed beadle to see that you don't and to lock the gates when the shops close. *Open 08.30–17.30 Mon–Sat. Closed Sun.*
θ Piccadilly Circus
🚌 3, 6, 9, 12, 13, 14, 15, 15B, 19, 22, 22B, 38, 53, 88, 159, 509

**Bush Theatre**
Bush Hotel, Shepherd's Bush Green W12. 01-743 3388. Well-known fringe theatre, its curtain-less stage and raked seating occupying the floor above the busy pub. Originally established to attract the non-theatre-going public, its new productions now often transfer to the West End. *Performances Tue–Sun.*
θ Shepherd's Bush
🚌 11, 12, 49, 72, 88, 105, 207, 220, 237, 260, 283, 295

## Cabinet War Rooms   *3O4*

Clive Steps, King Charles St SW1. 01-930 6961. The secret war-time HQ of Churchill's Cabinet now open to the public. The six-acre labyrinth of corridors and rooms underneath the heart of government Whitehall are fully equipped with genuine war-time furniture and fittings. *Open 10.00–17.50 Tue–Sun. Closed Mon & Nat Hols.* Charge.
⊖ Charing Cross, Westminster
🚌 3, 11, 12, 24, 29, 53, 77, 77A, 88, 109, 159, 170, 184, C1

## Café du Commerce

Business Efficiency Centre, 3 Lime-harbour E14. 01-538 2030. Busy, glossy venue in which to enjoy business breakfasts (newspapers provided) and light but elegant lunches. London Yard, at the same address, serves lavish dinners to the soft sounds of a string quartet. Wise to book for both. Café *open 08.00–17.00 Mon–Fri;* London Yard *open 19.00–23.00 Mon–Fri.* Docklands Light Railway: Crossharbour
🚌 D5, D6, P14

## Café Royal   *3N3*

68 Regent St W1. Grill Room 01-439 6320. The lush, plush rococo Grill Room has been refurbished to echo the days when Rex Whistler, Oscar Wilde and Aubrey Beardsley were regulars. Formal service, elaborate English and French dishes, a remarkable wine cellar. There is also a Bar and Brasserie for lighter eating and the pleasant Daniel's Wine Bar. Grill *open LD Mon–Fri; D Sat;* Brasserie *open 12.00–24.00 Mon–Sat;* Wine Bar *open 10.00–14.30 & 18.00–23.30 Mon–Fri, 18.00–23.30 Sat.*
⊖ Piccadilly Circus
🚌 3, 6, 9, 12, 13, 14, 15, 15B, 19, 22, 22B, 38, 53, 88, 159, 509

## Camden Lock   *1A3*

Where Chalk Farm Rd crosses Regent's Canal, NW1. The lock itself is pretty – attractive canalside walks go in either direction and art and craft shops surround a cobbled courtyard. At weekends an itinerant market flourishes with stalls crammed with antiques, junk and bric-a-brac. The market has a food stand by the entrance – and here too is Dingwalls lively music club.
⊖ Camden Town, Chalk Farm
🚌 24, 31, 68, 168

## Camden Palace

1a Camden High St NW1. 01-387 1428. Spacious and lively disco which attracts the young and trendy and has different theme nights, so find out what the theme is before turning up! *Open to 02.30 Tue–Sat & Sun.*
⊖ Mornington Crescent (closed Sat & Sun)
🚌 24, 27, 29, 68, 134, 135, 168, 214, 253

## Camden Passage

Islington High St N1. Puts Islington on the tourist map. A narrow paved street lined with small antique shops, both general and specialist, with unexpected arcades opening off it filled with yet more treasures. There are silver, lace, furniture, prints, fob watches, snuff and snuff boxes, porcelain, militaria, maps, jewellery and more. Market stalls reinforce the shops on Wednesday morning and all Saturday, and on Thursday and Friday second-hand book stalls take over. There are some good restaurants here, too. *Open 09.00–18.00 Mon–Sat. Market stalls 08.00–16.00 Wed & Sat; 09.00–17.00 Thur & Fri.*

θ Angel

🚌 4, 19, 30, 38, 43, 73, 153, 171, 171A, 214, 263A, 277, 279, 279A

### Canary Wharf

Isle of Dogs E14. Currently a vast building site as the largest commercial development in Western Europe rises around the quay which once docked ships from the Canary Islands.

Docklands Light Railway: West India Quay, Heron Quays

🚌 D5

### Cannon Cinema (1,2)  3M4

135 Shaftesbury Av W1. 01-836 8861. Current releases.

θ Leicester Square

🚌 14, 19, 22, 22B, 24, 29, 38, 176

### Cannon Cinema  3L1
### Baker Street

Station Approach, Marylebone Rd NW1. 01-935 9772. Modern cinema with two screens adjacent to Baker Street tube station. New releases, long runs and adult movies. *Late shows Fri & Sat.*

θ Baker Street

🚌 2A, 2B, 13, 18, 27, 30, 74, 82, 113, 159

### Cannon Cinema Bayswater

98 Bishop's Bridge Rd W2. 01-229 4149. Three screens. Long-running films and new releases. *Late shows Fri & Sat.*

θ Royal Oak, Paddington

🚌 7, 15, 27, 36

### Cannon Cinema Chelsea  5X2

279 King's Rd SW3. 01-352 5096. Four screens showing new releases.

θ Sloane Square

🚌 11, 19, 22, 49, 219

### Cannon Cinema Fulham Rd

Fulham Rd SW10. 01-370 2636. Five screens. Current releases.

θ South Kensington (then bus 14, 45)

🚌 14, 45

### Cannon Cinema Hampstead

Pond St NW3. 01-794 4400. Three screens showing new releases. *Late shows Fri & Sat.*

θ Belsize Park

🚌 24, 46, 168, 268, C11

🚉 Hampstead Heath

### Cannon Cinema  3N4
### Haymarket

Haymarket SW1. 01-839 1527. Three screens showing long-running releases and new releases. *Late shows Fri & Sat.*

θ Piccadilly Circus

🚌 3, 6, 9, 12, 13, 14, 15, 15B, 19, 22, 22B, 38, 53, 88, 159, 509

### Cannon Cinema  3M3
### Oxford Street

Oxford St W1. 01-636 0310. Five screens showing general releases. *Late shows Fri & Sat.*

θ Oxford Circus, Tottenham Court Road

🚌 3, 6, 7, 8, 10, 12, 13, 15, 15B, 16A, 25, 53, 73, 88, 113, 135, 137, 159, 176, 503, 509, C2

### Cannon Cinema  3N4
### Panton Street

Panton St SW1. 01-930 0631. Four small cinemas under one roof showing very new releases.

θ Piccadilly Circus

🚌 3, 6, 9, 12, 13, 14, 15, 15B, 19, 22, 22B, 38, 53, 88, 159, 509

### Cannon Cinema  3N3
### Piccadilly

215–217 Piccadilly W1. 01-437

3561. Two screens. Popular releases. *Late shows Fri & Sat.*
⊖ Piccadilly Circus
🚌 3, 6, 9, 12, 13, 14, 15, 15B, 19,
22, 22B, 38, 53, 88, 159, 509

**Cannon Cinema**          **3M4**
**Tottenham Court Rd**
Tottenham Court Rd W1. 01-636
6148. Three screens. New releases
and long-runners. *Late shows Fri &
Sat.*
⊖ Tottenham Court Road
🚌 7, 8, 10, 14, 14A, 19, 22, 22B,
24, 25, 29, 38, 55, 73, 134, 176,
503

**Cannon Premiere Cinema   3N4**
Swiss Centre, Leicester Sq WC2.
01-439 4470. New releases in this
complex of four cinemas. *Late
shows Fri & Sat.*
⊖ Leicester Square, Piccadilly
Circus
🚌 3, 6, 9, 11, 12, 13, 14, 15, 15B,
19, 22, 22B, 24, 29, 38, 53, 88,
159, 176, 509

**Cannon Royal Cinema     3N4**
35–37 Charing Cross Rd WC2.
01-930 6915. Long-running British
and American releases. *Late shows
Fri & Sat.*
⊖ Leicester Square
🚌 24, 29, 176

**Cannon Street Station    4T4**
Cannon St EC4. Information on
01-928 5100. Rebuilt in 1965, with
office accommodation above, the
station serves the south-east London suburbs, Kent and East
Sussex. *Station closed Sat & Sun.*
⊖ Cannon Street (Mon–Fri only)
🚌 6, 9, 11, 15, 15B, 17, 21, 43,
76, 95, 133, 149, 501, 513
🚆 Cannon Street (Mon–Fri only)

**Canonbury Tower**
Canonbury Pl N1. 01-226 5111.
Just round the corner from one of
London's most beautiful squares is
this 16thC building with a romantic
history of an elopement, a father's
wrath and the timely intervention of
Queen Elizabeth I. It has recently
been taken over by a Trust, which is
refurbishing it and will conduct
regular tours (tea by arrangement)
and which also hires out the rooms
for small functions. Telephone for
details. The bottom of the Tower is
the HQ of the Tavistock Repertory

Company which puts on eighteen
shows a year – a mixture of musicals and modern drama with the
occasional Shakespeare. Book on
01-226 5111.
⊖ Highbury and Islington
🚌 4, 19, 30, 38, 43, 73, 171A,
263A, 271, 277, 279, 279A

**Carlyle's House**          **5Y1**
24 Cheyne Row SW3. 01-352 7087.
Thomas Carlyle, formidable 'sage
of Chelsea' and author of – among
other works – 'The History of the
French Revolution', lived here with
his wife Jane from 1834 until their
respective deaths. The interior of
their modest 18thC house has been
so successfully preserved that
there is an eerie sense of his im-
minence. His desk, books, manuscripts and letters are in the skylit
attic study, built as a haven from
distracting sounds but a failure,
since it had the curious effect of
magnifying them. *Open 11.00–
17.00 Wed–Sat; 14.00–17.00 Sun.
Closed Mon, Tue & Nov–Mar.*
Charge.
⊖ South Kensington (then bus 45,
49, 219)
🚌 39 (direct), or 11, 22 to King's
Road or 19, 45, 49, 219 to Cheyne
Walk

**Carnaby Street**          **3M3**
W1. A paved pedestrian precinct of
boutiques, Indian emporia and nov-
elty shops thrumming with taped
light rock and packed with young
tourists. The sign from Regent
Street shows a couple from the
Swinging Sixties – but the street
has moved with the times. Still
lively, though with a more
aggressive 80s flavour.
⊖ Oxford Circus
🚌 3, 6, 7, 8, 10, 12, 13, 15, 15B,
16A, 25, 53, 73, 88, 113, 135, 137,
159, 176, 503, 509, C2

**Cartier**                 **3M2**
175 New Bond St W1. 01-493
6962. Top class internationally
famous jeweller and goldsmith – by
appointment to HM the Queen and
to the Queen Mother. *Open 09.30–
17.30 Mon–Fri; 10.00–16.00 Sat.*
⊖ Bond Street
🚌 25

**Cecil Court**             **3M4**
W1. Pedestrian precinct lined with

specialist and antiquarian book and print shops, linking St Martin's Lane with Charing Cross Road.

θ Leicester Square
▦ 24, 29, 176

### The Cenotaph 304
Whitehall SW1. Sir Edwin Lutyen's movingly simple memorial to the dead of two World Wars. The annual Service of Remembrance takes place here in November.

θ Westminster
▦ 3, 11, 12, 24, 29, 53, 77, 77A, 88, 109, 159, 170, 184, C1

### Central Music Library
160 Buckingham Palace Rd SW1. 01-798 2192. (Westminster City Libraries). Books on music, music scores and parts, music periodicals. *Open 09.30–19.00 Mon–Fri, 09.30–17.00 Sat.* Free.

θ Victoria
▦ 11, 39, C1

### Charbonnel et Walker 3N3
28 Old Bond St W1. 01-629 4396. Founded by Mlle Charbonnel in 1874 and still producing luscious hand-made chocolates presented in beautiful boxes. By appointment to HM the Queen. *Open 09.00–17.30 Mon–Fri; 10.00–16.00 Sat.*

θ Green Park, Piccadilly Circus
▦ 9, 14, 19, 22, 25, 38

### Charing Cross Hotel 3N5
Strand WC2. 01-839 7282. The Bet-

jeman Carvery is open for lunch and dinner every day. Help yourself to traditional British beef, lamb and pork with all that goes with them – Yorkshire pudding and roast potatoes for example. *Open LD Mon–Sun.*

θ Charing Cross, Embankment
▦ 1, 3, 6, 9, 11, 12, 13, 15, 15B, 22B, 24, 29, 53, 77, 77A, 88, 109, 159, 170, 176, 184, 509
⇌ Charing Cross

### Charing Cross Road 3M4
### & Bloomsbury
W1. Charing Cross Road is an excellent hunting ground for books, new and second hand, specialised and popular. Further north in Bloomsbury there are more, including the University (and general) bookstore, Dillons, and several specialist print and map shops.

θ Charing Cross, Leicester Square
▦ 24, 29, 176

### Charing Cross Station 3N5
Strand WC2. Information on 01-928 5100. Built in 1864 to serve the south-east London suburbs and Kent. The cross itself, in the station forecourt, is a replica of the last of the 'Eleanor crosses', set up by Edward I to mark the resting places of his Queen's cortège as it journeyed from Nottingham to Westminster Abbey.

θ Charing Cross, Embankment
▦ 1, 3, 6, 9, 11, 12, 13, 15, 15B, 22B, 24, 29, 53, 77, 77A, 88, 109, 159, 170, 176, 184, 509
⇌ Charing Cross

### Charlton House
Charlton Rd SE7. 01-856 3951. Perfect small red brick Jacobean manor house built 1607–12, with fine ceilings and staircase and some bizarre chimney pieces. Now occupied by an active Community Centre whose staff will conduct a tour when circumstances permit – lunchtime or between *16.00* and *18.00* are usually best. Telephone manager for appointment.

▦ 53, 54, 75
⇌ Charlton

### Chartered Insurance 4S4
### Institute Museum
20 Aldermanbury EC2. 01-606 3835. In the days before the Fire Brigade the insurance companies

did the job – but each would only douse flames on a building bearing its own fire mark. Here you may inspect these marks and the fire-fighting equipment used on the property they protected. Parties should give advance warning – there is very little space! *Open 09.15–17.00 Mon–Fri. Closed Sat, Sun & Nat Hols. Free.*

&#x398; Bank

&#x2709; 4, 8, 22, 22B, 25, 141, 501, 502, 509

## Charterhouse    4R3

Charterhouse Sq EC1. 01-253 9503. Originally a Carthusian monastery, then a private mansion, endowed as a school in 1611. The school moved to Surrey in 1872, and Charterhouse is now a residential home for retired gentlemen. Among the impressive rooms are the Elizabethan Dining Hall with hammerbeam roof and the magnificent Great Chamber. *Open Apr–Jul 14.45 Wed. Guided tours only.* Groups should book. Charge.

&#x398; Barbican

&#x2709; 4, 279, 279A, 509

## Chelsea Barracks    5X3

Chelsea Bridge Rd SW3. Sleek early 60s building which is one of the homes of the Coldstream, Grenadier, Scots and Welsh Guards. Some weekdays they parade at *10.20* and leave at *10.55* to relieve the Guard at Buckingham Palace. On other days and at weekends they leave from Wellington Barracks at *11.00.* The National Tourist Information Centre, (telephone 01-730 3488), has details of their movements.

&#x398; Sloane Square

&#x2709; 11, 39, 137

## Chelsea Bridge    5Y3

SW3. Seven hundred feet of handsome suspension bridge linking Chelsea with Battersea Park. It was rebuilt in the 1930s, 60 years after Albert Bridge, and is regularly repainted to enliven its distinctive structure.

&#x398; Sloane Square (then bus 137)

&#x2709; 137

## Chelsea Cinema

King's Rd SW3. 01-351 3742. Good films, spacious seating.

&#x398; Sloane Square

&#x2709; 11, 19, 22

## Chelsea Old Church, All Saints    5Y1

Chelsea Embankment SW3. The modern brick exterior comes as a shock – the church was bombed in 1941 and restored in the 50s – but inside it is rich in evocative memorials; the 17thC Sara Colville rises in her shroud, Lord and Lady Dacre are commemorated in baroque splendour, there are wall plaques to Henry James and William de Morgan. The chapel, which was built by Sir Thomas More in 1528, incorporated a 14thC archway.

&#x398; South Kensington (then bus 45, 49, 219)

&#x2709; 19, 39, 45, 49, 219

## Chelsea Old Town Hall    5X1

King's Rd SW3. 01-352 1856. The venue for the Chelsea Antiques Fair in March and September and the Chelsea Arts Society and Craftsmen's Fair in October. Also houses the Registrar's offices, Citizens Advice Bureau, Information Office, an indoor swimming pool and sports centre, and the local library. The attractive building was put up in the 1880s by John Brydon, its Ionic façade added in 1908 by Leonard Stokes.

&#x398; Sloane Square (then bus)

&#x2709; 11, 19, 22, 49

## Chelsea Physic Garden    5Y2

Royal Hospital Rd SW3. 01-352 5646. This is the second oldest Botanical Garden in the UK – only the one at Oxford is older. It was founded by the Society of Apothecaries in 1673. Plants are grown for research and teaching purposes and seeds exchanged on a world-wide scale. It also houses an extensive collection of culinary and medicinal herbs and the largest olive tree in Britain. *Open Apr–Oct 14.00–17.00 Wed & Sun or by appointment.* Charge.

⊖ Sloane Square

🚌 39

### Chelsea Royal Hospital 5X2

Royal Hospital Rd SW3. 01-730 0161. Unique retirement home founded by Charles II for aged and infirm soldiers – the 'Chelsea Pensioners' – whose scarlet frock coats and black tricorns dazzle summer visitors. The building of 1682 is by Wren, the stables and small museum of 1814–17 are by Sir John Soane. The pleasant grounds hold the famous massed blooms of the Chelsea Flower Show each May. *Open 10.00–12.00 & 14.15–16.00 Mon–Fri; 14.00–16.00 Sun. Closed Sat.* Free.

⊖ Sloane Square

🚌 11, 39, 137

### Cheshire Cheese, Ye Olde 4S2

145 Fleet St EC4. 01-353 6170. Rambling, low ceiling'd and atmospheric old inn with three smallish bars and three small restaurants, all with oak tables and sawdusted floor. The 14thC crypt of Whitefriars Monastery, still intact beneath the cellar bar, is hired out for parties. Famous for good, rich game puddings in autumn and winter. *Open 11.00–15.00 & 17.00–23.00 Mon–Sat. Closed Sun.*

⊖ Blackfriars

🚌 4, 6, 9, 11, 15, 15B, 171A, 502, 509, 513

### Chessington World of Adventures

Leatherhead Rd, Chessington, Surrey. 03727 27227. Sixty-five acres of zoo on the outskirts of London. Spectacular family rides set in specially designed areas – The Mystic East, Circus World, Calamity Canyon, The Fifth Dimension. A monorail travels overhead giving a marvellous view of the children's zoo, the bird garden and the polar bear plunge. *Open Apr–Oct 10.00–18.00 Mon–Sun.* Zoological gardens only *open* (at reduced price) *Oct–Apr 10.00–17.00 Mon–Sun. Closed Xmas day.* Charge.

⊖ Richmond (then bus 71)

🚌 71, Summer Suns only 72

🚉 Chessington South

### Cheyne Walk 5Y1

SW3. This picturesque riverside road with its appealing Georgian houses and ferocious modern traffic is part of the heart of old Chelsea. Great names keep its magic alive. George Eliot died at No 4, Rossetti and Swinburne lived at No 16, Whistler worked his way through 21, 96 and 101, Mrs Gaskell was born at 93 and Turner spent his later years at 119.

⊖ South Kensington (then bus 45, 49, 219)

🚌 19, 39, 45, 49, 219

### Chicago Pizza Pie Factory 3M2

17 Hanover Sq W1. 01-629 2669. Eat American deep-pan pizzas surrounded by Chicago paraphernalia including tapes of the local radio station and US football videos flown in weekly. *Open to 23.30 (Sun to 22.30).* No credit cards.

⊖ Oxford Circus

🚌 3, 6, 7, 8, 10, 12, 13, 15, 15B, 16A, 25, 53, 73, 88, 113, 135, 137, 159, 176, 503, 509, C2

### Chinatown    3N4

Soho W1. Chinatown lies in the southern part of Soho, in the angle formed by Charing Cross Road and Shaftesbury Avenue, with its heart in Gerrard Street and Newport Place. The area, which is home to a thriving Chinese community, is benefiting from the slow but steady facelift programme covering the whole of Soho, and its latest acquisition is the authentic Chinese Pavilion in Newport Place, created by Chinese builders from materials brought over from China. Here you will find the densest concentration of Chinese restaurants in London, as well as shops selling Chinese foods, arts and crafts, and here Chinese New Year is celebrated, usually in February, in customary manner, with dancing lions and a huge paper dragon.
⊖ Leicester Square, Tottenham Court Road
🚌 14, 19, 22, 22B, 24, 29, 38, 176

### Chiswick House

Burlington La W4. 01-995 0508. A lovely Palladian villa, designed in 1725–9 by the third Earl of Burlington as a gallery where fine pictures were hung and artists and writers entertained. The attractive grounds with canals, orangery and Italian garden, and the almost baroque splendour of the interior, were all designed by William Kent, who used perspective painting to great effect on the inside of the dome of the central salon making it appear higher than it actually is. Pleasant garden cafeteria. *Open 09.30– 18.00 (16.00 in winter) Mon–Sat; 14.00–16.00 Sun.* Charge.
⊖ Hammersmith (then bus 290)
🚌 290, E3
🚉 Chiswick

### Chiswick Mall

W4. The name 'Chiswick' is said to derive from 'cheese farm'. No farms now, just lovely 17th and 18thC riverside houses between Strand-on-the-Green near Kew Bridge and Hammersmith Bridge. An extremely pleasant walk punctuated by excellent old riverside hostelries.
⊖ Hammersmith (then bus 290)
🚌 290

### Christie, Manson & Woods    3N3

8 King St, St James's SW1. 01-839 9060. Internationally famous and fully comprehensive fine art auctioneers in whose premises works of art and large sums of money have changed hands since 1766. Sales generally begin at *11.00* and continue after lunch. *Open 09.00– 16.45 Mon–Fri. Closed Sat & Sun.*
⊖ Green Park
🚌 9, 14, 19, 22, 25, 38

### Christie's South Kensington    2J5

58 Old Brompton Rd SW7. 01-581 2231. A less expensive younger brother of the St James's branch, dealing in paintings and furniture, toys, cars, jewellery, wine and furs. *Open 09.00–19.00 Mon & Wed; 09.00–17.00 Tue, Thur & Fri. Closed Sat & Sun.*
⊖ South Kensington
🚌 14, 30, 45, 49, 219

### City Airport

Gate 20, King George V Dock, Connaught Rd E16. General flight info: 01-474 5555. The 50-seater de Havilland Dash-7 aircraft of Brymon Airways and Eurocity Express ferry passengers to and from destinations on the Continent and in the UK. Also has a Brasserie and a Business Centre.
🚌 276
🚉 Silvertown

### Clarence House    3O3

Stable Yard SW1. Built by Nash in 1825 for the Duke of Clarence who

later became William IV, and now the London residence of Queen Elizabeth the Queen Mother. On 4th August, her birthday, a lone piper plays on the lawn outside. Not open to the public.
θ Green Park, St James's Park
🚌 9, 14, 19, 22, 25, 38

### Claridge's 3M2
Brook St W1. 01-629 8860. Quiet luxury and comfort in this traditional hotel. There is a 30s atmosphere in the restaurant with its haute cuisine and distinguished wine list, a good Smörgasbord in the Causerie, and a touch of class in the comfortable lounge where liveried footmen serve sandwiches and pastries until *17.30* when they change their livery and take orders for cocktails.
θ Bond Street
🚌 25

### Cleopatra's Needle 3N5
Victoria Embankment SW1. One of a pair of obelisks from an Egyptian tomb, c1450 BC, a gift from Egypt, set up here in 1877 and nothing to do with the lady herself. Two 'time capsule' jars beneath the pedestal contain some things the Victorians felt would interest future archaeologists – including a box of hairpins and Bradshaw's Railway Timetable.
θ Embankment, Temple (not Sun)
🚌 1, 3, 6, 9, 11, 12, 13, 15, 15B, 22B, 24, 29, 53, 77, 77A, 88, 109, 159, 170, 176, 184, 509 to Trafalgar Square

### Cockney Pride 3N3
6 Jermyn St SW1. 01-930 5339. Nostalgic reconstruction of a Victorian cockney pub, where real ale is served with the bangers and mash. Live and lively Cockney bands play in the big bar every night. *Open Mon–Sun.*
θ Piccadilly Circus
🚌 3, 6, 9, 12, 13, 14, 15, 15B, 19, 22, 22B, 38, 53, 88, 159, 509

### Cockpit Theatre 1D1
Gateforth St NW8. 01-262 7907. A purpose-built youth arts workshop, with an adaptable studio theatre, where avant-garde drama and music are offered by visiting youth theatre groups. No productions from mid-July to September when the building is given over to local

youth projects. Coffee bar in the foyer. *Open 09.00–22.30 Mon–Sat. Closed Sun & two weeks at Christmas.*
θ Marylebone, Edgware Road
🚌 159

### Coliseum 3N4
St Martin's La WC2. 01-836 3161. The English National Opera has been based since the 1960s in this splendidly lavish theatre designed by Oswald Stoll in 1904, with the first revolving stage in Britain and a majestic arched and columned interior. International ballet companies perform for limited seasons when the ENO is on its summer tours.
θ Leicester Square, Charing Cross
🚌 1, 3, 6, 9, 11, 12, 13, 15, 15B, 22B, 24, 29, 53, 77, 77A, 88, 109, 159, 170, 176, 184, 509

### Comedy Theatre 3N4
Panton St SW1. 01-930 2578. Small proscenium arch theatre originally built for comic opera, now offering the normal West End mix of comedy and drama.
θ Piccadilly Circus
🚌 3, 6, 9, 12, 13, 14, 15, 15B, 19, 22, 22B, 38, 53, 55, 88, 159, 509

**Commonwealth Institute**    **2H2**
230 Kensington High St W8. 01-603
4535. Behind a forest of flagpoles
stands what appears to be a glass
and concrete tent. Inside are three
levels of exhibition galleries illustrating the cultural and economic
life not only of the Commonwealth
but of the continents of Asia and
Africa as well. There is a library and
resource centre, an adaptable
theatre-cum-cinema, an art gallery,
a book and gift shop, coffee bar and
restaurant – and frequent lively car-
nivals or festivals. *Open 10.00–
17.30 Mon–Sat; 14.00–17.30 Sun.
Closed Nat Hols.* Free.
⊖ High Street Kensington
🚌 9, 10, 27, 28, 31, 33, 49, C1

**Connaught Hotel**    **3N2**
Carlos Pl W1. 01-499 7070. Dignified and distinguished, its panelled dining room and à la carte Grill
still enjoy an unrivalled reputation
for excellent English and French
cuisine. Book well in advance.
⊖ Bond Street
🚌 25

**Courtauld Institute**    **3L4**
**Galleries**
Woburn Sq WC1. 01-580 1015. The
Institute's collection of rich and rare
paintings is made up of Samuel
Courtauld's bequest, The Princes
Gate Collection, which includes
works by Rubens and Tiepolo and
early Dutch and Flemish art, the
collection of Lord Lee of Fareham,
the Roger Fry bequest of 19thC and
20thC British and French paintings,
the Witt collection of Old Master
drawings and the Gambier-Parry
bequest of early Italian paintings.
Due to lack of wall space, only part
of the collection is on show – but
there's plenty to see. *Open 10.00–
17.00 Mon–Sat; 14.00–17.00 Sun.
Closed Nat Hols.* Charge.
⊖ Russell Square, Goodge Street
🚌 68, 77, 77A, 168, 188

**Covent Garden**    **3N4**
WC2. Originally designed in the
1630s by Inigo Jones, as a residential square to be served by St Paul's
Church, on land owned by the Earls
of Bedford. Although a general market was busy here as early as the
17thC, the present market buildings, including the Floral Hall by
E. M. Barry, were not constructed

until the early 19thC. The land was
sold by the Bedford family in 1918.
In the early 1970s the market, by
then dealing wholesale in fruit and
vegetables, moved to Nine Elms,
the area was refurbished, two small
antique and general markets began
to trade and in came The London
Transport Museum and numerous
small shops selling clothes, herbs,
books and luxury goods. Here are
the Puffin and Penguin Bookshops,
Culpepers, a Body Shop, shops for
candles and curries, kites and
coffee. The Punch and Judy pub
stands near the site of the first
puppet show, and there are plenty
of places to eat including the Bar
Crêperie, the Crusting Pipe, the
Rock Garden and Tuttons. Street
entertainers enliven the piazza
most days and into the evening.
Attractive and fun, the area is now
London's nearest equivalent to the
Left Bank in Paris.
⊖ Covent Garden
🚌 1, 6, 9, 11, 13, 15, 15B, 77,
77A, 170, 176, 509 (all go to the
Strand)

**Covent Garden General**    **3M4**
**Store**
111 Long Acre WC2. 01-240 0331.
Modish household effects and
attractive gifts – lots of basketry,

china and enamelled tinware. Also a healthy salad bar which opens one hour after the shop opens and closes one hour before the shop. *Open Mon–Sat 10.00–24.00; Sun 11.00–19.00.*
⊖ Covent Garden
🚌 1, 6, 9, 11, 13, 15, 15B, 77, 77A, 170, 176, 509 (all go to the Strand)

### Crafts Council Gallery 3N4
12 Waterloo Pl SW1. 01-930 4811. The Crafts Council is a national body set up to encourage and promote craftwork throughout England and Wales. To this end it administers grants and loan schemes, runs an education programme, and mounts four major exhibitions a year in its Gallery. There is also an Information Service, with a well-stocked colour slide library, and a bookstall. *Open 10.00–17.00 Tue–Sat; 14.00–17.00 Sun. Closed Mon.* Usually free.
⊖ Piccadilly Circus, Charing Cross
🚌 1, 3, 6, 9, 11, 12, 13, 14, 15, 15B, 19, 22, 22B, 24, 29, 38, 53, 77, 77A, 88, 159, 170, 176, 184, 509

### Craftsman Potters Shop 3M3
Marshall St W1. 01-437 7605. Beautiful and interesting pottery, hand-made by craftsmen, and also books, tools and information about relevant exhibitions. *Open 10.00–17.30 Mon–Sat. Closed Sun.*
⊖ Oxford Circus, Piccadilly Circus
🚌 3, 6, 9, 12, 13, 15, 15B, 53, 88, 159, 509

### Cranks Restaurant 3M3
8 Marshall St W1. 01-437 9431. Stone-ground excellence at this earliest of London's health food restaurants. Light piney decor, soft baroque background music, juices, infusions, vegetable dishes, salads and sticky cakes. *Open 08.00–22.30 Mon–Fri; 09.00–22.30 Sat. Closed Sun.*
⊖ Oxford Circus, Piccadilly Circus
🚌 3, 6, 9, 12, 13, 15, 15B, 53, 88, 159, 176

### Criterion Theatre 3N3
Piccadilly Circus W1. 01-930 3216. A listed building and London's only underground theatre in the strictly physical sense. You even go down to the Upper Circle, through a lobby

still decorated with original Victorian tiles. One of the Wyndham theatres (others are Albery, Donmar Warehouse, Piccadilly and Wyndham's) and theatre tours are available.
⊖ Piccadilly Circus
🚌 3, 6, 9, 12, 13, 14, 15, 15B, 19, 22, 22B, 38, 53, 88, 159, 509

### Crosby Hall 5Y1
Cheyne Walk SW3. 01-352 9663. Incorporates the magnificent 15thC dining hall of the City mansion of Sir John Crosby. It was transplanted piecemeal to this site in 1910. Serves as a residence for The British Federation of University Women. Telephone for appointment to view. Free.
⊖ South Kensington (then bus 45, 49, 219)
🚌 19, 39, 45, 49, 219

### Crystal Palace
SE19. 01-778 7148. Paxton's wondrous glass building known as the Crystal Palace, the centrepiece of The Great Exhibition of 1851, was removed here from its original site in Hyde Park and burnt to the ground in 1936. The 70-acre hillside park, with its wide views, has a National Youth and Sports Centre with an Olympic-size swimming pool and a fine modern sports stadium, as well as an artificial ski slope. The boating and fishing lake has four islands which are inhabited by 20 large replicas of prehistoric reptiles, including a wistful iguanadon, designed by Richard Owen in 1854, and there are real live animals of a small and strokable kind in the

children's zoo. *Open 08.00– ½ hour before dusk.*
⊖ Brixton (then bus 2A, 2B, 3, 3A)
🚍 2A, 2B, 3, 3A, 49, 63, 108B, 122, 137, 157, 227
⚇ Crystal Palace

**Culpeper House**　　　**3N2**
21 Bruton St W1. 01-629 4559. Fragrant herbalist offering herb jellies and dried herbs, loose or in packs and sachets, pot pourri, pomanders, pure cosmetics, nutmegs, honeys and spices. *Open 09.30–18.00 Mon–Fri; 10.00–17.00 Sat. Closed Sun.*
⊖ Oxford Circus
🚍 3, 6, 7, 8, 10, 12, 13, 15, 15B, 16A, 25, 53, 73, 88, 113, 135, 137, 159, 176, 503, 509, C2

**Cuming Museum**
Newington District Library, Walworth Rd SE17. 01-703 3324. The quaint and personal collection of Richard Cuming and his son, begun in 1872, to which have been added items of local interest disinterred from beneath Southwark during archaeological digs and the sinking of new foundations. Among the treasures are charms to cure rheumatism, a now static dancing bear and some 12thC carvings from Southwark Cathedral. *Open 10.00–17.30 Tue–Sat; 14.00–17.00 Sun. Closed Mon & Nat Hols. Free.*
⊖ Elephant and Castle
🚍 12, 35, 40, 45, 68, 171, 176, 184, 185A

**Curzon Cinema Mayfair**　　**3N2**
Curzon St W1. 01-499 3737. Deliciously comfortable surroundings in which to watch quality new releases. Good coffee on sale in the foyer. It's wise to book.
⊖ Hyde Park Corner
🚍 2A, 2B, 9, 10, 14, 16, 19, 22, 25, 30, 36, 38, 52, 52A, 73, 74, 82, 137, 503, 506

**Curzon Cinema West End**　　**3M4**
93 Shaftesbury Av WC2. 01-439 4805. New West End releases.
⊖ Leicester Square
🚍 14, 19, 22, 22B, 24, 29, 38, 176

**Curzon Phoenix**　　**4M4**
Phoenix Theatre, Charing Cross Rd WC2. 01-240 9661. Similar films as other Curzon venues.
⊖ Tottenham Court Road
🚍 14, 19, 22, 22B, 24, 29, 38, 176

**Cutler Street Market**　　**4S6**
Aldgate end of Goulston St EC1. The centre of the coin world – also gold-related items, such as jewellery and watches and stamps. *Open 07.00–14.00 Sun.*
⊖ Aldgate
🚍 5, 15, 22A, 25, 40, 42, 44, 67, 78, 100, 253, 510

**Cutty Sark**
King William Walk SE10. 01-858 3445. One of the great sailing tea clippers, built in 1869, now stands in dry dock waiting for visitors to admire her accommodation and rigging. Next to her is Gipsy Moth IV in which Sir Francis Chichester sailed around the world in 1966. *Both ships open 10.00–18.00 Mon–Sat; 12.00–18.00 Sun. (Closed 17.00 in winter.) Charge.*
⊖ Surrey Docks (then bus 1, 188) Docklands Light Railway: Island Gardens (then by foot tunnel)
🚍 1, 177, 180, 188, 286
⚇ Greenwich

# D

**Daily Mail**     **4T2**
Harmsworth Printing Ltd, Surrey Quays Rd SE16. 01-938 6000. Tours of the new print works. Minimum age 14, groups of 12. Contact General Production Manager.
Θ Surrey Docks
🚌 181, P11, P14

**Davenport's Magic Shop**     **3N5**
7 Charing Cross Underground Shopping Arcade, Strand WC2. 01-836 0408. The splendid Davenport's, who recently moved to this address, are still a reliable source of sneezing powder, masks, tricks, practical jokes, puzzles and the elaborate deceptions used by professional conjurers. They also publish books on magic and conjuring and have a large section of antiquarian books on the subjects. *Open 09.30–17.30 Mon–Fri; 09.30–16.00 Sat. Closed Sun.*
Θ Charing Cross
🚌 1, 3, 6, 9, 11, 12, 13, 15, 15B, 22B, 24, 29, 53, 77, 77A, 88, 109, 159, 170, 176, 184, 509

**David Shilling Hats**     **1D3**
44 Chiltern St W1. 01-935 8473. The most eccentric of David Shilling's designs are modelled annually by his mother at Royal Ascot; indeed the three of them, mother, son and hat, have become a national institution. He will make you a simple little number in a few hours – an extravaganza takes a bit longer. Appointment wise if you want the man himself. *Open 09.00–18.00 Mon–Fri. Closed Sat & Sun.*
Θ Baker Street
🚌 2A, 2B, 13, 18, 27, 30, 74, 82, 113, 159

**Debenham's**     **3M2**
344–8 Oxford St W1. 01-580 3000. Another one of the major department stores in Oxford Street, this one has been recently refurbished, with a new atrium as centrepiece. Not only can you buy everything you might need to clothe the family and furnish the home, you can also stock up on shares from the Debenham Share Centre on the third floor. For refreshment, try the self-service restaurant or the waitress-service café, both on the second floor. *Open 09.30–18.00 (to 20.00 Thur) Mon–Sat. Closed Sun.*
Θ Bond Street
🚌 6, 7, 8, 10, 12, 13, 15, 16A, 25, 73, 88, 113, 135, 137, 159, 503

**Design Centre**     **3N4**
28 Haymarket SW1. 01-839 8000. The Design Council is an arbiter of taste and quality, awarding its distinctive triangular marks of approval to British goods which come up to its high standards. Here you can visit changing exhibitions of the newest of the approved and there is a card index to direct you to retail outlets. Pleasant café which closes half an hour before the shop. *Open 10.00–18.00 Mon & Tue; 10.00–20.00 Wed–Sat; 13.00–18.00 Sun. Free.*
Θ Piccadilly Circus
🚌 3, 6, 9, 12, 13, 14, 15, 15B, 19, 22, 22B, 38, 53, 88, 159, 509

### Design Museum 4U6

Butler's Wharf, 45 Curlew St SE1. 01-403 6933. Opened in July 1989 and sponsored by the Conran Foundation this new museum's range of exhibits includes furniture, cars, gadgets and graphics and aims to make the public more aware of design. Looks at designs past, present and futuristic through permanent and temporary exhibitions. Also has a bookshop, café, restaurant, library and lecture theatre. *Open 11.30–18.30 Tue–Sun. Closed Mon. Charge.*
⊖ London Bridge
🚌 42, 47, 78, 188, P11

### Diamond Centre 3M2

10 Hanover St W1. 01-629 5511. This is where to be dazzled by the largest collection of diamonds and other precious stones in London, and to learn about the progress of a diamond from rough stone to glittering gem. Admission charge includes a memento – a brilliant-cut stone in a presentation wallet. *Open 09.30–17.30 Mon–Fri, 09.30–13.30 Sat.*
⊖ Oxford Circus
🚌 3, 6, 7, 8, 10, 12, 13, 15, 15B, 16A, 25, 53, 73, 88, 113, 135, 137, 159, 176, 503, 509, C2

### Dickens House Museum 3L5

48 Doughty St WC1. 01-405 2127. Charles Dickens lived and worked here from April 1837 to December 1839. In that relatively short time he finished the last five chapters of 'Pickwick Papers', most of 'Oliver Twist', 20 monthly instalments of 'Nicholas Nickleby' and the first few pages of 'Barnaby Rudge', and so established his reputation as a writer. The museum was founded by The Dickens Fellowship, who publish 'The Dickensian' three times a year, which is packed with fascinating information. Also houses the best Dickens library in the world (an appointment is necessary to see the library). *Open 10.00–17.00 Mon–Sat. Last admission 16.30. Closed Sun & Nat Hols. Charge.*
⊖ Russell Square, Chancery Lane (not Sun)
🚌 17, 19, 38, 45, 55, 171, 171A, 243, 259, 505

### Dickens Inn 4U6

St Katharine's Way E1. 01-488 1226. Fine views of the yacht marina and Tower Bridge from this artfully converted warehouse. Exposed beams, antique furniture, a brass-topped bar and sawdust on the floor. Pub grub in The Tavern Room on the ground floor; traditional English and classical French dishes in the first-floor Pickwick Room; fish in various forms and sauces in the top-floor Dickens Room. *Tavern open normal licensing hours Mon–Sun. Restaurants open LD Mon–Sun.*
⊖ Tower Hill
Docklands Light Railway: Tower Gateway
🚌 15, 42, 78, 100, 510, Sat & Sun 25

### Dickens Old Curiosity Shop 4S1

13–14 Portsmouth St WC2. 01-405 9891. Tudor-style building which is believed to have inspired Dickens' 'Old Curiosity Shop'. Sells antiques and souvenirs. *Open 09.30–17.30 Mon–Fri; 10.00–16.00 Sat, Sun & Nat Hols. Closed Good Fri & Xmas.*
⊖ Holborn, Aldwych
🚌 68, 77, 77A, 168, 171, 188

### Dickins & Jones 3M3

Regent St W1. 01-734 7070. Large fashion store with a good stock of British and continental men's and women's clothes, cosmetics and perfumes, knitting wools, costume jewellery, and with an excellent

underwear and lingerie department. There is also a shopping adviser, a hairdressing salon, the Rose Restaurant, and three coffee shops. *Open 09.30–18.00 (to 19.00 Thur) Mon–Sat. Closed Sun.*
⊖ Oxford Circus
🚌 3, 6, 12, 13, 15, 15B, 53, 88, 159, 509, C2

### Dillons The Bookstore   1D5
82 Gower St WC1. 01-636 1577. Lushly refurbished and still expanding, London's leading academic booksellers have now devoted half the store to general books. Enlarged sections on travel, arts, biography, literature; also classical music, antiquarian and bargain books. Some 5½ miles of books and nearly 200,000 titles. *Open 09.00–17.30 Mon & Wed–Fri; 09.30–17.30 Tue & Sat.*
⊖ Euston Square
🚌 10, 14, 14A, 18, 24, 29, 30, 73, 134, 253

### Dingwall's Club   1A3
Camden Lock, Chalk Farm Rd NW1. 01-267 4967. Barge-horse stables, near a busy weekend market, converted into a lively music club and dance venue with burger-style restaurant. Varied contemporary music from Monday–Sunday evening and at lunchtime on Saturday. *Open LD Mon–Sat, D Sun. Closed L Sun.*
⊖ Camden Town
🚌 24, 31, 68, 168

### Dino's Restaurant   2J5
1 Pelham St SW7. 01-589 3511. Long-established eatery, with a bustling Italian atmosphere, in which to enjoy breakfasts, grills, pasta, veal and chicken dishes all day and all evening. *Open 08.30–23.45 Mon–Sun.*
⊖ South Kensington
🚌 14, 30, 45, 49, 74, 219, 503, C1

### Docklands
The 8½ square miles of London's Docklands is made up of several areas, each with its own character. On the north bank lie the Royal Docks, the distinctive bulge of the Isle of Dogs, Wapping, Limehouse and St Katharine's Dock, while the extensive Surrey Docks are strung along the south bank. The system

of enclosed docks which grew up from about 1800 turned the Port of London into a thriving commercial centre. Modernisation of cargo handling, among other factors, led to the docks' decline and they closed between 1967 and 1981. The entire area is now the subject of an ambitious, and controversial, programme of regeneration under the London Docklands Development Corporation (LDDC) and has become 'Europe's largest building site'. However, there is plenty in the area worth seeing – dock machinery, Dickensian wharves, riverside taverns, 18thC churches, city farms, and striking modern architecture on a grand scale.
Docklands Light Railway: all stations from Tower Gateway
🚌 277, D5, D6, D7, P14

### Dominion Theatre   1E5
Tottenham Court Rd W1. 01-580 9562. Huge theatre which sometimes functions as a cinema and occasionally stages rock concerts. The late Lord Olivier made a celebrated appearance here in hologram form in the musical 'Time'.
⊖ Tottenham Court Road
🚌 7, 8, 10, 14, 14A, 19, 22, 22B, 24, 25, 29, 38, 55, 73, 134, 176, 503

### Donmar Warehouse   3M4
41 Earlham St WC2. 01-240 8230. Comfortable studio theatre which welcomes touring companies, mounts its own productions and is

a mixture of fringe venue and small legitimate West End theatre. One of the Wyndham theatres (others are Albery, Criterion, Piccadilly and Wyndham's) and theatre tours are available.

⊖ Leicester Square

🚌 14, 19, 22, 22B, 24, 29, 38, 176

**Dorchester Hotel**  *3N1*
Park La W1. 01-629 8888. Luxury and efficiency in this large, 285-room hotel. Eat English regional and national dishes in the Grill Room or dine and dance in the rococo Terrace Restaurant. There is also a light, airy bar and The Promenade which serves teas to piano accompaniment. Note: The hotel will be closed for refurbishment until April 1990.

⊖ Hyde Park Corner

🚌 2A, 2B, 10, 16, 30, 36, 73, 74, 82, 137, 503, 506

**Downing Street**  *3O4*
SW1. 17thC town houses built by Sir George Downing. No 10, with the policeman at the door, is the official residence of the Prime Minister, No 11 is that of the Chancellor of the Exchequer.

⊖ Westminster

🚌 3, 11, 12, 24, 29, 53, 77, 77A, 88, 109, 159, 170, 184, C1

**Dragon Gate**  *3N4*
7 Gerrard St W1. 01-734 5154. The first and probably the best Szechuan restaurant in London. Sliced pork with garlic and chilli, tea-smoked duck, pancakes or almond curd are just some of the delights to be sampled. *Open to 23.00.*

⊖ Leicester Square

🚌 24, 29, 176

**Draper's Company Hall**  *4S4*
Throgmorton Av EC2. Information from City Information Centre, St Paul's Churchyard EC4, 01-606 3030 extn 2456. The City Livery Hall dates from 1667 but was largely rebuilt in 1870. Tours to see the fine staircase and collection of silver plate may be booked in advance.

⊖ Bank, Liverpool Street

🚌 6, 8, 9, 11, 22, 22B, 149

**Drury Lane, Theatre Royal**  *3M5*
Catherine St WC2. 01-836 8108. Known as 'Drury Lane', although the entrance is around the corner. This is the richly decorated successor to three earlier theatres on the site. Famous for lavish musicals – 'Oklahoma', 'My Fair Lady', '42nd Street' – and for one of the best-loved theatre ghosts, The Man in Grey, who appears where building work uncovered a male skeleton, and whose presence is said to herald a successful show.

⊖ Covent Garden

🚌 1, 4, 6, 9, 11, 13, 15, 15B, 68, 77, 77A, 168, 170, 171, 171A, 176, 188, 502, 505, 509, 513

**Duchess Theatre**  *3M5*
Catharine St WC2. 01-836 8342. The new home of the Players' Theatre which presents regularly changed programmes of authentic Victorian music hall.

⊖ Covent Garden, Aldwych (rush hours only)

🚌 1, 4, 6, 9, 11, 13, 15, 15B, 68, 77, 77A, 168, 170, 171, 171A, 176, 188, 502, 505, 509, 513

**Duke of York's Theatre**  *3N4*
St Martin's La WC2. 01-836 5122. Attractive small theatre, with a domed auditorium – the first theatre to stage 'Peter Pan' and many other J. M. Barrie offerings.

⊖ Leicester Square

🚌 1, 3, 6, 9, 11, 12, 13, 15, 15B, 24, 29, 53, 77, 77A, 88, 109, 159, 170, 176, 184, 509

which is bathed in amber light and has a slightly eerie sense of expectancy. The collection includes important works by Rembrandt, Rubens, Gainsborough, Cuyp, Watteau, Murillo, Poussin, Hogarth and Van Dyck. *Open 10.00–13.00; 14.00–17.00 Tue–Sat; 14.00–17.00 Sun. Closed Mon & Nat Hols.* Charge.
⊖ Brixton (then bus 3, 3A or P4)
🚌 3, 3A, P4
⇌ West Dulwich, North Dulwich

**Dulwich Park**
SE21. 01-693 5737. A favourite garden of the late Queen Mary, wife of George V, which is quite spectacular in early summer when the rhododendrons and azaleas are in bloom. There is a pleasant boating lake, tennis courts, and a marked trail among the trees. *Open 07.30–dusk.* Free.
⊖ Brixton (then bus P4, 37 to North Dulwich Station)
🚌 P4, 37 (to North Dulwich Station), 12, 78, 176, 185 (to The Plough)
⇌ West Dulwich, North Dulwich

**Dumpling Inn**      **3N4**
15a Gerrard St W1. 01-437 2567. Small, simple but lively Peking and Cantonese restaurant – excellent pork dumplings, prawns in chilli sauce, fried seaweed. *Open LD Mon–Sun.*
⊖ Leicester Square
🚌 24, 29, 176

**Dulwich College Picture Gallery**
College Rd SE21. 01-693 5254. England's first purpose-built art gallery, designed by Sir John Soane, with natural light washing down from above. Incorporates a mausoleum for the benefactors

# E

### Earl's Court Exhibition Hall     2K2

Warwick Rd SW5. 01-385 1200. The 19-acre Exhibition Hall, designed by Howard Crane in 1937, regularly fills its mighty space with shows which attract visitors from all over the world. In January – the largest Boat Show in Europe; in February – Crufts judges pick Top Dog; in March – the Ideal Home Exhibition; in July – the Royal Tournament; in August – the Motor Cycle Show; in October, in odd-numbered years, the Motor Show; in December the farm machinery and puzzled livestock of the Smithfield Show. Bars and Buffet. Charge.
⊖ Earl's Court
🚌 30, 31, 74, C3

### East End

Extending from the borders of the City eastwards, north of the river, this old part of London has been traditionally associated with slums, poverty, docks, warehouses, warm-hearted Cockneys, vibrant street markets and night-time violence. It was in the Whitechapel district that for three grisly months in 1888 Jack the Ripper committed his hideous crimes and achieved international notoriety.

Proximity to the docks has meant that for centuries the East End has been an immigrant area and each ethnic group has left its imprint – from the 17thC Huguenot weavers who settled in Spitalfields, to the 19th and early 20thC huge influx of Jewish refugees from Eastern Europe, to today's industrious, Asian community.

Extensive bomb damage during the last war paved the way for new building developments which have changed the landscape of the area. And further developments are currently taking place as the East End experiences the spin-off effects from the commercial revival of the whole Docklands area.

The famous Petticoat Lane market is still lively (and worth a visit on

Sunday morning) and many of the East End pubs still go in for regular and spontaneous sing-songs. There are also some interesting cultural centres including the Bethnal Green Museum of Childhood, the Geffrye Museum and the Whitechapel Art Gallery. Blooms Jewish restaurant is on-hand for sustenance of a salt-beef kind!
⊖ Aldgate, Aldgate East, Bethnal Green, Mile End, Shadwell, Shoreditch, Stepney Green, Wapping, Whitechapel Docklands Light Railway: all stations from Tower Gateway
🚌 6, 8, 10, 15, 15B, 25 (from Central London)

### Economist Building     3N3

25 St James's St SW1. Alison & Peter Smithson, 1964–6. A very beautiful and harmonious group of buildings with its own raised piazza. The design was intended to demonstrate a general principle for the redevelopment of dense commercial areas and is a rare example of new buildings in an area with a traditional street pattern.
⊖ Green Park, Piccadilly Circus
🚌 9, 14, 19, 22, 25, 38

### Elfin Oak 2G3

Near Black Lion Gate, Kensington Gardens W2. An aged stump from Richmond Park, carved by Ivor Innes in the 1930s into a magic world of clambering gnomes, winged fairies, tiny animals and birds. Iron railings protect it from loving hands.

⊖ Queensway, Bayswater

🚌 12, 88

### El Vino's Wine Bar 4S2

47 Fleet St EC4. 01-353 6786. Something of an institution. Musty and masculine haunt of lawyers and journalists, who are required to wear jacket, collar and tie at all times. Ladies were not permitted to buy drinks at the bar until 1982. Excellent French and German wine list, snacks and a restaurant for cold lunches in the cellar. *Open Mon–Fri & L Sat, closed Sat eve & all Sun.*

⊖ Temple (not Sun), Chancery Lane (not Sun), Blackfriars

🚌 4, 6, 9, 11, 15, 15B, 171A, 502, 509, 513

### Eltham Palace

Off Court Yd, Eltham SE9. 01-859 2112. A royal palace beloved of kings from Henry III to Henry VIII. Henry IV was married here – though Joan of Navarre was not present at the time since it was a proxy affair. Rebuilding in the 1930s, and the fact that it is now HQ of the Institute of Army Education, has done for the atmosphere, rather, but the restored Banqueting Hall with its hammerbeam roof and oriel windows is splendid. *Open 10.30–12.15 & 14.15–18.00 Thur & Sun. Closed Mon–Wed, Fri & Sat & 16.00 in winter.*

🚌 21, 61, 124, 126, 132, 160, 161, 228, 286, 328, B1, B16

🚊 Eltham

### Empire Ballroom

Leicester Sq WC2. 01-437 1446. Resident band provides the music. Very crowded. Diner serving burgers, steaks and salads. *Open to 03.00 Mon–Sat, to 01.30 Sun.*

⊖ Leicester Square

🚌 24, 29, 176

### Empire Cinema (1, 2, 3) 3N4

Leicester Sq WC2. 01-437 1234. Cavernous 'movie palace' with adjustable seats, perfect vision, Dolby stereo. Shows new releases – booking advisable.

⊖ Leicester Square

🚌 24, 29, 176

### Endell Street Place 3M4

27–29 Endell St WC2. 01-240 1060. The large, glass-roofed gallery contains small glass-fronted shops in which crafts people create and sell. Woodcarving, spinning, painting and potting are among the crafts represented. *Open 10.00–18.00 Mon–Sat.*

⊖ Covent Garden

🚌 7, 8, 19, 22, 22B, 25, 38, 55, 503

### Epping Forest

Essex. Six thousand acres of natural woodland stretching from Chingford to Epping. This is mixed woodland with hornbeam, oak, ash, maple, beech and birch trees, sheltering a flourishing range of natural wildlife – a shade too flourishing in the case of the grey squirrels. Large enough to get thoroughly lost, though a detailed map of the area will enable you to find two ancient British camps – Loughton Camp and Ambersbury Banks – each at least 2,000 years old. *Open 24 hours. Free.*

⊖ Loughton (then local bus, Theydon Bois)

🚊 Chingford

### Eros  3N3

Piccadilly Circus W1. The famous arrow-firing cherub, by Sir Alfred Gilbert in 1892, cleaned up by the GLC in 1985, is not Eros at all but the Angel of Christian Charity, a memorial to the philanthropic Lord Shaftesbury.

⊖ Piccadilly Circus

🚌 3, 6, 9, 12, 13, 14, 15, 15B, 19, 22, 22B, 38, 53, 88, 159, 509

### L'Escargot  3M3

48 Greek St W1. 01-437 2679. Brasserie on ground floor, restaurant and banqueting room above. Snails parade around the periphery of the carpet – in the pile, that is – and the decor is 1920ish. Retains many features of the old Escargot. Booking essential. *Open L Mon–Fri, D Mon–Sat. Closed Sun.*

⊖ Tottenham Court Road

🚌 14, 19, 22, 22B, 24, 29, 38, 176

### Euston Station  1C5

Euston Rd NW1. Information on 01-387 7070. Modern structure, set back from the road behind lawns and a large forecourt, which dispatches trains north to Birmingham and Manchester, Liverpool, Glasgow and Inverness.

⊖ Euston, Euston Square

🚌 10, 14, 14A, 18, 30, 68, 73, 77, 77A, 168, 188

⪼ Euston

---

**London Transport 24-hour information service**
For any information on travel in Greater London – routes, fares, times – telephone 01-222 1234 at any time of the day or night.

## Fenchurch Street Station   *4T5*
Railway Pl, Fenchurch St EC3. Information on 01-283 7171. Victorian rail terminal, built in 1841, from which trains leave for Tilbury and Southend.
⊖ Tower Hill
▆▆▆ 40, 44, 100, 510
⇌ Fenchurch Street

## Fenton House
Hampstead Grove NW3. 01-435 3471. Built c1693, its early history is unknown. It was bought by a merchant called Philip Fenton in 1793 and, though it passed through other hands, kept his name. It was bequeathed to the National Trust in 1952 by its last owner, Lady Binning, together with her pictures, furniture and European and Chinese porcelain. It also houses the Benton Fletcher collection of early musical instruments, most in such good working order that you may well tour the house to the background strains of harpsichord or virginal. *Open Mar 14.00–18.00 Sat & Sun only; Apr–Oct 11.00–18.00 Sat–Wed. Last admissions 17.00. Closed Oct–Feb.*
⊖ Hampstead
▆▆▆ 46, 210, 268

## Finsbury Park
N4. 01-263 5001. 115 acres opened in 1869. This is a great sporting park – soccer, cricket, fishing, bowling, tennis, boating. Also two children's playgrounds, nursery, tea-room, car park and an athletics track. London plane trees predominate. The oldest aqueduct in London runs through the park and there is a reservoir underground. *Open 06.30–½ hour after sunset.*
⊖ Finsbury Park
▆▆▆ 4, 19, 29, 141, 171A, 221, 253, 279, 279A

## Fishmonger's Hall   *4T4*
London Bridge EC4. 01-626 3531. The Worshipful Company of Fishmongers still carry out the task assigned to them in the Charter granted by James I – to check the quality of fish brought into London.

Magnificent Banqueting Hall and many items of interest including paintings and the Book of Ordinances dated 1509. Write or telephone to book a tour. Free.
⊖ London Bridge
▆▆▆ 17, 21, 35, 40, 43, 44, 47, 48, 133, 501, 505, 510, 513, P3, P11

## Fitness Centre   *3M4*
11–12 Floral St WC2. 01-836 6544. Aerobics, stretch, rock, jazz, ballet, tap, karate, sauna, steam room. Gymnasium with nautilus and free weights, health bar and swimming pool. No membership requirement.
⊖ Covent Garden
▆▆▆ 24, 29, 176

## Flamsteed House
Old Royal Observatory, Greenwich Park SE10. 01-858 1167. Built by Wren and topped by the octagon room observatory, it has been furnished more or less as it may have been when the first Astronomer Royal lived in it. A series of modern galleries built on at the back show the history of time-keeping, navigation and surveying by means of displays of elegant instruments, with a ticking, whirring section of clocks and watches below. *Open 10.00–18.00 Mon–Sat; 14.00–17.30 Sun. Closes 17.00 in winter.*

⊖ New Cross, New Cross Gate
(then bus 53)
🚌 53, 54, 75
⇌ Maze Hill

**Flanagan's Fish Parlour      1D3**
100 Baker St W1. 01-935 0287.
Blithely phoney Victorian dining
rooms – with booths and sawdust,
Cockney songs, breezy service,
spirited pianist, and Irish stew, fish
and chips, spotted dick and custard
to eat. *Open LD Mon–Sun.*
⊖ Baker Street
🚌 2A, 2B, 13, 18, 27, 30, 74, 82,
113, 159

**Fleet Street      4S2**
EC4. London's 'street of ink' (or
'shame') has been associated with
printing since the days of Caxton.
Despite the mounting exodus of
the major newspaper groups, a few
national and many provincial newspapers still have their offices in or
near it.
      Where Fleet Street leaves the
City, past the two dragon guar-
dians, it enters the world of the law
because all around are the four Inns
of Court (Middle and Inner Temple,
Lincoln's Inn and Gray's Inn), and
the Royal Courts of Justice.
      This is an historic area, with nu-
merous pubs and wine bars all
heavily patronised by the last remaining journalists and by lawyers.

⊖ Blackfriars, Chancery Lane (not
Sun), Temple (not Sun), Aldwych
(Mon–Fri rush hours only)
🚌 4, 6, 9, 11, 15, 15B, 171A, 502,
509, 513

**Florence Nightingale      3O5
Museum**
On the same site as St Thomas'
Hospital, 2 Lambeth Palace Rd SE1.
01-620 0374. New museum featur-
ing a collection of objects which
belonged to Florence Nightingale.
*Open 10.00–16.00 Tue–Sat.*
⊖ Westminster, Waterloo
🚌 76, 77, 170, 507, Sun only 159

**Floris      3N3**
89 Jermyn St SW1. 01-930 2885.
Perfumiers to the Court of St
James since the reign of George IV.
Their very English flower perfumes
have matching toiletries and there
are gruffer preparations for men.
*Open   09.30–17.30   Mon–Fri;
09.30–16.00 Sat. Closed Sun.*
⊖ Piccadilly Circus
🚌 3, 6, 9, 12, 13, 14, 15, 15B, 19,
22, 38, 53, 88, 159, 509

**Fortnum and Mason      3N3**
181 Piccadilly W1. 01-734 8040.
World-famous, decorous department store with floor-walkers in
morning dress, a food hall full of
bottled exotica and delicatessen
delicacies, superb hampers, and,
upstairs,   designer   collection
clothes. Watch the outside clock on
the hour when four-foot-high figures of Messrs F and M emerge
from doors and bow to each other
to 18thC airs. The spacious Fountain Restaurant is *open 09.00–
23.30 Mon–Sat.* Store *open 09.00–
17.30 Mon–Fri; 09.00–17.00 Sat.
Closed Sun.*
⊖ Piccadilly Circus
🚌 9, 14, 19, 22, 25, 38

**Fortune Theatre      3M5**
Russell St WC2. 01-836 2238.
Small theatre still remembered as
the home of 'Beyond the Fringe' in
the 60s. Now presents musicals
and modern drama.
⊖ Covent Garden
🚌 1, 4, 6, 9, 11, 13, 15, 15B, 68,
77, 77A, 168, 170, 171, 171A,
176, 188, 502, 505, 509, 513

**Foundling Hospital      4Q1
(Thomas Coram Foundation
for Children)**
40 Brunswick Sq WC1. 01-278
2424. The charitable foundation,

set up by a sea captain in the 18thC to give shelter to homeless children, now functions as an adoption and fostering agency for children with special needs. Good collection of paintings, many by, or of, past governors. There are three Hogarths, a Gainsborough, original Handel scores and sad cases of trinkets left with children by destitute mothers. *Open 10.00–16.00 Mon–Fri. Closed Sat & Sun & during conferences – telephone first.* Charge.
⊖ Russell Square
🚌 68, 77, 77A, 168, 188, 503

### Foyles 3M4

119 Charing Cross Rd WC2. 01-437 5660. The largest of London's bookshops with an immense and wide-ranging stock, arranged rather perversely by publisher rather than author or subject. Paying for a book, once you've found it, can actually entail queuing three times. *Open 09.00–18.00 Mon–Wed, Fri & Sat; until 19.00 Thur. Closed Sun.*
⊖ Tottenham Court Road
🚌 14, 19, 22, 22B, 24, 29, 38, 176

### Freemason's Hall 3M5

Gt Queen St WC2. 01-831 9811.

This is the third hall on the site, built in 1927–33. Visitors, not all of them Masons, may see the Processional Corridor, The Grand Temple and the Museum, all rich with symbolism. Guided tours hourly, on the hour, from 11.00–16.00. The library, with ts comprehensive collection of Masonic works, is open to students of the subject. *Open 10.00–17.00 Mon–Fri; 10.00–13.00 Sat.* Free.
⊖ Covent Garden, Holborn
🚌 68, 77, 77A, 168, 188

### Freud's House Museum

20 Maresfield Gdns NW3. 01-435 2002. This is where Sigmund Freud lived after his escape from the Nazis in Vienna in 1938 until his death just over a year later. His daughter Anna continued to reside and work in the house, preserving her father's study and library as he had left them until her own death in 1982. The house has been maintained in its original style, adorned with distinctive Viennese painted furniture. Freud's study holds the famous analytical couch and chair, as well as his impressive collection of books and antiquities. Upstairs Anna Freud's room has a display of awards for her own work in the field of psychology. Freud's former bedroom, with letters and newspaper cuttings, now serves as a display room for temporary exhibitions on various aspects of psychology. The reception area sells copies of the Freud Penguin Library along with a number of postcards and souvenirs. *Open 10.00–17.00 Mon–Sat; 13.00–17.00 Sun. Closed Xmas.* Charge.
⊖ Finchley Road
🚌 13, 46, 82, 113

### Fulham Palace

Fulham Palace Rd SW6. The oldest visible parts of the calm two-storey house and intimate collegiate courtyard are Tudor. Used as ecclesiastical offices and not visitable, though the extensive riverside grounds are open to the public, and contain a magical herb garden discovered through a narrow Tudor arch. Fourteen past bishops lie in the nearby yew-shadowed churchyard of All Saints. *Open 09.00–½ hour before dusk.* Free.
⊖ Putney Bridge
🚌 14, 22, 39, 74, 220, C4

# G

## Gallipoli                    4S5
8 Bishopsgate Churchyard EC2. 01-588 1922. Once a subterranean Turkish bath, with gold decor and tiles, now a restaurant with twice nightly belly dancing and Turkish and French food. The minimum charge means you can't eat on the cheap. *Open LD (till late) Mon–Sat. Closed Sun.*
⊖ Liverpool Street
🚍 5, 6, 8, 22, 22A, 22B, 35, 47, 48, 78, 100, 149, 243A, 263A, 505

## Garrard & Co                    3N3
112 Regent St W1. 01-734 7020. Garrards are the Crown Jewellers – is there any more to be said? Fine jewellery, antique and modern silver and gold, by appointment to HM the Queen and to the Queen Mother. *Open 09.00–17.30 Mon–Fri; 09.00–17.00 Sat. Closed Sun.*
⊖ Piccadilly Circus
🚍 3, 6, 13, 15, 15B, 53, 88, 159, 509

## Garrick Theatre                    3N4
Charing Cross Rd WC2. 01-379 6107. Built in 1897, named for the actor David Garrick, and said to be haunted by Arthur Bourchier, one of its earliest actor-managers. Puts on varied programmes.
⊖ Leicester Square, Charing Cross
🚍 1, 3, 6, 9, 11, 12, 13, 15, 15B, 22B, 24, 29, 53, 77, 77A, 88, 109, 159, 170, 176, 184, 509

## Gate Cinema Notting Hill    2G2
Notting Hill Gate W11. 01-727 4043. The first Gate to open and to set the tone for showing outstanding films. *Late show Sat.* Membership at door.
⊖ Notting Hill Gate
🚍 12, 27, 28, 31, 52, 52A, 88

## Gatwick Airport
Horley, Surrey. 0293 28822. Busy international airport with an 800-foot-high viewing gallery from which to watch most types of aircraft, including light planes. *Gallery open 09.00–19.50 Mon–Sun. Closes dusk in winter.* Charge.
Green Line 727, 747, 777
🚆 Gatwick Airport

## Le Gavroche                    3N1
43 Upper Brook St W1. 01-408 0881. One of the best restaurants in London, renowned for its luxurious atmosphere, imaginative haute cuisine, magnificent wine list, faultless service. It is essential to book – and to be prepared for very high prices. *Open LD Mon–Fri. Closed Sat & Sun.*
⊖ Marble Arch
🚍 2A, 2B, 10, 16, 30, 36, 73, 74, 82, 137, 503, 506

## Gay Hussar                    3M3
2 Greek St W1. 01-437 0973. Intimate and sophisticated Hungarian restaurant in Soho, with some well-known politicians and publishers among its loyal devotees. Chilled wild cherry soup, roast saddle of carp and orange curd pancakes might be the order of the day. Booking essential. *Open LD Mon–Sat. Closed Sun.*

⊖ Tottenham Court Road
🚌 14, 19, 22, 22B, 24, 29, 38, 176

## Geffrye Museum 4Q6
Kingsland Rd E2. 01-739 8368. Named for a past Lord Mayor of London whose bequest founded the almshouses, built in 1715. These attractive buildings were converted into a museum of English furniture and woodwork early this century. It is arranged as a series of fully furnished period rooms so that you can assess the development of design from Georgian England to the 1930s. School visits are encouraged and projects and activities arranged in the holidays. *Open 10.00–17.00 Tue–Sat; 14.00–17.00 Sun. Closed Mon & Xmas.* Free.
⊖ Liverpool Street (then bus)
🚌 22, 22B, 48, 67, 149, 243, 243A

## General Trading Company 5W2
144 Sloane St SW1. 01-730 0411. China, glass, small items of furniture and up-market gifts are available from this well-known repository of Royal and high society wedding lists. *Open 09.00–17.30 Mon–Fri; 09.00–14.00 Sat. Closed Sun.*
⊖ Knightsbridge, Sloane Square
🚌 19, 22, 137, C1

## Geological Museum 2J5
Exhibition Rd SW7. 01-589 3444. The National Museum of Earth Science is a part of the Institute of Geological Sciences. Its collections are drawn from all over the world, though with one floor devoted entirely to British geology. Riveting displays of fossils, the world-famous gem and ornamental stone collection, a piece of moon rock, a stirring earthquake simulator, the Treasures of the Earth exhibition, and Story of the Earth which describes the origin of the whole universe. *Open 10.00–18.00 Mon–Sat; 14.30–18.00 Sun. Charge. Free from 16.30–18.00 Mon–Fri.*
⊖ South Kensington
🚌 14, 30, 45, 49, 74, 219, C1

## George Inn 4U4
77 Borough High St SE1. 01-407 2056. London's only remaining galleried coaching inn, first mentioned in John Stow's 'History of London' in 1590 and rebuilt, after fire damage, in 1676. Patronised by Dickens and featured in 'Little Dorrit'. Brief seasons of classical plays and medieval combats are staged in the courtyard in summer – enquire for times and dates. There are two bars, a wine bar, an à la carte restaurant and functions are catered for. *Open LD Mon–Sun.*
⊖ London Bridge
🚌 17, 21, 35, 40, 43, 44, 47, 48, 133, 501, 505, 510, 513, P3, P11

## The Glasshouse 3M4
65 Long Acre WC2. 01-836 9785. Watch glass being blown in the workshop from the observation area. Telephone for details. *Open 10.00–17.30 Mon–Fri; 11.00–16.00 Sat. Closed Sun.*
⊖ Covent Garden
🚌 14, 19, 22, 22B, 24, 29, 38, 176

## Globe Theatre 3M3
Shaftesbury Av W1. 01-437 3667. Built in 1906, designed by W. G. R. Sprague with a French flavour and reproduction Regency staircase. Known for a wide variety of plays but especially 'quality' comedies.
⊖ Piccadilly Circus
🚌 14, 19, 22, 22B, 38

**Goldsmiths Hall**                    **4S4**
Foster La EC2. Information from
City Information Centre, St Paul's
Churchyard EC4, 01-606 3030.
Classical-style palazzo rebuilt in
1835 by Philip Hardwick for the
company whose duty it is to assay
gold and silver plate and stamp it
with its own leopard-head hallmark.
Occasional exhibitions and regular
tours. Enquire at telephone number
above.
⊖ St Paul's
▥ 4, 8, 22, 22B, 25, 141, 501,
502, 509

**Good Friends**
139–141 Salmon La E14. 01-987
5541. One of the best of the
'Friends' group of Cantonese restaurants. Large, simple, reliable –
unlicensed, bring your own wine.
*Open LD Mon–Sun.*
Docklands Light Railway:
Limehouse, West Ferry
▥ 5, 15, 15B, 40, P14

**Goodwins Court**                    **3N4**
Just off St Martin's La WC2. Neat
and complete row of bow-fronted
18thC shops.
⊖ Leicester Square
▥ 24, 29, 176

**Gordon's Wine Cellar**              **3N5**
47 Villiers St WC2. 01-930 1408. A
300-year-old cellar with a main bar
and a tunnel-shaped inner sanctum.
Only Quasimodo could be truly
comfortable hunched against the
damp curvature of the ancient
stone walls, yet the candlelit
atmosphere is so pleasant that customers return again and again.
Good selection of wines, sherries,
ports and madeiras; tempting hot
and cold buffet. *Open Mon–Fri to
21.00. Closed Sat & Sun.*
⊖ Charing Cross, Embankment
▥ 1, 3, 6, 9, 11, 12, 13, 15, 15B,
22B, 24, 29, 53, 77, 77A, 88, 109,
159, 170, 176, 184, 509

**The Grapes**
76 Narrow St E14. 01-987 4396.
Atmospheric riverside pub with
good bar snacks and an upstairs
fish restaurant of high renown. Said
to be The Six Jolly Fellowship
Porters 'of dropsical appearance' in
Dickens' 'Our Mutual Friend'. *Open
LD Mon–Sat. Closed Sun.*
Docklands Light Railway:
Limehouse, West Ferry
▥ 5, 15, 15B, 40

**Gray's Inn**                        **4R1**
Holborn WC1. 01-405 8164. En-
trance from passage next to 22
High Holborn. An Inn of Court since
the 14thC, although the oldest surviving buildings are 17thC. Francis
Bacon had chambers here from
1577 until his death. It is said that
he laid out the gardens and planted
the Catalpas, now exceedingly
venerable and supported on
crutches. *Gardens open on summer weekday afternoons; Hall
open by written application to the
Under Treasurer. Free.*
⊖ Chancery Lane (not Sun),
Holborn
▥ 8, 17, 19, 22, 22B, 25, 38, 45,
46, 55, 171, 171A, 243, 259, 501,
505

**Great Eastern Hotel**               **4S5**
Liverpool St EC2. 01-283 4363. The
City Gates Bar and Restaurant – in
this the City's only hotel – is *open
every day all day* for full breakfasts,
light lunches, coffees or teas. There
is also the Entrecôte Restaurant
which is *open Mon–Fri only,* at
lunchtime, for steak and apple pie,
Brasserie Lynn offering fish dishes
from *Mon–Fri at lunchtime,* and
Balls Bros Wine Bar, *open LD
Mon–Fri, closes 20.00.*
⊖ Liverpool Street
▥ 5, 6, 8, 9, 11, 22, 22A, 22B, 35,
47, 48, 78, 100, 133, 149, 243A,
263A, 279A, 502, 505, 509
⇌ Liverpool Street

### Great Ormond Street Hospital for Sick Children    4R1

Great Ormond St WC1. 01-405 9200. Founded in 1851, this was England's first hospital for children – who were rarely admitted to general hospitals.

θ Russell Square

🚌 68, 77, 77A, 168, 188, 503

### Green Park    3O2

SW1. A simple green space with trees for shade and deckchairs for comfort. Henry VIII enclosed it as a deer park and later, in the 18thC, the fashionable gentry strolled within its bounds. The delicate gates opposite Buckingham Palace were made by Jean Tijou around 1690. *Open 05.00–24.00.* Free.

θ Green Park

🚌 9, 14, 19, 22, 25, 38

### Greenwich

SE10, SE3. Royal Greenwich once had a palace – in fact Henry VIII was born here. It was rebuilt, principally by Wren, as a Royal Naval College and is now the Royal Naval College. Greenwich remains rich in history, much of it within the beautiful royal park which sweeps down to the river. Here are the National Maritime Museum, and the Old Royal Observatory where you can see the Zero Meridian from which Greenwich Meantime is calculated. In dry dock by the waterside are 'Cutty Sark' and Sir Francis Chichester's 'Gipsy Moth'.

Greenwich Theatre offers new and classic plays and has an art gallery, too. There are concerts in the Wren Chapel of the Royal Naval College from October to April and again during the Greenwich Festival in June. The Festival itself attracts numerous visitors to its concerts, events and exhibitions which involve most possible venues in the area, including the open air. See separate entries for all the above.

θ Surrey Docks (then bus 1, 188), New Cross (then bus 177)
Docklands Light Railway: Island Gardens (then via foot tunnel)

🚌 1, 177, 180, 188, 286

≠ Greenwich

Boats from Westminster and Charing Cross Piers

### Greenwich Theatre

Crooms Hill SE10. 01-858 7755. Purpose-built with a large ground floor restaurant which has a bar in one corner and a wine bar in the other. Upstairs an airy space houses changing exhibitions of paintings. The theatre itself mounts a season of seven plays a year – new plays, revivals and classics, often with famous names in the cast.

θ Surrey Docks (then bus 1, 188), New Cross (then bus 177)
Docklands Light Railway: Island Gardens (then via foot tunnel)

🚌 1, 177, 180, 188, 286

≠ Greenwich

### Grosvenor House Hotel    3N1

Park La W1. 01-499 6363. Unobtrusive luxury in this large hotel with extensive banqueting facilities, its own garage, shopping arcade, swimming pools, restaurants and coffee house. The exclusive restaurant 90 Park Lane has nouvelle cuisine, The Pavilion is a coffee house-cum-brasserie with afternoon teas, and the informal Pasta Vino e Fantasia has fresh pasta daily.

θ Marble Arch

🚌 2A, 2B, 10, 16, 30, 36, 73, 74, 82, 137, 503, 506

### Guildhall    4S4

Off Gresham St EC2. 01-606 3030. The City is governed from this primarily 15thC building with a façade by George Dance, 1789, and later restoration by Sir Giles Gilbert Scott. You may view the medieval Great Hall unless a council meeting is in progress. The library is wonderfully rich in works on London and the art gallery has occasional exhibitions from visiting art societies.

*Open   09.30–17.30   Mon–Sat.
Closed Sun.* Free.
⊖ Bank
🚍 6, 8, 9, 11, 15B, 21, 22, 22B,
25, 43, 76, 133, 141, 149, 279A,
501, 502

**Guildhall Art Gallery**   *4S4*
Aldermanbury EC2. 01-606 3030.
Has its own entrance by the side of
the Guildhall and uses its two floors
of exhibition space to display the
works of professional artists in a
programme of 10 or 12 different
shows a year. Pictures are usually
for sale. *Opening times vary.
Closed between exhibitions.* Free.
⊖ Bank
🚍 6, 8, 9, 11, 15B, 21, 22, 22B,
25, 43, 76, 133, 141, 149, 279A,
501, 502

**Guinness World of**   *3N3*
**Records Exhibition**
Trocadero, Piccadilly W1. 01-439
1791. For those who like to go to
extremes – compare yourself with
the tallest man and smallest
woman, use VDUs to check your
knowledge of sporting records,
watch videos of people eating more
than anyone else, diving from
higher into less water than anyone
else, and collecting more bees on
the chin than ever before recorded.

Plentiful cafés and other facilities in
the encompassing Trocadero complex. *Open 10.00–21.30 Mon–
Sun.* Charge.
⊖ Piccadilly Circus
🚍 3, 6, 9, 12, 13, 14, 15, 15B, 19,
22, 22B, 38, 53, 88, 159, 509

**The Gun**
27 Coldharbour E14. 01-987 1692.
Engaging old pub with three bars
and a large balcony overhanging the
river. Good bar lunches but no food
in the evenings or at weekends.
*Open Mon–Sun; L Mon–Fri only.*
Docklands Light Railway: South
Quay
🚍 D5, D6, D7, 277

**Gunnersbury Park Museum**
Gunnersbury Park, Pope's La W5.
01-992 1612. The fine rooms of this
one-time home of a branch of the
Rothschild family are used for a
series of regularly changing exhibitions on local history, archaeology
and topography. There is also a
transport collection of aged bikes
and chariots and a fully equipped
Victorian kitchen. The grounds are
now a public park with a lakeful of
waterfowl, a pleasant café, and a
'Temple' used for musical enter-
tainments and lectures (summer
only). *Open 13.00–17.00 Mon–Fri;
14.00–18.00 Sat, Sun & some Nat
Hols. Closed mornings, 24–26 Dec,
Good Friday & 16.00 in winter.*
Free.
⊖ Acton Town (then bus E3)
🚍 E3

**Guy's Hospital**   *4U4*
St Thomas St SE1. 01-407 7600.
General hospital founded by
Thomas Guy in the early 18thC.
Famous names who worked here
include Richard Bright, Thomas
Addison and Thomas Hodgkin,
each of whom discovered the dis-
ease now named after him. 24hr
casualty.
⊖ London Bridge
🚍 17, 21, 35, 40, 43, 44, 47, 48,
133, 501, 505, 510, 513, P3, P11

# H

## Habitat 1D5
196 Tottenham Ct Rd W1. 01-631 3880. Not so much a shop, more a way of life! Modern furniture, household goods and kitchen equipment in brightly coloured, simple but striking designs. Also has other branches. *Open 10.00– 18.00 Mon; 09.30–18.00 Tue, Wed & Fri; 09.30–19.30 Thur; 09.00– 18.00 Sat. Closed Sun.*
⊖ Warren Street
🚌 10, 14, 14A, 18, 24, 27, 29, 30, 73, 134, 135, 176, 253

## Hainault Forest
Essex. 01-500 3106. Once a part of the great forest of Essex, known as Waltham Forest, this area is now a country park of 1,100 acres of extensive woodland with a lake, two 18-hole golf courses, a playing field and facilities for angling, riding, picnicking, cross-country running and orienteering. *Open 24 hours. Free.*
⊖ Hainault (then bus 247)
🚌 247 (also 62 at certain times)

## Half Moon Pub
93 Lower Richmond Rd, Putney SW15. 01-788 2387. Large pub with spacious back room where a wide range of music is played nightly and at Sunday lunchtimes. Top names sometimes billed here. *Open LD Mon–Sun.*
⊖ Putney Bridge
🚌 22, 265, C4

## Ham House
Richmond, Surrey. 01-940 1950. A richly baroque Stuart house on the banks of the Thames outside Richmond, now administered by the Victoria and Albert Museum and offering the best glimpse of 17thC life at that social level to be found anywhere in England. Portraits by Lely and Kneller, tapestries, cabinets of miniatures, Chinese porcelain, fine pieces of furniture and attractive formal gardens, in which the Orangery has become a pleasant tea room. The 20-minute audio visual show in the Gentleman's Parlour is a good place to start the tour. *Open 11.00–17.00 Tue–Sun. Closed Mon, Nat Hols & 16.00 in winter. Charge.*
⊖ Richmond (then bus 71)
🚌 71
≷ Richmond

## Hamleys 3M3
188–196 Regent St W1. 01-734 3161. London's largest toy shop with four floors richly stocked with delights for all ages – from dolls to electronic games, tiny pocket-money novelties to vast model railway set-ups. *Open 09.00–17.30 (to 20.00 Thur) Mon–Sat. Also open some Nat Hols.*
⊖ Oxford Circus
🚌 3, 6, 12, 13, 15, 15B, 53, 88, 159, 509, C2

## Hampstead Heath
NW3. The 790 acres of the heath sprawl over sandy hills and dip into wooded valleys. Dick Turpin ranged over it and drank, or hid, in most of the inns on its borders. There are wonderful views over London from here, especially from Jack Straw's Castle, rebuilt in the 60s on the site of the pub where Dickens once drank. The 16thC Spaniard's Inn, once the residence of the Spanish Ambassador to the Court of James I, is equally famous, as is Kenwood

House with its collection of fine pictures from the Iveagh Bequest and its lakeside concerts in summer. As well as its natural features, the Heath has 10 tennis courts, an Olympic running track and grass skiing. The August Bank Holiday Fair is well worth a visit. *Open 24 hrs.*

⊖ Hampstead
🚌 24, 46, 168, 210, 268

**Hampstead Theatre Club**
Swiss Cottage Centre, Avenue Rd NW3. 01-722 9301. One of the leading club theatres which has acquired a respectability at variance with its controversial and experimental productions. Has passed several excellent productions on to the West End and to television. Bar and coffee bar.

⊖ Swiss Cottage
🚌 13, 31, 46, 82, 113, 268, C11

**Hampstead Village**
NW3. High society came to the country village of Hampstead in the 18thC when a mineral spring was discovered and thought to have healing properties, and most of the attractive houses and alleyways date from this period. Constable lived and worked here and so did Keats and Galsworthy. Still very much a village, and still popular with writers and artists of all persuasions.

⊖ Hampstead
🚌 46, 210, 268

**Hampton Court Palace**
Hampton Court, Middx. 01-977 8441. Begun by Cardinal Wolsey in 1514, enlarged by Henry VIII, repaired by Charles II, extended by Sir Christopher Wren under William and Mary, with further interior decoration carried out on the orders of Queen Anne, George I and George II. The State Apartments were first opened to the public by Queen Victoria.

Vast and grand, on a prime riverside site, its sweeping grounds contain the famous Maze. Interior treasures include paintings by Giorgione, Titian, Tintoretto and early primitives, wall and ceiling paintings by Thornhill, Vanbrugh and Verrio, 16th and 17thC tapestries, the Chapel Royal, the magnificent Tudor Great Watching Chamber, and the Great Hall with its superb hammerbeam roof.

The Cartoon Gallery was badly damaged by fire in 1986 and will be closed to the public for some years. Rebuilding and restoration work inevitably limit the tour, but most of the Palace is still accessible. There is also a licensed restaurant and cafeteria. *Open Mar–Oct 10.00–18.00 Mon–Sun; Nov–Feb 10.00–16.30 Mon–Sun.* Last admissions *30 mins* before closing time. Note that the Maze and some other parts of the Palace are closed from *Nov–Mar.* Charge.

⊖ Hammersmith (then bus 267)
🚌 111, 131, 216, 267
Green Line 715, 718
≠ Hampton Court

**Hard Rock Café**    *3O2*
150 Old Park La W1. 01-629 0382. One of London's most popular, long-established hamburger joints. Vast room on two levels with huge wooden tables and non-stop blaring rock music. The hamburgers and steaks are excellent – all prime meat. Expect a very long queue outside or have a drink at the bar while you wait. *Open LD Mon–Sun.*

⊖ Hyde Park Corner
🚌 2A, 2B, 9, 10, 14, 16, 19, 22, 25, 30, 36, 38, 52, 52A, 73, 74, 82, 137, 503, 506

**Harrods**    *2H6*
Knightsbridge SW1. 01-730 1234. World-famous department store which prides itself on selling virtu-

ally everything – furniture, musical instruments, superb men's, ladies' and children's fashions, up-to-the-minute styles in the Way In boutique, expensive fabrics from Switzerland, Italy and France, gemstones, silver, books and exotic pets. There are also the magnificent marbled Edwardian food halls where displays of fish have become an art form, a restaurant and various cafés and juice bars. *Open 09.00–18.00 Mon, Tue & Thur-Sat; 09.30–19.00 Wed. Closed Sun.*
⊖ Knightsbridge
🚌 9, 10, 14, 19, 22, 30, 52, 52A, 74, 137, 503, C1

**Harvey Nichols**  *3O1*
Knightsbridge SW1. 01-235 5000. Major department store with stylish clothes from top British, American and continental designers, housewares, home furnishings, haberdashery and perfumery. Harvey's Restaurant, the Zone Café or The Coffee Shop for coffees, lunches and teas. *Open 10.00–20.00 Mon–Fri; 10.00–18.00 Sat. Closed Sun.*
⊖ Knightsbridge
🚌 9, 10, 14, 19, 22, 30, 52, 52A, 74, 137, 503, C1

**Hatchards**  *3N3*
187 Piccadilly W1. 01-439 9921. Reliable and knowledgeable bookshop established in 1797, with a calm and dignified atmosphere. Good stock of books on most subjects, apart from academic or technical. Large paperback section downstairs, excellent children's section upstairs, also rare and art books. *Open 09.00–17.30 Mon–Fri; 09.00–13.00 Sat. Closed Sat afternoon & Sun.*
⊖ Piccadilly Circus
🚌 9, 14, 19, 22, 38

**Hatfield House**
Hatfield, Herts. 070 72 62823. A mellow and completely preserved Jacobean mansion with a magnificent interior built in 1607–11 by Robert Cecil, 1st Earl of Salisbury. It is still the home of the Cecil family. The Tudor Old Royal Palace nearby was the home of Queen Elizabeth I. Superb collection of 16th, 17th and 18thC portraits, manuscripts and relics. Lavish Elizabethan banquets are held all year round, enquire on 070 72 62055. *Open Mar–Oct 12.00–17.00 Tue–Sat; 14.00–17.30 Sun; 11.00–17.00 Nat Hols. Closed Oct–Mar.* Charge.
Green Line 797
➤ Hatfield

**Haymarket (Theatre Royal)**  *4N4*
Haymarket SW1. 01-930 9832. Founded in the 18thC as 'the little theatre in the Hay', it moved in the 1820s to the present building with its grand Palladian Nash exterior and pretty gilded interior. Sometimes enlivened by the ghost of Mr Buckstone, Queen Victoria's favourite actor-manager, who no doubt approves of the policy to present plays of quality.
⊖ Piccadilly Circus
🚌 3, 6, 9, 12, 13, 14, 15, 15B, 19, 22, 22B, 38, 53, 88, 159, 509

**Hay's Galleria**  *6U5*
Tooley St SE1. The façades of the Victorian warehouses which surrounded Hay's Dock have been retained and the dock filled in to form the floor of the Galleria – billed as 'London's new shopping and eating experience'. A wonderful kinetic sculpture-cum-fountain, the Navigators, is the centrepiece of an elegant and lofty arcade with a barrel-

vaulted glass roof. Off this are to be found a range of up-market High Street shops, a wine bar, a brasserie and a pub-brasserie. Galleria *open 06.00–23.30 Mon–Sat; 06.00–22.30 Sun.* Shops *open 09.00–17.30 Mon–Sat;* eating places *open LD Mon–Sun (wine bar closed Sun).*
⊖ London Bridge
🚍 17, 21, 35, 40, 43, 44, 47, 48, 133, 501, 505, 510, 513, P3, P11

### Hayward Gallery 3N5
South Bank SE1. 01-928 3144. Can be picked out from the rest of the South Bank complex by the kinetic sculpture it wears on its head. Administered by the Arts Council who mount major changing exhibitions of British, American and European art. *Open 10.00–20.00 Mon–Thur; 10.00–18.00 Fri & Sat; 12.00–18.00 Sun.* Charge.
⊖ Waterloo
🚍 1, 4, 68, 76, 149, 168, 171, 171A, 176, 188, 501, 502, 505, 507, 513, C1, P11

### Heals 1D5
196 Tottenham Court Rd W1. 01-636 1666. Three famous floors of furniture, furnishings and home accessories – the best of British and continental designs. Also a flower shop and a restaurant which opens 30 mins later and closes 30 mins earlier than the shop. *Shop open 10.00–18.00 Mon; 09.30–18.00 Tue, Wed & Fri; 09.30–19.00 Thur; 09.00–18.00 Sat.* Closed Sun.

⊖ Goodge Street, Warren Street
🚍 10, 14, 14A, 18, 24, 27, 29, 30, 73, 134, 135, 176, 253

### Heathrow Airport (London Heathrow)
01-759 4321. Major international airport, extremely busy, with a viewing terrace above Queen's Building (between Terminals 1 & 2) from which to watch the planes. There is also a roof garden, a small children's play area and several levels of refreshments. *Viewing terrace open 10.00–18.00 Mon–Sun; closes 16.00 in winter.* Charge.
⊖ Heathrow Terminals 1, 2, 3, and Heathrow Terminal 4
🚍 105, 111, 140, 202, 223, 285, U5, Airbus A1, A2

### Heinz Gallery 1E3
RIBA Drawings Collection, 21 Portman Sq W1. 01-580 5533. The Royal Institute of British Architects' extensive collection of drawings may be viewed by appointment from *10.00–13.00 Mon–Fri.* From time to time, there are public exhibitions arranged around specific themes. *Exhibitions open 11.00–17.00 Mon–Fri; 10.00–13.00 Sat. Closed between exhibitions, except by appointment.* Free.
⊖ Marble Arch
🚍 2A, 2B, 13, 30, 74, 82, 113, 159

### Henry VIII's Wine Cellar 3O4
Whitehall SW1. This Tudor wine cellar, built for Cardinal Wolsey, is, in company with the Banqueting House, a remnant of the Tudor Palace of Whitehall. *Guided tours on Sat afternoon from Mar–Sep.* Apply in writing to the Department of the Environment, Room 10/14, St Christopher House, Southwark St SE1. 01-928 3666, extn 4673.
⊖ Charing Cross
🚍 3, 11, 12, 24, 29, 53, 77, 77A, 88, 109, 159, 170, 184

### Her Majesty's Theatre 3N4
Haymarket SW1. 01-930 6606. A fine Victorian baroque theatre founded by Sir Herbert Beerbohm Tree. Successful productions include 'West Side Story', 'Fiddler on the Roof' and 'Amadeus'.
⊖ Piccadilly Circus
🚍 3, 6, 9, 12, 13, 15, 15B, 22B, 53, 88, 159, 509

## Highgate
NW3. Attractive largely 18thC hill-top village whose residents are on a level with the cross on top of St Paul's. It shares with Hampstead an arty-literary reputation; Coleridge and A. E. Housman lived here.
⊖ Archway (then bus)
🚌 143, 210, 271

## Highgate Cemetery
Swains La N6. Everyone thinks of Karl Marx, and his tomb is here, in the newer eastern section, along with George Eliot, Herbert Spencer and Sir Ralph Richardson. In the older western section is the great Egyptian gateway (which has loomed menacingly in Hammer House of Horror movies), with wondrous funerary sculpture, ivy-clad mourners, hovering angels and native woodland rich in wild flowers and birds. *Open 09.00–17.00 Mon–Sat; 14.00–17.00 Sun. Closes 16.00 in winter. Tours on the hour from 10.00–15.00.*
⊖ Archway
🚌 143, 210, 271

## Hilton Hotel 3O2
22 Park La W1. 01-493 8000. Modern luxurious hotel overlooking Hyde Park. The Roof Restaurant has splendid views, buffet lunches and dinner dances. There are also two bars, the British Harvest Restaurant, serving local ingredients, in season; a discotheque called 22 Park Lane, and Trader Vic's with its South Seas decor, Asian cuisine,

and cocktails decorated with floating flowers.
⊖ Hyde Park Corner
🚌 2A, 2B, 10, 16, 30, 36, 73, 74, 82, 137, 503, 506

## Hippodrome 3N4
Hippodrome Corner WC2. 01-437 4311. Peter Stringfellow's most lavish night club with rainbow-laser ceiling, smoke machines, a huge video machine, flying speakers, a magic stage, six bars including the exclusive Star Bar, a restaurant, live dancing acts nightly, three live bands a week, and a young clientele of wonderful weirds, juvenile aristos and pop stars. Selective and idiosyncratic admission vetting. *Open 21.00–03.00 nightly.*
⊖ Leicester Square
🚌 24, 29, 176

## Hispaniola
The Thames at Victoria Embankment, Charing Cross WC2. 01-839 3011. A floating restaurant. Romantic setting and good Spanish food on upper or lower deck.
⊖ Embankment
🚌 1, 3, 6, 9, 11, 12, 13, 15, 15B, 22B, 24, 29, 53, 77, 77A, 88, 109, 159, 170, 176, 184, 509 (to Trafalgar Square)

## HMSO Bookshop 4S1
49 High Holborn WC1. 01-211 5656. The retail outlet for the publications of Her Majesty's Stationery Office. This is where to buy the venerable 'Hansard' – the verbatim record of the daily proceedings in both chambers of the Houses of Parliament. Also carries National Heritage publications, regional guides, some Ordnance Survey maps, and publications from the EEC, the UN, and other overseas bodies. *Open 08.30–17.15 Mon–Fri; 08.30–13.00 Sat.*
⊖ Chancery Lane (not Sun)
🚌 8, 17, 18, 22, 22B, 25, 45, 46, 171A, 243, 259, 501

## HMV Record Store 3M3
150 Oxford St W1. 01-631 3423. The biggest record store in the world with a comprehensive stock of music of every kind. Two vast floors of records, compact discs, videos, cassettes, books, T-shirts and stereo accessories. Also has a Ticketmaster outlet. *Open 09.30–*

*19.00 (to 20.00 Thur) Mon–Sat. Closed Sun.*
θ Oxford Circus
⊞ 7, 8, 10, 25, 73, 176, 503

### Hogarth's House

Hogarth La, Great West Rd W4. 01-994 6757. This was William Hogarth's country house from 1749 until the night before he died 15 years later and it contains an un-rivalled collection of prints, 'visual writings' satirising the life of his day. 'The Harlot's Progress' and 'Marriage à la Mode' are here, to-gether with jolly 'Beer Street' and dismal 'Gin Lane'. *Open 11.00– 18.00 Mon & Wed–Sat; 14.00– 18.00 Sun. Closed Tue, Good Fri & 16.00 Oct–Apr.* Free.
θ Hammersmith (then bus 290), Turnham Green (then walk)
⊞ 290

### Holiday Inn, Marble Arch    3M1

134 George St W1. 01-723 1277. Modern hotel with 241 rooms, a conference capacity for 150 and its own swimming pool and sauna. Le Brasserie Village is open all day, every day.
θ Marble Arch
⊞ 2A, 2B, 6, 7, 8, 10, 12, 15, 16, 16A, 30, 36, 73, 74, 82, 88, 135, 137, 503, 506

### Holiday Inn, Mayfair    3N2

3 Berkeley St W1. 01-493 8282. Modern hotel but with Louis XV-style interior. There are 189 rooms and a conference capacity for 100 delegates. The Berkeley Room, a silver service restaurant, is *open daily from 07.00–23.30.*
θ Green Park
⊞ 9, 14, 19, 22, 25, 38

### Holland Park    2G1

W8. Once the private park of Hol-land House, a Jacobean mansion which was the seat of the Whig Foxes – Lords Holland from the 18thC. Largely destroyed in World War II, the remaining wing is a youth hostel. The Orangery and Ice House hold changing exhibitions of paintings and ceramics from March to November, and the Court Theatre in the courtyard presents opera and ballet during July. This area, with its attendant Dutch and rose gardens, is floodlit every night. The northern part is 28 acres of verdant woodland where tree-creepers, owls and green wood-peckers live among 3,000 species of trees and plants. *Area around house closes 24.00. Rest of park closes at dusk.*
θ Holland Park, High Street Kensington
⊞ 9, 10, 12, 27, 28, 31, 33, 49, 88, C1

### Holy Trinity Church    2H6

Brompton Rd SW7. 01-581 8255. Behind Brompton Oratory stands this Victorian Gothic parish church, consecrated in 1892. The choir, of mainly professional singers, can be heard at Sunday morning family service at 10.30; there is also a well-attended informal service at 18.30 on Sunday.
θ South Kensington
⊞ 14, 30, 74, 503, C1

### Holy Trinity Church    5W3

Sloane Square SW1. 01-235 3383. A living and lovely church and also a memorial to the Arts and Crafts Movement of the 1890s. The graceful design is by J. D. Sedding and the east window was planned by Burne-Jones with glass by William Morris. Occasional con-certs. Donation welcome.
θ Sloane Square
⊞ 11, 19, 22, 137, C1

### Honourable Artillery Company    4R4

Armoury House, City Rd EC1. 01-606 4644. Victorian castellated fortress (1857) hides the Georgian

(1735) headquarters of the oldest regiment in the British Army. Supplies the Guard of Honour for Lord Mayor's shows and for Royalty visiting the City. *Open 12.00–18.00 Mon–Fri.* Free.
⊖ Old Street
🚌 43, 214, 263A

**Horniman Museum**
100 London Rd SE23. 01-699 2339. Given to the LCC (London County Council) in 1901 by Frederick Horniman of the famous tea firm, together with his personal collection of ethnography and natural history. Though enlarged since, it has retained the special charm peculiar to such places with its masks and stuffed tigers, mummies and musical instruments and temporary exhibitions on lives and lifestyles. In the aquarium there are tree frogs, piranhas and a working beehive. There is an animal enclosure and nature trail in the park at the back. *Open 10.30–18.00 Mon–Sat; 14.00–18.00 Sun. Closed Xmas.* Free.
🚌 12A, 12B, 63, 78, 176, 185, 185A, P4
⇌ Forest Hill

**Horse Guards** **3O4**
Whitehall SW1. The building is by William Kent, 1750–60, and Horse Guards Parade is the scene of the ceremony of Trooping the Colour

on or near the Queen's official birthday on 11th June. A daily spectacle is the changing of the Queen's Life Guard, on their splendid black horses, *at 11.00 Mon–Sat & 10.00 Sun.*
⊖ Westminster, Charing Cross
🚌 3, 11, 12, 24, 29, 53, 77, 77A, 88, 109, 159, 170, 184

**House of Fraser** **2H3**
63 Kensington High St W8. 01-937 5432. Barkers no more, but this landmark store has been lavishly refurbished to show off both its beautiful art deco features and its quality merchandise. Cosmetics and fragrance hall, up-market fashions, household and electrical goods, bureau de change, restaurant. *Open 09.30–19.00 Mon–Fri; 09.00–18.00 Sat.*
⊖ High Street Kensington
🚌 9, 10, 27, 28, 31, 33, 49, 52, 52A, C1

**House of Fraser** **3M2**
318 Oxford St W1. 01-629 8800. Department store with fashions for men, women and children including top designer labels and upmarket high street fashions. Also has an accessories department, Astral sports and household goods. Café, restaurant, export scheme, shopping advisor. *Open 09.30–18.00 Mon–Wed & Fri; 09.30–20.00 Thur; 09.00–18.00 Sat.*
⊖ Bond Street
🚌 6, 7, 8, 10, 12, 13, 15, 16A, 25, 73, 88, 113, 135, 137, 159, 503

**House of St Barnabas** **3M3**
1 Greek St W1. Early Georgian town house at one corner of Soho Square with fine wood carving and rococo plasterwork inside. Now owned by a charity caring for London's destitutes. *Open Mon morning & Thur afternoon.* Donation appreciated.
⊖ Tottenham Court Road
🚌 7, 8, 10, 14, 14A, 19, 22, 22B, 24, 25, 29, 38, 55, 73, 134, 176, 503

**Houses of Parliament** **3P4**
St Margaret St SW1. 01-219 3000. More properly the New Palace of Westminster, by Barry and Pugin 1840–68. The grand and glorious Gothic structure was built around the 11thC Westminster Hall,

whose 14thC timber roof rivals any in Europe. Still has royal status. Tour the building when the house is not sitting or listen from the Strangers Gallery when it is. Write to your MP for an invitation, or join the queue outside. *Open 09.00–17.50 Mon–Sat. Closed Sun*. Free.

⊖ Westminster

🚌 3, 11, 12, 24, 29, 53, 77, 77A, 88, 109, 159, 170, 184, C1

### Hyatt Carlton Tower     3P1
Cadogan Pl SW1. 01-235 5411. Sophisticated hotel, with a high standard of cuisine and service. Ambitious, largely French menu in the Chelsea Room, notable roast beef in the Rib Room and a new addition – The Peak Health Club.

⊖ Sloane Square

🚌 11, 19, 22, 137, C1

### Hyde Park     3N1
W2. The most informal of the royal parks, appropriated by Henry VIII from the Abbot of Westminster and used as a royal hunting ground until

it was opened to the public during the reign of James I. The Great Exhibition of 1851 was staged here, in Paxton's Crystal Palace which originally stood between Knightsbridge and Rotten Row.

A wild bird sanctuary, various sporting facilities, the fine artificial lake called the Serpentine with its Lido, hire-boats and restaurants at either end, and the famous Speaker's Corner are among the Park's many attractions. Sadly, many of the magnificent trees fell victim to the storm of October 1987, but a replanting programme is underway.

The Household Cavalry Review is held here in spring, the London to Brighton Veteran Car Rally begins 'ere in autumn, and military bands ilay rousing music on summer Sunlays.

➔ Marble Arch, Lancaster Gate, 4yde Park Corner

🚌 2A, 2B, 6, 7, 8, 9, 10, 12, 14, 15, 16, 16A, 19, 22, 25, 30, 36, 38, 52, 52A, 73, 74, 82, 88, 135, 137, 503, 506

### Hyde Park Corner     3O1
Consists of Constitution Arch at the top of Constitution Hill, and the Ionic screen of three classical-style triumphal arches at the entry to Hyde Park, by Decimus Burton, 1825. Admire too the Duke of Wellington's house, once known as 'Number One, London'.

⊖ Hyde Park Corner

🚌 2A, 2B, 9, 10, 14, 16, 19, 22, 25, 30, 36, 38, 52, 52A, 73, 74, 82, 137, 503, 506

---

**London Transport 24-hour information service**
For any information on travel in Greater London – routes, fares, times – telephone 01-222 1234 at any time of the day or night.

## ICA    3N4
### (Institute of Contemporary Arts)
12 Carlton House Ter SW1. 01-930
0493. Recorded information 01-930
6393. The three galleries hold three
simultaneous exhibitions of paintings, drawings or photographs. The
cinema screens foreign, avant-
garde and unusual films and there is
a children's cinema club at weekends. The cinematheque shows
low-budget films and videos and
there is also a video library. The
studio theatre changes shape to
suit productions and there are
lunchtime and evening talks and
seminars. Fully licensed healthfood
restaurant. *Open 12.00–23.00
Mon–Sun. Galleries close 20.00.*
Charge (for day or annual membership).
⊖ Charing Cross, Piccadilly Circus
🚌 3, 6, 9, 12, 13, 15, 15B, 53, 88,
159, 509

## Imperial War Museum    3P6
Lambeth Rd SE1. 01-735 8922.
An extremely popular national
museum on all aspects of warfare –
military and domestic – concerning
Britain and the Commonwealth
from 1914. It has recently under-
gone a major redevelopment programme. Housed in the central
portion of the old Bethlehem Royal
Hospital for the Insane – or Bedlam.
There is also an art gallery, film
shows at weekends, and reference
departments of documents, film,
photographs, printed books and
sound records, open for study by
appointment. The museum's two
out-stations are 'HMS Belfast' in
the Port of London and Duxford
Airfield in Cambridge. *Open 10.00–
18.00 Tue–Sat; 14.00–17.30 Sun.
Closed Mon, Nat Hols & 17.00 in
winter.* Free.
⊖ Lambeth North
🚌 3, 44, 109, 159, 510

## Inn on the Park Hotel    3O2
Park La W1. 01-499 0888. Luxurious modern hotel of international
standing, with views over Hyde
Park and two restaurants, the ele-

gant Four Seasons and the less formal Lanes. Despite its relative new-
ness, it has much of the charm and
comfortable appeal of an older
establishment.
⊖ Hyde Park Corner
🚌 2A, 2B, 9, 10, 14, 16, 19, 22,
25, 30, 36, 38, 52, 52A, 73, 74, 82,
137, 503, 506

## Inns of Chancery    4S2
Before the 18thC, a student of law
had first to go through one of the
nine Inns of Chancery then existing.
They have now mostly disap-
peared. Staple Inn, High Holborn
remains a fine Elizabethan building.
Others survive only as names:
Clifford Inn, Thavies Inn and Fur-
nival Inn.
⊖ Chancery Lane (not Sun)
🚌 8, 17, 18, 22, 22B, 25, 45, 46,
171A, 243, 259, 501

## Intercontinental Hotel    3O2
Hyde Park Corner W1. 01-409
3131. Good modern hotel, in a central location with 500 rooms, conference facilities, its own Fitness
Club and Sauna, and three restaurants – the Coffee House,

Hamilton's Restaurant and Night-club and Le Soufflé with its Michelin star.
⊖ Hyde Park Corner
🚌 2A, 2B, 9, 10, 14, 16, 19, 22, 25, 30, 36, 38, 52, 52A, 73, 74, 82, 137, 503, 506

## Island Gardens DLR Terminus & Shop

Isle of Dogs E14. The DLR terminal is a magnet for tourists because Greenwich, across the river, looks beautiful from here and can actually be reached by way of the foot tunnel. Shop *open 11.00–16.00 Mon–Fri; 11.00–17.00 Sat & Sun.*
Docklands Light Railway: Island Gardens
🚌 277, D7, P14

## Isle of Dogs

E14. Not strictly an island, but a peninsula formed by a loop in the river. The land was regularly flooded until a system of drainage ditches was introduced in the 17thC – 'Dogs' may be a corruption of 'Dikes' – and was unpopulated until the coming of the Docks in the early 19thC. Nevertheless there is a strong sense of community among the islanders, partly borne of the isolation imposed by limited transport links with the rest of East London.

Major change began in 1981 when the Government-inspired and -funded London Docklands Development Corporation (LDDC) established an Enterprise Zone in the centre, with financial incentives to attract developers and businesses, among them the massive new international financial centre at Canary Wharf.

Improved communications – with the Docklands Light Railway

as the star of the show – make it easy now to visit this extraordinary area with its mix of locals and in-comers, its controversial hi-tech buildings and thriving city farm, its revamped docks and derelict corners, its old traditions and new money.
Docklands Light Railway: West India Quay, Island Gardens and all stations between
🚌 277, D5, D6, D7, P14

## Ismaili Centre                    2J5

1–7 Cromwell Gdns SW7. Founded by His Highness, the Aga Khan, the architecturally acclaimed Ismaili Centre is the principal Islamic Cultural and Religious Centre in London. Within it is the Zamana Gallery (see p. 136), an independent exhibition area with its own entrance in Cromwell Rd. *Centre not open to public.*
⊖ South Kensington
🚌 14, 30, 45, 49, 74, 219, 503, C1

# J

## Jack Straw's Castle
North End Way NW3. 01-435 8885.
Rebuilt in the 1960s on the site of
the original pub, which was named
for Wat Tyler's comrade who was
hanged outside. Unusual weather-
board frontage, marvellous views
over Hampstead Heath, a sunny
courtyard, snack bar, cocktail bar
and upstairs Carvery. *Open LD
Mon–Sat & L Sun. Closed D Sun.*
⊖ Hampstead
🚌 210, 268

## Jaeger                          3M3
204 Regent St W1. 01-734 8211.
Famous for well-cut, smart English
clothes. A reliable source of cashmere, camel-hair coats and pure
wool knitteds. Also cocktail and
evening wear. Men's clothes, too.
*Open 09.30–18.00 Mon, Wed, Fri
& Sat; to 19.00 Thur. Closed Sun.*
⊖ Oxford Circus
🚌 3, 6, 12, 13, 15, 15B, 53, 88,
159, 509, C2

## Jewel Tower                     3P4
Old Palace Yd SW1. Discreet
amidst the Gothic finery of Westminster Abbey and the Houses of
Parliament stands this 14thC frag-
ment of the old Palace of Westminster. Once Edward III's treasure
house, it now displays medieval
carvings. *Open 10.00–17.30 Mon–
Sat. Closed Sun. Free.*
⊖ Westminster
🚌 3, 11, 12, 24, 29, 53, 77, 77A,
88, 109, 159, 170, 184, C1

## Jewish Museum                   15C
Woburn House, Tavistock Sq WC1.
01-388 4525. A small museum in an
upstairs room of the Jewish Com-
munal Centre, with a collection of
Jewish ceremonial art illustrating
Jewish life, history and religion, particularly in Britain. Two audio-visual
programmes on Judaism are
shown at varying times, often to
suit visiting groups. *Open 10.00–
16.00 Sun & Tue–Thur; 10.00–
16.00 Fri in summer; 10.00–12.45
Fri in winter. Closed Mon, Sat, Jew-*

*ish & Nat Hols.* Donations welcome.
⊖ Euston, Euston Square
🚌 10, 14, 14A, 18, 30, 68, 73, 77,
77A, 168, 188

## Joe Allen's                     3M5
13 Exeter St WC2. 01-836 0651.
Fashionably crowded, especially after the theatre, this large converted
warehouse restaurant follows the
pattern of its New York and Paris
counterparts. Dim lights, slick and
friendly service, killer cocktails,
blackboard menu of steak, chilli,
spinach salad, pecan pie. Reservations wise. *Open LD Mon–Sun.*
⊖ Charing Cross (then any bus
along the Strand)
🚌 1, 4, 6, 9, 11, 13, 15, 15B, 68,
77, 77A, 168, 170, 171, 171A,
176, 188, 501, 502, 505, 509, 513

## John Lewis                      3M2
Oxford St W1. 01-629 7711. De-

partment store with the largest dress fabric department in Europe, a large furnishing fabric department, furniture, china, glass, bureau de change, export bureau and interpreters. Prides itself on being 'never knowingly undersold'. The Place to Eat has seven different service counters with seven different menus and there is also a Coffee Shop. Many branches. *Open 09.00–17.30 Mon–Wed, Fri & Sat; 09.30–20.00 Thur.*
⊖ Bond Street, Oxford Circus
🚌 3, 6, 7, 8, 10, 12, 13, 15, 15B, 16A, 25, 53, 73, 88, 113, 135, 137, 159, 176, 503

### Dr Johnson's House 4S2
17 Gough Sq, off Fleet St EC4. 01-353 3745. The industrious Dr J. lived here from 1748–59 and it was in the attic that much of the famous 'Dictionary' was compiled, with the help of six copyists. The furnishings and effects include a first edition of the great work, contemporary portraits, and the last will and testament. *Open 11.00–17.30 Mon–Sat. Closed Sun, Nat Hols & 17.00 in winter.* Charge.
⊖ Chancery Lane (not Sun), Blackfriars
🚌 4, 6, 9, 11, 15, 15B, 17, 45, 63, 76, 141, 171A, 502, 509, 513

### Julie's Bar
137 Portland Rd W11. 01-727 7985. Downstairs is a wooden, mirrored bar, upstairs an intimate, informal lounge and a small glassed-in balcony piled with Persian rug cushions. Wines mostly French, hot dishes and salads always available, also traditional Sunday lunch and proper cream teas. *Open 10.00–23.00 Mon–Sat; 10.00–22.30 Sun.*
⊖ Holland Park
🚌 12, 88

# K

## Keats House

Wentworth Pl, Keats Grove NW3. 01-435 2062. A pair of semi-detached houses in which Keats spent much of his most prolific period, 1818–21. This is where he wrote 'Ode To A Nightingale', 'Lamia', 'La Belle Dame Sans Mercie', 'On A Grecian Urn', and became engaged to Fanny Brawne next door. There is a wealth of memorabilia – letters, pictures and annotated books. The Keats Memorial Library is open by appointment only. *Open 14.00–18.00 Mon–Fri; 10.00–17.00 Sat. Closed Sun.* Free.
⊖ Hampstead
🚌 24, 46, 168, C11
≷ Hampstead Heath

## Kensal Green Cemetery

Harrow Rd W10. Its 56 acres of splendid stone and marble tombs trace the decline of the 'classic' and the introduction of the Gothic style. Wilkie Collins, the two Brunels, Princess Sophia, the Duke of Sussex, G. K. Chesterton, Thackeray and Trollope lie here.
🚌 18, 52
≷ Kensal Green

## Kensington Gardens　　2G4

W8. 01-937 4848. Originally laid out as the private gardens of Kensington Palace, this lovely spread of 275 acres of tree-lined walks, luxuriant flower beds and the man-made

Long Water and Round Pond adjoins Hyde Park. It is the most endearingly fey of London's royal parks, and probably the one that appeals most to children, with its Elfin Oak, ornamental ducks and swans, pets' cemetery and statue of Peter Pan. *Open 07.30–dusk.* Free.
⊖ Queensway, High Street Kensington
🚌 9, 10, 12, 33, 49, 52, 52A, 88, C1

## Kensington High Street　　2H2

Has a similar range of shops to Oxford Street, including a House of Fraser Department Store, but, though busy, is less frenetic. The smaller and more unusual shops are in the side roads.
⊖ High Street Kensington
🚌 9, 10, 27, 28, 31, 33, 49, 52, 52A, C1, C3

## Kensington Market　　2H3

Kensington High St W8. Large shop front behind which are grouped a complex of stalls selling off-beat clothes, jewellery, antiques and records. Stallholders prepared to buy, sell and barter. *Open 10.00–18.00 Mon–Sat.*
⊖ High Street Kensington
🚌 9, 10, 27, 28, 31, 33, 49, 52, 52A, C1, C3

## Kensington Palace　　2G3

Kensington Gardens W8. 01-937 9561. Queen Victoria and Queen Mary were born here, and this is where Victoria received the news of her accession. The Prince and Princess of Wales, Princess Margaret, Prince Michael of Kent and the Duke and Duchess of Gloucester still have apartments in the private wings. Bought in 1689 by William III, house and gardens are rich in the work of the famous who refurbished them – William Kent, Sir Christopher Wren, Grinling Gibbons, Nicholas Hawksmoor. There are also paintings from the royal collection, busts, furniture and ornaments and the Court Dress

Collection. *Open 10.00–17.00 Mon–Sat; 14.00–17.00 Sun. Closed some Nat Hols.* Charge.
θ Queensway, High Street Kensington, Notting Hill Gate
🚌 9, 10, 12, 33, 49, 52, 52A, 88, C1

## Kentish Town City Farm
1 Cressfield Clo, off Grafton Rd NW5. 01-482 2861. Horses, pigs, chickens, sheep, goats, rabbits, a nature area and an exhibition. Children have reasonably close encounters with the animals and may see work in progress if they arrive at the appropriate times. *Open 09.30–17.30 Mon–Sun. Closed Xmas.* Free.
🚌 24, 46 (to Queens Crescent), C11 (to Gospel Oak)
⇌ Gospel Oak

## Kenwood House
Hampstead La NW3. 01-348 1286/7. A fine Adam house at the edge of Hampstead Heath with lawns that slope down to a lake. Bequeathed to the nation by the first Earl of Iveagh, together with his collection of paintings which includes works by Gainsborough, Reynolds, Vermeer, Rembrandt, Frans Hals, Van Dyck and Turner. Music and poetry recitals are held in the Orangery on spring and autumn evenings, and in summer symphony concerts compete with the birdsong at the lakeside (details on 01-633 1707). *Open 10.00–19.00 Mon–Sun. Closes 16.00 or 17.00 in winter.* Free.
θ Archway (then bus 210), Golders Green (then bus 210)
🚌 210

## Kew Bridge Steam Museum
Green Dragon La, Brentford, Middx. 01-568 4757. Engines in steam at the weekend, static during the week. Working forge, Victorian machine shop, tea room. *Open 11.00–17.00 Mon–Sun.* Charge.
θ Gunnersbury (then bus 237, 267)
🚌 65, 237, 267
⇌ Kew Bridge

## Kew Gardens
Kew Rd, Richmond, Surrey. 01-940 1171. More properly – the Royal Botanical Gardens, Kew. An important research institute and a wonderful sight with more than 25,000 species and varieties of plants grown over its 300 acres. An arboretum, alpine, water and rhododendron gardens, magnificent cast-iron and glass palm house and temperate house by Decimus Burton, the Princess of Wales Conservatory with its ten climatic zones, each with appropriate vegetation, and a library of rare books on botany and exploration. Two attractive cafeterias. *Open 09.30–dusk (or 18.00 Mon–Sat).* Small charge.
θ Kew Gardens
🚌 7, 27, 65, 90

## Kew Palace
Kew Gardens, Richmond, Surrey. 01-940 7333. The Dutch House, as it is sometimes called, was built in 1631 for the merchant Samuel Fortrey. In 1802 George III and Queen Charlotte used it while they awaited the building of a new summer palace, which was never completed. The Queen loved the chunky brick house and died here in 1818. There are portraits, furniture and royal knick-knacks and, outside, formal gardens laid out in the 1960s in 17thC style. *Open 11.00–17.30 Mon–Sun. Closed Oct–Mar, Good Fri & May Day.* Charge.
θ Kew Gardens
🚌 7, 27, 65, 90

## King's Cross Station    1B6
Euston Rd NW1. Information on 01-278 2477. Mainline station built by Cubitt in 1851 and topped by the clock tower from the original Crystal Palace. The trains go to many points north, including Leeds, York, Newcastle and Edinburgh.

⊖ King's Cross, St Pancras
🚌 10, 14, 14A, 17, 18, 30, 45, 46, 63, 73, 77A, 214, 221, 259, C11
⇌ King's Cross

### King's Head Theatre
115 Upper St N1. 01-226 1916. Arguably the best-known of the pub theatres, presenting musicals, reviews, new plays, revivals. Buy a ticket for performance only, or for a meal as well, in which case you watch the show from your table. The pub itself has live music seven nights a week. *Open LD Mon–Sun. Theatre Mon–Sat lunchtime & eve.*
⊖ Angel
🚌 4, 19, 30, 38, 43, 73, 171, 171A, 263A, 277, 279, 279A

### King's Road                5X1
Chelsea SW3. Once a private royal track from St James's towards Hampton Court Palace, much later one of the places where the Swinging Sixties swung. Still exciting, especially on a Saturday when the young and colourful fill the boutiques and antique shops and drink coffee and wine at pubs and pavement cafés. An essential stop on the shopping circuit for the latest fashions, which are often the last word! Indigenous wildlife includes flame-coated Chelsea pensioners and flame-haired punks.
⊖ Sloane Square
🚌 11, 19, 22, 45, 49

### Knightsbridge                301
Originally a village with a bridge upon which two knights are said to have met in mortal combat. The bridge crossed the River Westbourne, which now flows underground. Famous as an expensive shopping area – the big names are Harrods, fairy-lit and lusciously stocked, and Harvey Nichols, but there are also smaller and equally smart shops along Knightsbridge itself and in Beauchamp Place which leads off Brompton Road to the south. Knightsbridge Barracks, next to Hyde Park, is the London home of the Household Cavalry, who can be spotted early in the morning exercising their horses in the Park.
⊖ Knightsbridge
🚌 9, 10, 14, 19, 22, 30, 52, 52A, 74, 137, 503, C1

**London Transport 24-hour information service**
For any information on travel in Greater London – routes, fares, times – telephone 01-222 1234 at any time of the day or night.

# L

## Lamb and Flag            *3M4*
33 Rose St WC2. 01-836 4108. 300-year-old pub, once known as 'The Bucket of Blood' because of the bare fist fights upstairs – and perhaps too because Dryden got the once-over downstairs for writing satirical ballads about Charles II's mistress. Now a popular mellow bar. *Open normal licensing hours Mon–Sun.*
⊖ Leicester Square
🚌 24, 29, 176

## Lambeth Palace           *3P5*
SE1. Begun in the early 13thC, although most of the present structure with its castellated gatehouse and high protective wall is medieval. The London residence of the Archbishop of Canterbury for 700 years and *not open to the public* – although groups are occasionally admitted on application to the Secretary.
⊖ Victoria (then bus 76, 507, 510)
🚌 3, 44, 76, 77, 159, 170, 507, 510

## Lancaster House           *3O3*
Stable Yard, St James's SW1. Early 19thC town house, decorous without but lushly, ripely baroque within. Lavishly painted ceilings and breathtaking staircase. Used as a government hospitality centre. *Open Sat & Sun afternoons in summer. Closed Mon–Fri & winter.* Free.
⊖ St James's Park, Green Park
🚌 9, 14, 19, 22, 25, 38

## Langan's Brasserie        *3N2*
Stratton St W1. 01-493 6437. Large restaurant opened by Michael Caine and Peter Langan. Atmosphere of decaying splendour, sometimes eccentric service and a changing menu. If you don't spot a famous face you're just not trying. *Open L Mon–Fri; D Mon–Sat.*
⊖ Green Park
🚌 9, 14, 19, 22, 25, 38

## Laura Ashley             *3M3*
256–258 Regent St W1. 01-437

9760. Women and children's clothes in distinctive patterned cottons and subtly-coloured corduroys on one floor and furniture and furnishings on the other. Other branches. *Open       09.30–18.00 Mon–Wed & Fri; 09.30–20.00 Thur; 09.00–18.00 Sat.*
⊖ Oxford Circus
🚌 3, 6, 12, 13, 15, 15B, 53, 88, 159, 509, C2

## Law Courts               *4S2*
Strand WC2. 01-936 6000. An elaborate fairy-tale castle, with spire, turrets and statues, built by Street in 1874–80 to house the Royal Courts of Justice. Admission only to visitors aged 16 and over. *Open       10.00–16.00      Mon–Fri. Closed Sat & Sun.* Courts not in session *Aug & Sep,* apart from emergency cases, but open to public. Free.
⊖ Temple (not Sun), Charing Cross (then bus 6, 9, 11, 15, 15B)
🚌 4, 6, 9, 11, 15, 15B, 171A, 502, 509, 513

## Leadenhall Market          *4T5*
Gracechurch St EC3. Horace Jones built the superb glass and iron hall in

1881, on the site of the old Roman basilica and forum, which still shelters a lively general market. *Open 09.00–17.00 Mon–Fri.*

⊖ Bank, Monument

🚍 15B, 25, 35, 40, 47, 48, 505, 510

### Leather Lane Market 4R2

Leather Lane EC1. Once specialised in the sale of cured skins – now a busy general market, with lively patter from the stallholders and few leather stalls left. *Open 11.00–15.00 Mon–Sat.*

⊖ Farringdon, Chancery Lane (not Sun)

🚍 8, 17, 22, 22B, 25, 45, 46, 55, 63, 171A, 221, 243, 259, 501, 505

### Leicester Square 3N4

WC2. Pedestrianised and commercial, flanked by four major cinemas, the Swiss Centre and several eating places with their sights set on tourists. The first statue of Charlie Chaplin stands to the west, under trees raucous with starlings at dusk. London's Chinatown lies just behind, on the north side.

⊖ Leicester Square

🚍 24, 29, 176

### Leighton House 2H1

12 Holland Park Rd W14. 01-602 3316. Designed by Aitchison in 1865, in collaboration with Lord Leighton, as the latter's home and studio. Now an intimate museum of high Victorian art, with an exquisite Arab Hall on the ground floor and the finest collection of Leighton paintings in any one place. Music recitals, poetry readings, lectures and social functions are held in the barrel-vaulted studio above. *Open 11.00–17.00 Mon–Sat. Free.*

⊖ High Street Kensington (then bus)

🚍 9, 10, 27, 28, 31, 33, 49

### Liberty 3M3

Regent St W1. 01-734 1234. This architecturally remarkable department store, with its half-timbered façade and Tudor-style interior, is world-famous for its own distinctive printed fabrics. There are also china and glass departments, gifts made out of the famous fabrics, furniture, fashions, oriental carpets and fashion jewellery, including a Cobra & Bellamy section. *Open 09.30–18.00 Mon–Wed, Fri & Sat; to 19.00 Thur. Closed Sun.*

⊖ Oxford Circus

🚍 3, 6, 12, 13, 15, 15B, 53, 88, 159, 509, C2

### Light Fantastic Gallery of Holography 3M4

48 South Row WC2. 01-836 6423. A fascinating and constantly changing display of holograms. A hologram is a three-dimensional image produced by a laser on a specially treated plate. The objects on the plate move in relation to one another as you move the plate or walk past it. *Open 10.00–18.00 Mon–Sat; 11.00–18.00 Sun.*

⊖ Covent Garden

🚍 24, 29, 176

### Lillywhites 3N3

Lower Regent St SW1. 01-930 3181. Excellent general stock of top English and continental equipment and clothes for most sports, especially skiing, tennis, golf and cricket. For each sport, a pro is available to advise on purchases. *Open 09.30–18.00 Mon–Wed, Fri & Sat; to 19.00 Thur. Closed Sun.*

⊖ Piccadilly Circus

🚍 3, 6, 9, 12, 13, 14, 15, 15B, 19, 22, 22B, 38, 53, 88, 159, 509

### Lincoln's Inn 4S1

WC2. One of the four great Inns of Court, a compact Dickensian world

of squares, gardens and barristers' chambers, whose records go back to 1422. The 15thC Old Hall and the 17thC Chapel by Inigo Jones may be viewed on application to the Gatehouse in Chancery Lane.
θ Holborn, Chancery Lane (not Sun)
🚌 8, 17, 18, 19, 22, 22B, 25, 38, 45, 46, 55, 68, 77, 77A, 168, 171, 171A, 188, 243, 259, 501, 505

### Linley Sambourne House   2H2
18 Stafford Ter W8. Administered by The Victorian Society which was formed here (1 Priory Gdns W4, 01-994 1019). An unspoiled Victorian house. Linley Sambourne, who lived here from 1879–1910, was chief political cartoonist for 'Punch' and the decor and furnishings remain unchanged since he sat at the drawing board in his study. *Open Mar–Oct 10.00–16.00 Wed; 14.00–17.00 Sun. Groups by appointment.* Charge.
θ High Street Kensington
🚌 9, 10, 27, 28, 31, 33, 49, C1

### Little Angel Marionette Theatre
14 Dagmar Passage, Cross St N1. 01-226 1787. Marionettes are the puppets worked by strings – and this is their only permanent London venue. The excellent shows – at weekends and in the school holidays – are put on by the resident company or visiting puppeteers and are based on traditional folk tales. Booking essential.
θ Angel
🚌 4, 19, 30, 38, 43, 73, 171, 171A, 263A, 277, 279, 279A

### Little Venice
W2. A section of Regent's Canal, lined with brightly painted houseboats and flanked by large Victorian houses and plane trees which reflect in the green water. It was likened to Venice by the poet Robert Browning. There are pleasant pubs along here and something of an artists' colony.
θ Warwick Avenue
🚌 6, 18, 46

### Liverpool Street Station   4G5
Liverpool St EC2. Information on 01-283 7171. 19thC station built to serve the east and north-east London suburbs. Trains go to Cambridge, Colchester, Norwich and Harwich Harbour.
θ Liverpool Street
🚌 5, 6, 8, 9, 11, 22, 22A, 22B, 35, 47, 48, 78, 100, 133, 149, 243A, 263A, 279A, 502, 505, 509
⇌ Liverpool Street

### Lloyds Building   4T5
Lime St EC3. 01-623 7100. World-famous headquarters of the international insurance market, particularly concerned with shipping. In 1986 it moved to this new hi-tech monument in the City designed by Richard Rogers, who was jointly responsible for the Pompidou Centre in Paris. It looks a little like an oil refinery with its 12 storeys and 6 towers. The huge dealing room is housed in a 246-ft high atrium. The Lutine Bell is still rung on ceremonial occasions, once for bad news, twice for good. The visitors' viewing area is *open 10.00–14.30 Mon–Fri.* Minimum age 14. Free.
θ Bank, Monument
🚌 15B, 25

### London Apprentice
62 Church St, Old Isleworth, Middx. 01-560 1915. Famous 16thC Thames-side pub named for the apprentices from London's Docks who spent their one-day-off-a-year rowing down to it for a pint or so. Lovely interiors, flowery patio, good restaurant. *Open LD Mon–Sun.* Restaurant *closed L Sat.*
θ Gunnersbury (then bus 267)
🚌 37, 267
⇌ Isleworth (then bus 37)

**London Bridge** 4T4

SE1. Concrete construction completed in 1973. Its 1830s predecessor now spans an artificial lake in Arizona. The 13thC stone bridge which preceded that one bore houses and shops until 1762 and is famous from old woodcuts.

ө Monument, London Bridge

🚌 15, 17, 21, 35, 40, 43, 44, 47, 48, 133, 501, 505, 510, 513, P3, P11

**London Bridge Station** 4U5

Borough High St SE1. Information on 01-928 5100. 19thC station dispatching trains to the south and south-east London suburbs – Kent, Sussex, and East Surrey.

ө London Bridge

🚌 17, 21, 35, 40, 43, 44, 47, 48, 133, 501, 505, 510, 513, P3, P11

≠ London Bridge

**London Dungeon** 4U5

34 Tooley St EC1. 01-403 0606. Gruesomely realistic exhibition of the dark side of British history in a dank vaulted cellar. Sacrifices, tortures, plagues, murders, executions – everything you need for a really vivid nightmare or several. Unsuitable for those of a sensitive disposition. *Open 10.00–17.30 Mon–Sun; to 16.30 Oct–Apr.* Charge.

ө London Bridge

🚌 17, 21, 35, 40, 43, 44, 47, 48, 133, 501, 505, 510, 513, P3, P11

**London Experience** 3N3

Trocadero, Piccadilly W1. 01-734 0555. A 35-minute multi-media show on the history of London – film (including old news reel films), slides, video and special effects. High points are the Plague, the Great Fire, the Blitz and Jack the Ripper, but there is plenty of pageantry and glamour as well. *Shows every 40 mins from 10.20–22.20, Mon–Sun.* Charge.

ө Piccadilly Circus

🚌 3, 6, 9, 12, 13, 14, 15, 15B, 19, 22, 22B, 38, 53, 88, 159, 509

**London Hospital (Whitechapel)**

Whitechapel Rd E1. 01-247 5454. General hospital founded in 1740 and installed at its present site in 1757. Its medical school was begun in 1785 and relaunched in new buildings in 1854 – Dr Barnardo was

one of its students. Largely rebuilt since World War II, the hospital's 'out-posts' are London Hospital Mile End and London Hospital St Clements. *24-hr casualty.*

ө Whitechapel

🚌 25, 253

**London Mosque** 1C2

Hanover Gate NW1. The religious centre for London's Muslims is a graceful building on the edge of Regent's Park, completed in 1978.

ө Marylebone, Baker Street

🚌 13, 74, 82, 113

**London Pavilion** 3N3

Piccadilly Circus W1. Listed building redeveloped as (another) shopping and leisure complex. The elegant neo-classical exterior remains as it was originally but two extra storeys have been added and the whole topped with sculptures of classical maidens. The interior has the usual range of shops.

ө Piccadilly Circus

🚌 3, 6, 9, 12, 13, 14, 15, 15B, 19, 22, 22B, 38, 53, 88, 159, 509

**London Planetarium** 1D3

Marylebone Rd NW1. 01-486 1121. The beginner's guide to the universe – stars, planets, galaxies are represented every 40 minutes on the domed ceiling with full commentary. There are evening laser light shows in the adjoining Laserium (01-486 2242). *Open 11.00–16.30 Mon–Sun.* Charge. (Reduced combined ticket includes admission to Madame Tussaud's.)

ө Baker Street

🚌 2A, 2B, 13, 18, 27, 30, 74, 82, 113, 159

**London Stone**

Cannon St EC4. Set into the wall of the Bank of China opposite Cannon St Station. This is the Roman Millarium from which all road distances were measured.

ө Cannon Street

🚌 15, 513

**London Telecom Tower** 3L3

Maple St W1. 198 metres of telecommunications gadgetry and mast. Transmits radio, television and telephone signals around the country and, via a Goonhilly Down satellite link-up, around the world.

⊖ Goodge Street, Warren Street, Great Portland Street

🚌 10, 14, 14A, 18, 24, 27, 29, 30, 73, 134, 135, 253

## London Tourist Board & Convention Bureau   3P2

Victoria Station Forecourt SW1. 01-730 3488. Comprehensive travel and tourist information for London and England. Most languages spoken. Also instant hotel reservations, theatre and tour bookings, sales of tourist tickets, guidebooks and maps. *Open 09.00–20.30 Mon–Sun.*

⊖ Victoria

🚌 2, 2A, 2B, 11, 16, 24, 25, 29, 36, 36A, 36B, 38, 39, 52, 52A, 73, 76, 82, 185, 506, 507, 510, C1

≋ Victoria

## London Toy & Model Museum   2F4

23 Craven Hill W2. 01-262 7905. Restored Victorian house with an international collection of model trains, a collection of Victorian and Edwardian tin toys, a mock-up of a Victorian nursery and, in the garden, a carousel, two miniature working railways – electric and steam – and a 56-seater bus. There's a café too. *Open 10.00– 17.30 Tue–Sat; 11.00–17.30 Sun. Closed Mon.* Charge.

⊖ Lancaster Gate

🚌 12, 88

## London Transport Museum 3M5

The Piazza, Covent Garden WC2. 01-379 6344. Buses, trams, trolleybuses, tube trains, tickets, posters, photographs – in fact, everything you could want to see and know about London's public transport. The fascinating history of London's transport is told by way of audiovisual displays, working exhibits and gleamingly preserved historic vehicles of road and rail. Visitors are encouraged to try out some of the controls themselves. *Open 10.00– 18.00 Mon–Sun* (last admission 17.15). Charge.

⊖ Covent Garden

🚌 1, 6, 9, 11, 13, 15, 15B, 77, 77A, 170, 176, 509 (to the Strand)

## London Wall

Surviving parts of the Roman and medieval wall around the old city of London can still be seen at St

Alphage on the north side of London Wall EC2 (⊖ Moorgate); St Giles Churchyard Cripplegate EC1 (⊖ St Paul's); Jenny St EC3 (⊖ Fenchurch St); off Trinity Square EC3 (⊖ Tower Hill); and in the Tower of London (⊖ Tower Hill).

## Loon Fung Supermarket   3M4

42–44 Gerrard St W1. 01-437 7332. Large, family-run Chinese supermarket with fresh, canned, dried, preserved and frozen foods and an information counter to explain all. *Open 10.00–20.30 Mon–Sun.*

⊖ Piccadilly Circus, Leicester Square

🚌 14, 19, 22, 22B, 38

## Lord's Cricket Ground   1C1

St John's Wood Rd NW8. 01-289 1615. Thomas Lord's Marylebone Cricket Club – the MCC – was founded in 1787 in Dorset Square and moved here in 1814. This, the most famous cricket ground in the world, has a museum housed in the racquets court. *Open on match days only.* Charge.

⊖ St John's Wood

🚌 13, 74, 82, 113, 159

## Lumiere Cinema   3N4

St Martin's La WC2. 01-836 0691. Premiere-release cinema for quality films.

⊖ Leicester Square

🚌 24, 29, 176

## Lyric, Hammersmith

King St W6. 01-741 2311. Rebuilt in its original Victorian-style inside a modern block. There is also an adaptable studio theatre, a bar and a wine-bar style restaurant, and regular exhibitions of pictures and prints. Productions range from classic through to modern and fringe. Complex *open 10.00–23.00 Mon– Sat; 11.30–15.00 Sun.*

⊖ Hammersmith

🚌 9, 10, 11, 27, 33, 72, 91, 220, 266, 267, 283, 290, 295

## Lyric Theatre   3N3

Shaftesbury Av W1. 01-437 3686. The oldest theatre in Shaftesbury Avenue, built in 1888, presenting straight plays and comedies, usually by established writers.

⊖ Piccadilly Circus

🚌 14, 19, 22, 22B, 38

**M**

## Madame Tussaud's 3L1
Marylebone Rd NW1. 01-935 6861.
Tableaux of wax images of the
famous and notorious – royalty,
stars of sport, television and film,
politicians, murderers. The Chamber of Horrors has the original wax
casts made by Madame Tussaud
herself of heads severed during the
French Revolution. There is also a
life-size reconstruction of the gun
deck of Nelson's 'Victory' at the
height of the Battle of Trafalgar,
complete with sound, light and
smoke effects. *Open 10.00–17.30
Mon–Sun.* Charge (a special reduced price ticket includes admission to the London Planetarium
next door; the queue at Madame
Tussaud's can be avoided if you buy
one of the joint LT sightseeing tour
and visit to Tussaud's tickets at a LT
Travel Information Centre – see
p. 5 for details).
⊖ Baker Street
🚌 2A, 2B, 13, 18, 27, 30, 74, 82,
113, 159

## Man in the Moon
392 King's Rd SW3. 01-351 2876.
Very comfortable pub theatre in a
converted cold store. Enterprising
management presents predominantly modern plays – two different
productions each night. The pub itself is worth a visit – lovely engraved glass, real ale and lunchtime
snacks. Theatre *Tue–Sun.*
⊖ Fulham Broadway
🚌 11, 22

## Mansion House 4T4
Walbrook EC4. 01-626 2500. Fine
Palladian building, completed in
1752, which is the official residence
of the Lord Mayor of London and
scene of his annual banquets. The
Egyptian Hall – sumptuous, though
devoid of Egyptian architectural
features – is worth seeing. Apply in
writing for appointment to view.
Free.
⊖ Bank, Mansion House
🚌 6, 8, 9, 11, 15B, 21, 22, 22B,
25, 43, 76, 133, 149, 501

## Maples 3L3
145 Tottenham Court Rd W1.
01-387 7000. 50,000 square feet of
furniture in this store, stocking all
types and styles – including reproduction and modern. Oriental and
English carpets and rugs, soft furnishing fabrics and customer services which include curtain-making,
contract and design. *Open 09.00–
17.30 Mon–Sat. Closed Sun.*
⊖ Warren Street
🚌 10, 14, 14A, 18, 24, 27, 29, 30,
73, 134, 135, 253

## Mappin & Webb 3M3
170 Regent St W1. 01-734 3801.
Senior shop of a prestigious chain
selling high-quality jewellery and silver. *Open 09.00–17.30 Mon–Fri;
09.30–17.00 Sat. Closed Sun.*
⊖ Oxford Circus, Piccadilly Circus
🚌 3, 6, 12, 13, 15, 15B, 53, 88,
159, 509, C2

## Marble Arch 6M1
W2. This well-known arch, with its
finely-wrought gate, is now no
more than a landmark. It was originally designed by Nash as a gateway to Buckingham Palace, but

declared too narrow and moved here as an entrance to Hyde Park. It was then stranded by road widening in the early 1900s.
⊖ Marble Arch
🚌 2A, 2B, 6, 7, 8, 10, 12, 15, 16, 16A, 30, 36, 73, 74, 82, 88, 135, 137, 503, 506

### Marble Hill House
Richmond Rd, Twickenham, Middx. 01-892 5115. Standing in pleasant grounds near the Thames, this attractive English Palladian house was built for Henrietta Howard, mistress of George II and later Countess of Suffolk. The furnishings date from the Countess's time and there are portraits from the school of Van Dyck. Tea rooms in the coach house. *Open 10.00–17.00 Mon–Thur, Sat & Sun. Closed Fri & Xmas.* Free.
⊖ Richmond (then bus)
🚌 33, 37, 90, 202, 270, 290
⇌ St Margarets

### Marine Ices
Haverstock Hill NW3. 01-485 8898. Huge choice of Italian ice-cream and water ices. Also restaurant. *Open 10.30–23.00.*
⊖ Chalk Farm
🚌 31, 68, 168

### Marks & Spencer 3M1
458 Oxford St W1. 01-935 7954. The Marble Arch branch is one of the largest shops of many in this internationally-famous and popular high street chain which sells ladies', men's and children's clothes, home furnishings, foods and gifts. Clothes may be returned for exchange or refund (keep the receipt). *Open 09.00–20.00 Mon–Fri; to 18.00 Sat.*
⊖ Marble Arch
🚌 2A, 2B, 6, 7, 8, 10, 12, 15, 16A, 30, 73, 74, 82, 88, 135, 137, 503, 506

### The Marquee 3M3
105 Charing Cross Rd WC2. 01-437 6603. One of the original London rock clubs. Bars. *Open to 23.00 Mon–Sun.*
⊖ Tottenham Court Road
🚌 14, 14A, 19, 22, 24, 29, 38, 55, 176

### Martinware Pottery Collection
Southall Library, Osterley Park Rd, Middx. 01-574 3412. A room in the reference library displays some of the heavily distinctive bowls, heads and quizzically grotesque birds made by the Martin brothers in Southall from 1873–1923. *Open 09.00–19.30 Tue, Thur & Fri; 09.00–16.45 Wed & Sat. Closed Mon & Nat Hols.* Free.
⊖ Hounslow West (then bus 232), Hounslow Central (then bus 120)
🚌 105, 120, 195, 232, E5

### Maudsley Hospital
Denmark Hill SE5. 01-703 6333. Psychiatric hospital, founded by Dr Henry Maudsley and opened in 1916, which also specialises in drug dependency. *24-hr walk in emergency.*
🚌 40, 68, 176, 184, 185, 185A
⇌ Denmark Hill

### May Fair Intercontinental Hotel 3N2
Stratton St W1. 01-629 7777. Five-star deluxe hotel, a precious stone's throw from Berkeley Square, incorporating the Crystal Room ballroom, Le Chateau à la carte restaurant, a good Coffee Shop and the intimate May Fair Theatre.
⊖ Green Park
🚌 9, 14, 19, 22, 25, 38

**May Fair Theatre**     **3N2**
Stratton St W1. 01-629 3036.
Luxurious and intimate West
End theatre in the May Fair Inter-
continental Hotel, not open perma-
nently but taken by companies for
short seasons.
⊖ Green Park
🚌 9, 14, 19, 22, 25, 38

**Mayflower**
117 Rotherhithe St SE16. 01-237
4088. Tudor inn which was christ-
ened The Shippe but changed its
name when the 'Mayflower', which
set off from this part of the river,
reached America. You can stand on
the jetty and ponder on the Pilgrim
Fathers. Unusually, the pub is licensed to sell English and American postage stamps alongside the
more usual beers and spirits. Has a
seafood restaurant and bar snacks
are always available. *Pub open normal licensing hours Mon–Sun.
Restaurant open LD Mon–Sat & L
Sun; closed D Sun.*
⊖ Rotherhithe
🚌 47, 188, 225, P11, P14

**MCC Memorial Gallery**     **1C1**
Lord's Cricket Ground, St John's
Wood Rd NW8. 01-289 1611. Exhibition on the history of cricket
from its beginnings to the present
day housed in the old racquets
court. *Open 10.30–17.00 Mon–Sat
on match days. Other times by
appointment only.* Donation.
⊖ St John's Wood
🚌 13, 74, 82, 113, 159

**McDonald's**     **3N4**
57 Haymarket SW1. 01-930 9302.
Famous hamburger chain with
branches all over London. Spot-
lessly clean, fast service, mostly
takeaway but with seating areas for
those with nowhere to take it away
to. Also hot fruit pies, and milk
shakes almost too thick to climb up
the straw. *Open LD Mon–Sun.*
⊖ Piccadilly Circus
🚌 3, 6, 9, 12, 13, 14, 15, 15B, 19,
22, 38, 53, 88, 159, 509

**Mermaid Theatre**     **4T3**
Puddle Dock, Blackfriars EC4.
01-236 5568. Lord Bernard Miles'
creation, established in the late 50s
as an Elizabethan-style theatre
across the river from the site of
Shakespeare's Globe which is cur-

rently being reconstructed. Puts on
new plays, revivals, musicals,
riotous Christmas shows and children's shows. Well-equipped, with
a restaurant and two bars.
⊖ Blackfriars
🚌 45, 59, 63, 76, 141

**Metro 1 & 2**     **3M3**
11 Rupert St W1. 01-437 0757. Independent cinema showing first-
run films.
⊖ Piccadilly Circus
🚌 14, 19, 22, 22B, 38

**Middlesex Hospital**     **3L3**
Mortimer St W1. 01-636 8333.
Large general hospital, with a
cancer wing, which grew from the
tiny Middlesex Infirmary, founded
1745. Also has a Medical School
and Institutes of Pathology and Bio-
chemistry. *24-hr casualty.*
⊖ Goodge Street
🚌 135, C2

**Minema Cinema**     **2H6**
45 Knightsbridge SW7. 01-235
4225. Minimal in size but with maxi-
mum comfort – regular programmes of modern classics.
⊖ Knightsbridge
🚌 9, 10, 14, 19, 22, 30, 52, 52A,
74, 137, 503

**Mitre Hotel**
Hampton Court Bridge, Middx.
01-979 2264. A large and popular
pub, with an enormous riverside
garden. Bar snacks every day and
full meals in the Steak House Restaurant. *Open LD Mon–Sun.*
⊖ Hammersmith (then bus 267)
🚌 111, 131, 216, 267
Green Line 715, 718
≉ Hampton Court

**Mitre Tavern, Ye Olde**　　**4S2**
1 Ely Pl EC1. 01-405 4751. Built in
the 16thC by the Bishops of Ely to
house their servants and rebuilt in
the 18thC. Panelled walls, small
bars and gentle lighting. Elizabeth I
is said to have danced around the
old cherry tree, preserved in the
corner (it was out of doors at the
time). *Open Mon–Fri. Closed Sat &
Sun.*
⊖ Chancery Lane (not Sun),
Farringdon
🚌 8, 17, 22, 22B, 25, 45, 46,
171A, 221, 243, 259, 501

**The Monument**　　**4T5**
Monument St EC3. 01-626 2717.
Wren's monument to the Great Fire
of London. It is 202 ft high – the
distance from its base to the fire's
origin in Pudding Lane. 311 steps
lead to a literally breathtaking view
on top. *Open 08.00–17.00 Mon–
Sat.' Closed Sun.* (Sometimes
closed at short notice, please telephone first). Charge.
⊖ Monument
🚌 15, 21, 35, 40, 43, 47, 48, 133,
501, 505, 510, 513

**Morriss's Café**　　**4S3**
**Restaurant**
Old Bailey EC4. Small, friendly,
Italian-run café, with two pavement
tables and a few more inside. Sandwiches, salads, pizzas, cakes, hot
and cold drinks – to eat in or take
away. Breakfast served all day.
*Open 08.30–18.00 Mon–Fri.*
⊖ St Paul's
🚌 8, 22, 22B, 25, 501 (top), 4, 6,
9, 11, 15, 15B, 17, 76, 141, 502,
509, 513 (bottom)

**Moss Bros & Attitudes**　　**3N3**
88 Regent St W1. 01-494 0666.
Moved to Regent St in 1988 after
150 years in Covent Garden. Well-
known for classic menswear, including service uniforms. Attitudes

stocks cosmetics, women's designer clothes, jewellery and accessories. Also hires out men's
ceremonial and formal wear. Wise
to make hiring arrangements a
week in advance. *Open 09.00–
17.30 (to 19.00 Thur) Mon–Sat.
Closed Sun.*
⊖ Piccadilly Circus
🚌 3, 12, 13, 15, 15B, 53, 88, 159,
509, C2

**Mothercare**　　**3M1**
461 Oxford St W1. 01-629 6621.
From maternity clothes to clothes
and equipment for babies, toddlers
and children up to 11, all at competi-
tive prices. Several branches. *Open
09.30–18.00 Mon–Wed; 09.30–
19.30 Thur; 09.00–18.00 Fri & Sat
Closed Sun.*
⊖ Marble Arch, Bond Street
🚌 2A, 2B, 6, 7, 8, 10, 12, 13, 15,
16A, 30, 73, 74, 82, 88, 113, 135,
137, 159, 503

**Mudchute Farm**
Pier St E14. 01-515 5901. 32-acre
city farm, run by local people, with
beef cattle, ponies, sheep, goats,
pigs, poultry, rabbits and bees. The
venue for the annual Isle of Dogs
Agricultural Show. *Open 09.00–
17.00 Mon–Sun.* Free.
Docklands Light Railway:
Mudchute
🚌 277, D7, P14

**Museum of Garden**　　**3P5**
**History**
St Mary-at-Lambeth, Lambeth Palace Rd SE1. 01-261 1891. Housed
in a deconsecrated church, saved
from demolition by the Tradescant
Trust. The museum is a memorial
to the two Tradescants, father and
son, pioneering gardeners to

Charles I, who introduced numerous plants to this country and who are buried in the churchyard, next to Bligh of mutiny on the 'Bounty' fame. Garden of Tradescant imports is outside, the exhibition inside and there are plants and seeds for sale. *Open 11.00–15.00 Mon–Fri; 10.30–17.00 Sun. Closed Sat & from 2nd Sun in Dec to 1st Sun in Mar.* Donation welcome.

⊖ Waterloo

🚌 76, 77, 170, 507, Sun only 159

### Museum of London          4T6
London Wall EC2. 01-600 3699. Relics and reconstructions of the City of London from its Roman beginnings, through its Elizabethan and Dickensian stages to the present. Shops, docks and death masks, coronations, jewellery and the Great Fire, china, glass, weapons and the Lord Mayor of London's ceremonial coach. Licensed restaurant for hot dishes, snacks and other refreshments. *Open 10.00–18.00 Tue–Sat; 14.00–18.00 Sun. Closed Mon.* Free.

⊖ Barbican (not Sun), St Paul's

🚌 4, 141, 279A, 502

### Museum of Mankind          3N3
6 Burlington Gdns W1. 01-437 2224. The British Museum's Department of Ethnography, with huge collections of carvings, masks, clothing, weapons and artefacts from Africa, Australia, the Pacific Islands, the Americas and parts of Asia and Europe. Also film shows linked to current exhibitions, and a bookshop. *Open 10.00–17.00 Mon–Sat; 14.30–18.00 Sun. Closed Nat Hols.* Free.

⊖ Piccadilly Circus

🚌 9, 14, 19, 22, 38, 55

### Museum of the Moving          4U1
### Image
Under Waterloo Bridge, South

Bank SE1. 01-928 3535. Part of the South Bank Complex, this bright new museum charts the history of moving images from ancient cave paintings to film, television, video and hologram technology. Forty main exhibit areas plus changing exhibitions. Continuous programme of events in the Moving Image workshop – lectures, films, magic lantern shows. *Open 10.00–20.00 Tue–Sat; 10.00–18.00 Sun. Closed Mon.* Charge.

⊖ Waterloo

🚌 1, 4, 68, 76, 149, 168, 171, 171A, 176, 188, 501, 502, 505, 507, 513, C1, P11

### Musical Museum
368 High St, Brentford, Middx. 01-560 8108. The only musical museum in Europe that has 10 reproducing pianos and 3 reproducing pipe organs all under one roof (which still leaks). In all around 200 instruments, some of which will be played during the 1½-hr tour. *Open Apr–Oct 14.00–17.00 Sat & Sun; also Jun–Sep 14.00–17.00 Wed–Fri.* Donation. No small children.

⊖ Gunnersbury (then bus 267)

🚌 237, 267

## Nag's Head   3M5

10 James St WC2. 01-836 4678. Famous and lively Edwardian pub with a strong theatrical flavour. Real ale and good home-cooking, especially at Sunday lunchtime. *Open Mon–Sun (no food in the evenings).*
⊖ Covent Garden
🚌 24, 29, 176

## National Army Museum   5X2

Royal Hospital Rd SW3. 01-730 0717. The story of the British Army from 1485 to the present, of the Indian Army up to partition in 1947 and of other Commonwealth armies until the time of their independence, can be traced in the four galleries. There are uniforms, medals and decorations, weapons, models, dioramas, an art gallery and a shop for books and model soldiers. The books, manuscripts, maps, drawings and photographs stored in the reading room may be consulted on application to the Director. New cafeteria *open 10.30–16.30 Mon–Sat; closed Sun.* Museum *open 10.00–17.30*

*Mon–Sat; 14.00–17.30 Sun. Free.*
⊖ Sloane Square
🚌 39

## National Film Theatre   3N5

South Bank SE1. 01-928 3232. The two cinemas show rare foreign films, classic revivals, and run seasons specialising in the work of one director or one star. The bookshop is a must for serious students of movie history. The licensed buffet does a nice line in snacks. It is also a club; children have their own programmes on Saturdays.
⊖ Waterloo
🚌 1, 4, 68, 76, 149, 168, 171, 171A, 176, 188, 501, 502, 505, 507, 513, C1, P11

## National Gallery   3N4

Trafalgar Sq WC2. 01-839 3321. The imposing mid-19thC building by William Wilkins houses a rich collection of important paintings including many masterpieces. Here are pictures by Ucello and Botticelli, Titian, Veronese, Tintoretto, Bellini, Montegna, Rembrandt, Frans Hals, Cuyp, Rubens, Van Dyck, Caravaggio, Poussin, Turner, Constable, Gainsborough, Watteau, Fragonard, Canaletto, Tiepolo, El Greco, Velasquez, Murillo, Goya, Monet, Manet, Degas and Renoir. There is the cartoon and 'The Virgin of the Rocks' by Leonardo da Vinci, Goya's 'Duke of Wellington', Monet's 'Waterlillies', Philipe de Champaigne's sumptuous 'Cardinal Richelieu', Constable's 'Hay Wain', Turner's 'Fighting Temeraire'. If dazed by all the possibilities join a guided tour *(11.30 & 15.00 Mon–Fri; 14.00 & 15.30 Sat).* There are also lectures, audio-visual shows, special exhibitions, an interesting shop and a pleasant restaurant. *Open 10.00–18.00 Mon–Sat (till 20.00 Wed Jul–Sep); 14.00–18.00 Sun. Closed some Nat Hols.* Free.
⊖ Charing Cross
🚌 1, 3, 6, 9, 11, 12, 13, 15, 15B, 22B, 24, 29, 53, 77, 77A, 88, 109, 159, 170, 176, 184, 509

## National Maritime Museum

Romney Rd SE10. 01-858 4422. The world's largest museum on its subject. The beautiful buildings – the Queen's House by Inigo Jones at their centre – are set in a sloping riverside park with the Old Royal Observatory on the hill behind. Life-size displays and packed show-cases cover all imaginable aspects of Britain's maritime history. Ship-building, battles, trade and explora-tion – scale models, actual vessels, navigational instruments and weapons.

Up by the Old Royal Observatory is the house of the first Astronomer Royal, Flamsteed.

In the Meridian Building is a uni-que display of instruments used for measuring time and the beginnings of the understanding of space, as well as the famous Meridian line from which Greenwich Mean Time is measured. The bookshop is good and the Dolphin Coffee Shop res-torative. *Open 10.00–18.00 Mon–Sat; 14.00–17.00 Sun. Closed 17.00 Oct–Easter.* Charge which includes entry to Old Royal Obser-vatory.
⊖ Surrey Docks (then bus 1, 188) Docklands Light Railway: Island Gardens (then via foot tunnel)
🚌 1, 177, 180, 188, 286
➤ Maze Hill

## National Monuments Record 3N3

23 Savile Row W1. 01-734 6010. The historic architecture of England in a library of over a million photo-graphs, measured drawings and prints. Sign in at reception. *Open 10.00–17.30 Mon–Fri.*
⊖ Oxford Circus
🚌 25

## National Portrait Gallery 3N4

2 St Martin's Pl WC2. 01-930 1552. Fascinating collection of contem-porary portraits of major figures in British history – in which the sub-jects are more important than the quality of the painting. Spans from Richard II to Bob Geldof, with many important literary, political and sci-entific figures in between. The ground floor is devoted to the 20thC and includes some very re-cent and exciting revolving displays arranged by theme. Special exhibi-tions from time to time. *Open*

*10.00–17.00 Mon–Fri; 10.00–18.00 Sat; 14.00–18.00 Sun. Closed Nat Hols.* Free (occasional charge for special exhibitions).
⊖ Charing Cross
🚌 1, 3, 6, 9, 11, 12, 13, 15, 15B, 22B, 24, 29, 53, 77, 77A, 88, 109, 159, 170, 176, 184, 509

## National Postal Museum 4S3

King Edward St EC1. 01-239 5420. One of the most significant stamp collections in the world, above a major Post Office where current first day covers are on sale. Here are The Phillips Collection of 19thC British stamps; The Post Office Collection of all stamps issued un-der its aegis since 1840, plus proof sheets, designs, recent issues and the stamp archives of the Royal Mint. There is also The Berne Col-lection of almost every stamp or piece of postal stationery issued anywhere in the world since 1878. *Open 10.00–16.30 Mon–Thur; 10.00–16.00 Fri. Closed Sat, Sun & Nat Hols.* Free.
⊖ St Paul's
🚌 4, 8, 22, 22B, 25, 141, 501, 502, 509

## National Theatre 4U2

South Bank SE1. 01-928 2252.

Within the massive concrete structure are three theatres: the large Olivier with its open-thrust stage; the smaller Lyttelton with its proscenium arch; and the adaptable little Cottesloe. There are bars and coffee bars on every floor, the Lyttelton Buffet, and Ovations Restaurant and Wine Bar (01-928 2033 extn 531), bookshops, art gallery and live music often to be seen and heard in the foyer. *Open 10.00–23.00 Mon–Sat. Closed Sun.*
⊖ Waterloo
🚌 1, 4, 68, 76, 149, 168, 171, 171A, 176, 188, 501, 502, 505 507, 513, C1, P11

**Natural History Museum**   **2J5**
Cromwell Rd SW7. 01-589 6323. A cathedral-like, twin-towered building by Alfred Waterhouse, 1873–80, with a superb Romanesque interior housing the national collections of zoology, entomology, palaeontology, mineralogy and botany. Here are the famous dinosaur replicas backed up by push-button VDUs explaining their evolution, not to mention reptiles, scorpions, birds, mammals and minerals. The human biology display includes a walk-in womb, and other important presentations are Origin of Species, Man's Place in Evolution, Discovering Mammals, Introducing Ecology and British Natural History. Regular films, lectures, special exhibitions, and good gift and book shops. Small cafeteria. *Open 10.00–18.00 Mon–Sat; 14.30–18.00 Sun. Closed Nat Hols in winter & spring.* Charge.
⊖ South Kensington
🚌 14, 30, 45, 49, 74, 219, 503, C1

**Natural Shoe Store**   **3M4**
21 Neal St WC2. 01-836 5254. An idea that shouldn't be unusual, but is – foot-shaped shoes, for men, women and children. *Open 10.00–18.00 Mon, Tue & Sat; 10.00–19.00 Wed–Fri.*
⊖ Covent Garden
🚌 14, 19, 22, 22B, 24, 29, 38, 176

**Nat West Tower**   **4S5**
25 Old Broad St EC2. London's tallest building, designed by a master of architectural overkill, Richard Seifert. The Nat West logo is on the roof, visible only from the air.

⊖ Liverpool Street
🚌 6, 8, 9, 11, 22, 22B, 100, 149, 502, 509

**Neal's Yard**   **3M4**
A very wholesome corner of Covent Garden. Neal's Yard Bakery Co-operative (01-836 5199), Neal's Yard Farm Shop (01-836 1066), Neal's Yard Flour Mill (01-836 1082) and Neal's Yard Wholefood Warehouse, round the corner at 23 Short's Gardens (01-836 5151/2). Each shop has its own opening times, but all are trading between *11.00–17.00 Mon–Sat.*
⊖ Covent Garden
🚌 14, 19, 22, 22B, 24, 29, 38, 176

**Nelson's Column**   **3N4**
Trafalgar Sq WC2. The whole square commemorates Lord Nelson and his last, greatest naval victory at Trafalgar in 1805. The focal point is the 185-ft column topped by a statue of the Admiral and guarded by Landseer's four identical lions. At the base of the column are four bronze reliefs cast from French cannon captured in Nelson's famous battles.
⊖ Charing Cross
🚌 1, 3, 6, 9, 11, 12, 13, 15, 15B, 22B, 24, 29, 53, 77, 77A, 88, 109, 159, 170, 176, 184, 509

**New Charing Cross Hospital**
Fulham Palace Rd W6. 01-748 2040. General hospital, with attendant Medical School, opened on this site in 1973 although its predecessor was founded in 1818 in Suffolk Street under the name West London Infirmary and Dispensary. *24-hr casualty.*
⊖ Barons Court
🚌 11, 220, 283, 295

**New Covent Garden Market**    **5Y6**
Nine Elms SW8. 01-720 2211. London's foremost wholesale fruit, vegetable and flower market moved here from its previous Covent Garden site in 1974. *Open 04.00–12.00 Mon–Sun.*
⊖ Vauxhall
🚌 44, 170

**New London Theatre**    **3M5**
Drury Lane WC2. 01-405 0072. Can convert from a 900-seat conventional theatre to an intimate theatre-in-the-round within minutes. Opened 1972 on the site of the old Winter Gardens. The hit musical 'Cats' is well-established here.
⊖ Covent Garden
🚌 1, 4, 6, 9, 11, 13, 15, 15B, 68, 77, 77A, 168, 170, 171, 171A, 176, 188, 501, 502, 505, 509, 513

**New West End Synagogue**   **2F3**
St Petersburgh Pl W2. The twin cupolas of the imposing building give a somewhat Moorish air to this late 1870s version of early Gothic by Audesley and Joseph.
⊖ Queensway, Bayswater
🚌 12, 88

**Next**    **2H3**
54–60 Kensington High St W8. 01-938 4211. The largest of an ever-growing chain of shops selling bright, smart and competitively priced clothes for men, women and children, accessories, cosmetics, confectionery and home furnish-

ings. Also has The Paramount Restaurant and a sandwich bar. *Open 09.15–18.00 (to 20.00 Thur) Mon–Sat.*
⊖ High Street Kensington
🚌 9, 10, 27, 28, 31, 33, 49, 52, 52A, C1, C3

**North End Road Market**   **2K1**
W14. The basic necessities at low prices in an amiable and busy atmosphere – food, small household goods, clothes. *Open 09.00–17.00 (to 13.00 Thur) Mon–Sat.*
⊖ Fulham Broadway
🚌 11, 14, 28, 74, 91, 283, 295, C4

**North Woolwich Station Museum**
Pier Rd E16. 01-474 7244. Appealing railway museum in the original (restored) North Woolwich Station building, beside the functioning station. Photos, objects, rolling stock and a preserved Robert Stephenson and Hawthorn 0-6-OST. *Open 10.00–17.00 Mon–Sat; 14.00–17.00 Sun & Nat Hols.* Free.
🚌 69, 101, 262, 276
➤ North Woolwich

## Odeon Cinema 3N4
Haymarket SW1. 01-839 7697. Mainly new releases but also revivals in separate performances.
θ Piccadilly Circus
⊞ 3, 6, 9, 12, 13, 14, 15, 15B, 19, 22, 22B, 38, 53, 88, 159, 509

## Odeon Cinema 2H2
Kensington High St W8. 01-602 6644. Mainly new releases, some recent revivals.
θ High Street Kensington (then bus or walk)
⊞ 9, 10, 27, 28, 33, 49

## Odeon Cinema 3N4
Leicester Sq WC2. 01-930 6111. New releases. Booking wise.
θ Leicester Square
⊞ 24, 29, 176

## Odeon Cinema 3M1
Marble Arch W2. 01-723 2011. Claimed to be the most advanced cinema in Britain, with closed-circuit TV. Premières and blockbusters.
θ Marble Arch
⊞ 2A, 2B, 6, 7, 8, 10, 12, 15, 16, 16A, 30, 36, 73, 74, 82, 88, 135, 137, 503, 506

## Old Bailey 4S3
EC4. 01-248 3277. More properly, The Central Criminal Court. The impressive buildings are on the site of old Newgate Prison and some of its stones are incorporated in the lower walls. The public (only those age 14 and over) may watch the trials. *Open 10.30–13.00 & 14.00–16.00 Mon–Fri. Closed Sat & Sun.* Free.
θ St Paul's
⊞ 8, 22, 22B, 25, 501

## Old Bull & Bush
North End Way NW3. 01-455 3685. The famous pub of the Florrie Forde song. Drink on the forecourt and gaze at Hampstead Heath opposite.
θ Golders Green
⊞ 210, 268

## Old Royal Observatory
Greenwich Hill SE10. 01-858 4422. On a green hill above and behind the riverside National Maritime Museum. Among a group of buildings made up of the Great Equatorial Building with the world's seventh largest refracting telescope; the Altazimuth Pavilion; the South Building with its planetarium; and Flamsteed House and the Meridian Building, the only two which are open to the public. *Open 10.00–18.00 Mon–Sat; 14.00–17.00 Sun. Closes 17.00 Oct–Easter.* Charge (includes entry to Maritime Museum).
θ New Cross, New Cross Gate (then bus 53)
⊞ 53, 54 75
⇌ Maze Hill

## Old St Thomas's Hospital 4U4
## Operating Theatre
The Chapter House, St Thomas' St SE1. 01-407 7600. The only surviving early 19thC operating theatre in Britain. Also houses contemporary surgical instruments, pictures of people being separated from their

limbs, and a garret atop a spiral stair full of herbs dried by the hospital apothecary. *Open 12.30–16.00 Mon, Wed & Fri, or by appointment.* Charge.

⊖ London Bridge

🚌 17, 21, 35, 40, 43, 44, 47, 48, 133, 501, 505, 510, 513, P3, P11

⇌ London Bridge

## Old Vic Theatre                    4U2
Waterloo Rd SE1. 01-928 7616. Built in 1818 and run for many years by Lilian Baylis who presented opera, concerts and drama, especially Shakespeare. The home of the National Theatre Company from 1962–76, then of the Prospect Theatre Company. Refurbished in late Victorian style in the early 1980s by its Canadian purchaser, Ed Mirvish. Jonathan Miller is currently artistic director.

⊖ Waterloo

🚌 1, 4, 68, 76, 149, 168, 171, 171A, 176, 188, 501, 502, 505, 507, 513, C1, P11

⇌ Waterloo

## Olympia                           2J1
Hammersmith Rd W14. 01-603 3344. Gargantuan hall staging regular, popular shows and exhibitions. Among them are: the Fine Arts and Antiques Fair in early June; the Festival for Mind, Body and Spirit in late June; the Cat Club Show in early December and International Show Jumping in late December. Bars and snack bars inside. Charge.

⊖ Kensington Olympia, West Kensington (then walk)

🚌 9, 10, 27, 28, 33, 49, 91

## Open-Air Theatre                 1C3
Regent's Park NW1. 01-486 2431. Opened in 1933, renovated in 1975, and famous for its summer season of – mainly Shakespearean – plays.

⊖ Regent's Park, Great Portland Street

🚌 18, 27, 30, 135, C2

## Orange Tree Theatre
45 Kew Rd, Richmond, Surrey. 01-940 3633. Early Victorian pub with leaded windows and marble columns, above which is an 80-seat theatre in which the Richmond Fringe gives evening performances from September to April and rehearsed play readings during May. Pleasant restaurant in which it is wise to reserve dinner. *Open Mon–Sun. Restaurant closed Sun.*

⊖ Richmond

🚌 27, 65, Sun only 7

## Osterley Park House
Isleworth, Middx. 01-560 3918. An out-station of the Victoria and Albert Museum and one of the most perfect examples of 18thC decor and furniture in the country. Built by Sir Thomas Gresham in the 1570s, refurbished by Robert Adam in the 1760s, presented to the nation in 1949. Adam interior design, Gobelins tapestries, Reynolds portraits, lovely grounds and a cafeteria in the stable block. *Open 11.00–17.00 Tue–Sun. Closed Mon & winter Nat Hols.* Charge.

⊖ Osterley

🚌 91

## Oval Cricket Ground
Kennington Oval SE11. 01-582 6660. Stages Surrey county matches and a test match, usually in August. For latest scores of matches played here phone 01-735 4911.

⊖ Oval

🚌 3, 36, 36A, 36B, 59, 95, 109, 133, 155, 159, 185

## Oxford Street                     3M1
W1. Here is the largest choice of modern mass-produced clothes and shoes in London, sold through clothes chains such as C & A, Benetton, Next and Marks & Spencer and shoe chains such as Saxone, Dolcis, Derber and Ravel, all of which reappear periodically down its length. The street is also punctuated by large department stores – Selfridges, John Lewis and House of Fraser among them.

⊖ Oxford Circus (centre), Bond Street (centre), Marble Arch (western end), Tottenham Court Road (eastern end)

⊖ 2A, 2B, 3, 6, 7, 8, 10, 12, 13, 15, 15B, 16A, 25, 30, 53, 73, 74, 82, 88, 113, 135, 137, 159, 176, 503, 509, C2

# P

**Paddington & Friends** *1E2*
22 Crawford Pl W1. 01-262 1866.
Small shop which is a magnet for
the fans of Michael Bond's world-
famous Paddington Bear. Bears
and books and benefactions are
here, both large and small. *Open
10.00–17.00 Mon–Sat. Closed
Sun.*
⊖ Edgware Road
6, 7, 8, 15, 16, 16A, 18, 27, 36

**Paddington Station** *1E1*
Praed St W2. Information on
01-262 6767. Railway cathedral en-
gineering at its best, by Brunel, the
Gothic ornament by Wyatt and
Owen Jones and the adjoining
Renaissance-Baroque hotel by the
younger Hardwick. Trains go west
– to Bath, Bristol, Cardiff, Hereford,
Swansea, Devon and Cornwall.
⊖ Paddington
7, 15, 27, 36, 506
⪥ Paddington

**Palace Theatre** *3M4*
Shaftesbury Av W1. 01-437 6834.
Large and grand. Its first manager,
Richard D'Oyly Carte, intended it to
become the home of English opera,
but it staged music-hall, and, more
recently, such smash hit musicals
as 'Jesus Christ Superstar', 'Okla-

homa', 'Song and Dance', 'On Your
Toes' and 'Les Misérables'.
⊖ Leicester Square
14, 19, 22, 22B, 24, 29, 38,
176

**Palladium Theatre** *3M3*
8 Argyll St W1. 01-437 7373. Variety shows par excellence, international names, musical spectaculars
including 'Barnum' and 'La Cage aux
Folles' and the annual Royal Variety
Show.
⊖ Oxford Circus
3, 6, 7, 8, 10, 12, 13, 15, 15B,
16A, 25, 53, 73, 88, 113, 135, 137,
159, 176, 503, 509, C2

**Pall Mall** *3N4*
SW1. Early 19thC opulence, re-
flected in the cushioned world of
gentlemen's clubs. Here are the
Traveller's Club and the Reform
Club, both fine buildings by Sir
Charles Barry.
⊖ Piccadilly Circus
3, 6, 9, 12, 13, 14, 15, 15B, 19,
22, 22B, 38, 53, 88, 159, 509

**Pan Bookshop** *2K4*
158–162 Fulham Rd SW10. 01-373
4997. Revamped and refurbished,
London's original late night bookshop stocks most Pan paperbacks,
so if Pan have it in print you'll get it
here. Also other publishers' paperbacks, new hardbacks and coffee
table books. *Open 10.00–22.00
Mon–Sat; 13.00–21.00 Sun.*
⊖ South Kensington
14, 45

**Park Lane** *3N1*
W1. In the 18thC a select lane bor-
dered by small palaces and large
mansions, now a busy dual car-
riageway with some of the mansions taken over by luxury hotels –
The Dorchester, Grosvenor House
and the flashier (and newer)
London Hilton are all here.
⊖ Marble Arch (northern end),
Hyde Park Corner (southern end)
2A, 2B, 10, 16, 30, 36, 73, 74,
82, 137, 503, 506

**Passmore Edwards Museum**
Romford Rd E15. 01-519 4296. Collections of Essex archaeology, local history, geology and biology. Good collection of Bow porcelain. *Open 10.00–18.00 Mon–Fri; 10.00–13.00 & 14.00–17.00 Sat; 14.00–17.00 Sun & Nat Hols.* Free.
⊖ Stratford
🚌 25, 86

**Penguin Bookshop** 3N4
Unit 10, The Market, Covent Garden WC2. 01-379 7650. If by any chance a Penguin in print is not present, it can be summoned within a few days. Paperbacks from most other publishers and some hardbacks, too. *Open 10.00–20.00 Mon–Sat; 12.00–18.00 Sun.*
⊖ Covent Garden
🚌 6, 9, 11, 13, 15, 15B, 77, 77A, 170, 176, 509

**Penhaligon's** 3M5
41 Wellington St WC2. 01-836 2150. Traditional and pricey perfumes, hand-made fragrances and toilet waters based on English flowers either alone – Bluebell – or in groups – Victorian Posy. *Open 10.00–18.00 Mon–Fri; 10.30–17.30 Sat. Closed Sun.*
⊖ Covent Garden
🚌 1, 4, 6, 9, 11, 13, 15, 15B, 68, 77, 77A, 168, 170, 171, 171A, 176, 188, 502, 505, 509, 513

**Percival David Foundation** 1D5
**of Chinese Art**
53 Gordon Sq WC1. 01-387 3909. In 1950 Sir Percival David gave a fine library and a priceless collection of Sung, Yuan, Ming and Ch'ing dynasty Chinese ceramics to the University of London. They are housed here not solely for serious students but for anyone wanting to enjoy the cool serenity of their presence. *Open 10.30–17.00 Mon–Fri; Closed Sat & Sun.* Free.
⊖ Euston, Euston Square
🚌 10, 14, 14A, 18, 30, 68, 73, 77, 77A, 168, 188

**Peter Jones** 5W3
Sloane Sq SW1. 01-730 3434. One of the most architecturally successful of London's department stores with its clear curved glass frontage. Furniture and furnishing fabrics, glass, china, linen, clothes, interpreters and an airy, friendly restaurant and café at tree-top height. *Open 09.00–17.30 Mon, Tue, Thur–Sat; 09.30–19.00 Wed. Closed Sun.*
⊖ Sloane Square
🚌 11, 19, 22, 137, C1

**Peter Pan's Statue** 2G5
Near Long Water, Kensington Gardens W8. J. M. Barrie's famous celebration of arrested development here reproduced in bronze by Sir George Frampton. The nymphs and rabbits clambering up the pedestal are burnished as high as young fingers can reach to stroke.
⊖ High Street Kensington
🚌 9, 10, 33, 49, 52, 52A, C1

**Petticoat Lane Market** 4S6
Radiates from Middlesex St E1. Huge bustling complex, too famous now for amazing bargains, but lively and stocked with pretty well everything. Some of the side streets specialise – Brick Lane has furniture and electrical goods and Chilton Street has bicycles. *Open 09.00–14.00 Sun. Closed rest of week.*
⊖ Liverpool Street, Aldgate, Aldgate East
🚌 5, 6, 8, 11, 15, 22, 22B, 25, 35, 40, 42, 44, 47, 48, 67, 78, 100, 149, 243A, 253, 263A, 279A, 510

**Phoenix Theatre** 3M4
Charing Cross Rd WC2. 01-836 2294. Large theatre offering com-

edies, straight plays and musicals. It opened with 'Private Lives', and Noel Coward and Gertrude Lawrence both played here during the 30s.
⊖ Tottenham Court Road
🚌 14, 19, 22, 22B, 24, 29, 38, 176

**Photographer's Gallery**   *3M4*
8 Gt Newport St WC2. 01-831 1772. Lively exhibitions and good stocks of photographic books and postcards. Two doors down at No 5 is another gallery, prints for sale and a small coffee bar. *Open 11.00–19.00 Tue–Sat. Closed Sun & Mon.* Free.
⊖ Leicester Square
🚌 24, 29, 176

**Piccadilly Circus**   *3N3*
W1. Celebrated confluence of roads, originally by Nash, with Eros, the famous winged cherub, at its centre. Here you will find quality and tradition at Fortnum & Mason, Hatchard's, Simpson and Lilly-whites; also the historic Burlington Arcade. The Trocadero and the London Pavilion cater for the more up-to-date market, providing one-stop shopping, refreshment and entertainment, while Tower Records now dominates Piccadilly Circus from the old Swan & Edgar building.
⊖ Piccadilly Circus
🚌 3, 6, 9, 12, 13, 14, 15, 15B, 19, 22, 22B, 38, 53, 88, 159, 509

**Piccadilly Theatre**   *3N3*
Denman St W1. 01-437 4506. A pre-war theatre which turned into a cinema and showed the first season of 'talkies' in Britain. Transformed into a cabaret theatre in 1983.
⊖ Piccadilly Circus
🚌 3, 6, 9, 12, 13, 14, 15, 15B, 19, 22, 22B, 38, 53, 88, 159, 509

**Picketts Lock Centre**
Picketts Lock La N9. 01-803 4756. Large sports centre with facilities for soccer, hockey, tennis and golf and, indoors, gymnastics, badminton, squash, basketball, hockey, netball, volley ball, martial arts, roller-skating, shooting, bowls and swimming. There is also a sauna, sunbed, resident beautician, sportswear shop, fast food restaurant – and a campsite out at the back. Tuition available in most sports. *Open 09.30–22.00 Mon–Sun.*
🚌 W8
🚆 Lower Edmonton (then bus W8)

**Pineapple Dance Studio**   *3M4*
7 Langley St WC2. 01-836 4004. Qualified teachers for every type of dance imaginable from belly to break. Also gymnasium for weight training, hydro fitness, body control studios (Pilates technique), café-bar, resident osteopath and masseur.
⊖ Covent Garden
🚌 14, 19, 22, 22B, 24, 29, 38, 176

**Pizza Express**   *3L4*
30 Coptic St WC1. 01-636 3232. One of a well-known and reliable chain of Pizza restaurants serving thin pizzas with plentiful and varied toppings. *Open 12.00–24.00 Mon–Sun.* Other branches.
⊖ Russell Square, Tottenham Court Road
🚌 7, 8, 19, 22, 22B, 25, 38, 55, 503

**The Place**   *3M1*
17 Duke's Rd WC1. 01-387 0161. Small-scale independent theatre presenting varied programmes of contemporary dance.
⊖ Euston
🚌 10, 14, 14A, 18, 30, 68, 73, 77, 77A, 168, 188

**Players Theatre Club**   **3N5**
Duchess Theatre, Catherine St WC2. 01-836 8243. The Players is temporarily based at the Duchess – probably until the end of 1989 – while new premises are built in Villiers Street, near to its original home. The lively presentations of authentic Victorian Music Hall continue unabated – and there's a restaurant and bar to complete the evening. Full membership should be taken out in person *48 hrs* before the show – temporary membership at the door. *Open Tue–Sat. Closed Sun & Mon.*
⊖ Aldwych (peak hours only Mon–Fri)
🚌 1, 4, 6, 9, 11, 13, 15, 15B, 68, 77, 77A, 168, 170, 171, 171A, 176, 188, 502, 505, 509, 513

**Playhouse Theatre**   **3N4**
Northumberland Av WC2. 01-839 4401. Edwardian theatre used as a BBC studio and then closed in 1975. Restored to former glory and reopened in late 1987. Seats 800. Stages musicals, serious dramas and comedies.
⊖ Charing Cross
🚌 1, 3, 6, 9, 11, 12, 13, 15, 15B, 22B, 24, 29, 53, 77, 77A, 88, 109, 159, 170, 176, 184, 509

**Plaza Cinema (1, 2, 3, 4)**   **3N3**
..ower Regent St W1. 01-200 0200. Varied programmes – usually with new releases.
⊖ Piccadilly Circus
🚌 3, 6, 9, 12, 13, 14, 15, 15B, 19, 22, 22B, 38, 53, 88, 159, 509

**Polka Children's Theatre**
240 The Broadway, Wimbledon SW19. 01-543 4888. The shows often involve mime, puppets, masks, clowns and noisy audience participation. There is also an exhibition of toys, a small playground, workshops and classes for adults and children and the Polka Pantry for suitably gooey treats. *Open 09.30–16.30 Tue–Fri; 11.00–18.00 Sat. Closed Mon & Sun.*
⊖ Wimbledon
🚌 57, 93, 131, 155, 156, 163, 164, 200, 352

**Pollock's Toy Museum**   **3L3**
1 Scala St W1. 01-636 3452. Three rickety floors of small, creaking rooms packed with a magical mix of bygone toys, including Victorian cut-out theatres, puppets, ancient dolls, dolls' houses, tin toys and decrepit Teddy bears. Scale models and Pollock's own famous toy theatres are on sale on ground level. *Open 10.00–17.00 Mon–Sat. Closed Sun.* Charge.
⊖ Goodge Street
🚌 10, 14, 14A, 24, 29, 73, 134

**Poons**   **3N4**
27 Lisle St WC2. 01-437 4549. There are larger, smarter Poons – in Woburn Place and King Street – but this is the tiny, cramped, atmospheric seed from which they grew. The specialities of the house are wind-dried meats. *Open LD Mon–Sat. Closed Sun.*
⊖ Leicester Square
🚌 24, 29, 176

**Portobello Road Market**   **2F2**
W11. The famous welter of glorious junk lies heaped enticingly on stall after stall every Saturday. During the week the permanent antique shops come into their own. Abundant fruit and veg, too. *Open 09.00–17.00 Mon–Sat. Full market 09.00–17.00 Sat only.*
⊖ Ladbroke Grove, Notting Hill Gate
🚌 7, 15, 52, 52A

**Postman's Park**   **4S3**
Churchyard of St Botolph, Alders-

gate St EC1. A touching little corner of Victoriana. On the enclosing walls, Victorian tile tablets commemorate the courage of ordinary individuals. The glowering bronze minotaur in the centre is by Michael Ayrton.
- ⊖ Barbican (not Sun), St Paul's
- ⊞ 4, 8, 22, 22B, 25, 141, 279A, 501, 502, 509

**Primrose Hill**
NW8. 01-486 7905. This 200-ft-high grassy hill, with its fine views over London, is a minor royal park. The up-currents attract all manner of kite and glider enthusiasts.
- ⊖ Camden Town
- ⊞ 31, 74, C11
- ⇌ Primrose Hill

**Prince Charles Cinema**   *3N4*
Leicester Pl, Leicester Sq WC2. 01-437 8181. Small cinema showing new releases. *Late shows Fri & Sat.*
- ⊖ Leicester Square
- ⊞ 24, 29, 176

**Prince Edward Theatre**   *3M4*
Old Compton St W1. 01-734 8951. One-time cabaret spot, cinema and casino – now a large theatre showing hit musicals. 'Evita' was here. 'Chess' has since moved in.
- ⊖ Tottenham Court Road
- ⊞ 14, 19, 22, 22B, 24, 29, 38, 176

**Prince Henry's Rooms**   *3M6*
17 Fleet St EC4. 01-353 7323. Above the archway to Inner Temple Lane is the oldest domestic building in London, dating from 1610. The room which is open to visitors has a fine Jacobean ceiling and a small exhibition of Pepysiana, on loan from Pepys' house in Huntingdon. *Open 13.45–17.00 Mon–Fri; 13.45–16.30 Sat. Closed mornings & Sun.* Charge.
- ⊖ Temple (not Sun), Blackfriars
- ⊞ 4, 6, 9, 11, 15, 15B, 171A, 502, 509, 513

**Prince of Wales Theatre**   *3N4*
Coventry St W1. 01-839 5987. Rebuilt in 1937, this large modern theatre has housed many musicals including the revival of 'South Pacific'.
- ⊖ Piccadilly Circus

- ⊞ 3, 6, 9, 12, 13, 14, 15, 15B, 19, 22, 22B, 38, 53, 88, 159, 509

**Prospect of Whitby**
57 Wapping Wall E1. 01-481 1095. Historic and famous dockland tavern dating back to the reign of Henry VIII. Its famous customers have included the notorious Judge Jeffreys, Samuel Pepys and Rex Whistler. It has beams and wood panelling, a restaurant terrace overlooking the Thames, inventive à la carte menu upstairs, good bar snacks and live music nightly downstairs. *Open Mon–Sun. Restaurant closed L Sat, D Sun.*
- ⊖ Wapping
- ⊞ 100

**Public Records Office**   *3M6*
**Library**
Chancery La WC2. 01-405 0741. The search rooms contain legal documents and government archives from 'Domesday Book' to 1800. The ever-popular census returns are held at the Land Registry Building in Portugal St, nearby. *Open 09.30–17.00 Mon–Fri. Closed Sat & Sun.* Free.
- ⊖ Chancery Lane (not Sun), Temple (not Sun)
- ⊞ 4, 6, 9, 11, 15, 15B, 171A, 502, 509, 513

**Puffin Bookshop**   *3M5*
1 The Market, Covent Garden WC2. 01-379 6465. Not only Puffin Books but also books from other publishers, toys, stationery, cassettes, a reading corner, a Beatrix Potter Room and a special room for teenage books. *Open 10.00–20.00 Mon–Sat (to 18.00 Jan & Feb).*
- ⊖ Covent Garden
- ⊞ 14, 19, 22, 22B, 24, 29, 38, 176

**Purcell Room**   *4U1*
South Bank SE1. 01-928 3191. The smallest of the three South Bank concert halls, whose intimate atmosphere is ideal for chamber music and solo recitals. Bar and coffee bar – more facilities at the Royal Festival Hall nearby.
- ⊖ Waterloo
- ⊞ 1, 4, 68, 76, 149, 168, 171, 171A, 176, 188, 501, 502, 505, 507, 513 C1, P11

*Q*

## Queen Elizabeth I     *3M6*
St Dunstan-in-the-West, Fleet St EC4. Originally stood over Lud Gate. Made during the Queen's lifetime in 1586, it is one of London's oldest statues.
θ Aldwych (peak hours Mon–Fri only), Chancery Lane
🚌 4, 6, 9, 11, 15, 15B, 171A, 502, 509, 513

## Queen Elizabeth Hall     *4U1*
South Bank SE1. 01-928 3191. Shares its foyer with the Purcell Room and uses its larger space for symphony, orchestral and big band concerts. More facilities at the Royal Festival Hall nearby.
θ Waterloo
🚌 1, 4, 68, 76, 149, 168, 171, 171A, 176, 188, 501, 502, 505, 507, 513, C1, P11

## Queen Elizabeth's Hunting Lodge
Rangers Rd E4. 01-529 6681. Beautiful old Tudor building, now the Epping Forest Museum. Exhibition of the history of the royal forest. Interesting displays on wildlife, conservation, local archaeology and history, with animal tracks, butterflies, insects, birds, mammals, trees and flowers. *Open 14.00–18.00 (or dusk in winter) Wed–Sun. Closed Mon & Tue.* Charge.
🚌 97, 97A, 144, 179, 212, 313, 379
≢ Chingford

## Queen's Chapel     *3O3*
St James's Palace, Marlborough Rd SW1. Designed by Inigo Jones in 1623 for Charles I's Queen, Henrietta Maria. The coffered timber ceiling has been beautifully restored. Open on application to the Administrative Officer, Marlborough House SW1, or for occasional public services.
θ Green Park
🚌 9, 14, 19, 22, 25, 38

## Queen's Club
Palliser Rd W14. 01-385 3421. Stages matches in both tennis and real tennis. Real tennis events October–April. The Stella Artois Championship, the run-up event to Wimbledon, is staged here in the first two weeks of *June*.
θ Barons Court
🚌 28, 91 (to West Kensington)

## Queen's Elm     *2K5*
241 Fulham Rd SW3. 01-352 9157. The pub is so-called because Queen Elizabeth I took shelter under a nearby elm in 1567. Recent renovations and change of management have altered its character. The function room is now a games room, the clientèle are younger and the writers and publishers drink elsewhere. Hot and cold food at every session. *Open 11.00–23.00 Mon–Sat; usual licensing hours Sun.*
θ Fulham Broadway (then bus 14 or walk), South Kensington (then bus 14, 45 or walk)
🚌 14, 45

## Queen's Gallery     *5W4*
Buckingham Palace, Buckingham Palace Rd SW1. 01-930 4832 extn

351. The one-room gallery, formerly a private chapel, is reached through the Buckingham Palace Shop and gives no access to the rest of the palace. The priceless paintings and drawings of the royal collection make public appearances here in small, regularly changed exhibitions. *Open 10.30–17.00 Tue–Sat; 14.00–17.00 Sun. Closed Mon.* Charge.
⊖ Victoria
🚌 2, 2A, 2B, 11, 16, 24, 25, 29, 36, 36A, 36B, 38, 39, 52, 52A, 73, 76, 82, 185, 506, 507, 510, C1

**Queen's House**
National Maritime Museum, Romney Rd SE10. 01-858 4422. A Palladian masterpiece by Inigo Jones which is now the central building of the Maritime Museum. The House is closed for refurbishment until mid-1990. Ring for details.
⊖ Surrey Docks (then bus 1, 188) Docklands Light Railway: Island Gardens (then by foot tunnel)
🚌 1, 177, 180, 188, 286
🚆 Maze Hill

**Queen's Ice Skating Club**    *2F3*
17 Queensway W2. 01-229 0172. Glamorous rather disco-like atmosphere in which to show off the fancy footwork. Tuition available. *Open 10.00–12.00, 14.30–17.00, 19.00–22.00 Mon–Sun (to 22.30 Sat).* Charge (for membership and skate hire).
⊖ Queensway, Bayswater
🚌 12, 88

**Queen's Theatre**    *3M4*
Shaftesbury Av W1. 01-734 1166. Twin to the Globe. Particularly successful between the wars, but still presents good drama and varied productions.
⊖ Piccadilly Circus
🚌 3, 6, 9, 12, 13, 14, 15, 15B, 19, 22, 22B, 38, 53, 88, 159, 509

# R

## RAF Museum
Aerodrome Rd, Hendon NW9. 01-205 2266. This first national museum to cover all aspects of the RAF and its predecessor the RFC was opened in 1972 on a former wartime airfield. It has one of the world's finest collections of historic aircraft, as well as equipment, documents and paintings. It incorporates Battle of Britain Hall with British, German and Italian aircraft – Spitfire, Hurricane, Gladiator, Defiant, Blenheim, Messerschmitt, Heinkel, Junkers, Fiat. There is also a replica of the No 11 group ops room at RAF Uxbridge; Bomber Command Hall with its range of aircraft from World War I to an Avro-Vulcan of the post-war era; the only Halifax and Wellington left in the world; a B17 Flying Fortress; and a B25 Mitchell of the USAF. *Open 10.00–18.00 Mon–Sat; 14.00–18.00 Sun. Closed Nat Hols.* Charge.
⊖ Colindale
🚌 226

## Rangers House
Chesterfield Walk, Blackheath SE10. 01-853 0035. An attractive late 17thC villa, once home to the 4th Earl of Chesterfield and later to General Lord Wolsey. The Suffolk collection of portraits from Stuart and Jacobean England are painted in such detail that they serve as valuable reference material on contemporary court dress. Furniture and antique musical instruments of the same periods are gradually being acquired. *Open 10.00–17.00 Mon–Sun.* Free.
⊖ New Cross, New Cross Gate (then bus 53)
🚌 53, 54, 75
🚃 Maze Hill

## Regent's Park      1B2
NW1. 01-486 7905. Originally part of Henry VIII's royal hunting grounds, the park took its present handsome form when the Prince Regent appointed John Nash to connect it by way of Regent Street to the now demolished Carlton House. The design of 1812–26 was never completed, but the 470 acres of lawns and lakes were encircled by elegant Regency terraces and imposing gateways.

Here you will find the Grand Union Canal – called Regent's Canal at this point – the Zoo, a boating lake with 30 species of wildfowl, the London Mosque and, in the Inner Circle, Queen Mary's lovely rose gardens, with their bandstand and the Open Air Theatre (01-486 2431). In good weather you can watch performances, primarily of Shakespearean plays, *from May–Aug. Open 05.00–dusk.* Free.
⊖ Regent's Park, Baker Street, Great Portland Street
🚌 2A, 2B, 13, 18, 27, 30, 74, 82, 113, 135, 159, C2

## Regent Street      3H3
W1. One great curve of elegance when built by Nash in 1813, now almost entirely rebuilt into a sedate shopping street for good clothes, china, glass, toys, jewellery and tourism.
⊖ Piccadilly Circus, Oxford Circus
🚌 3, 12, 13, 15, 15B, 53, 88, 159, 509, C2

## Reject Shop      3L3
209 Tottenham Court Rd W1. 01-580 2895. Don't be put off by

the name. Most of the merchandise is perfect, although some has been rejected because of minuscule flaws. Kitchen equipment, china, glass, gifts, and household bits and pieces at very good prices. Branches in Beauchamp Place, Brompton Road and King's Road as well. *Open 09.30–18.00 (to 19.00 Thur) Mon–Sat. Closed Sun.*
⊖ Goodge Street
🚌 10, 14, 14A, 24, 29, 73, 134

### Renoir 1 & 2 1D6
Brunswick Sq WC1. 01-837 8402. Formerly The Gate, Bloomsbury but now redesigned and refurbished. Quality films, some subtitled.
⊖ Russell Square
🚌 68, 77, 77A, 168, 188, 503

### Richmond Ice Rink
Clevedon Rd, East Twickenham, Middx. 01-892 3646. Admission and skate-hire charge. *Open 10.00 (10.30 Sat)–12.30; 14.30–17.00; 19.30–22.00 (to 22.30 Fri & Sat) Mon–Sun.*
⊖ Richmond
🚌 33, 37, 90, 202, 270, 290

### Richmond Park
Surrey. 01-940 0654. A royal park of 2,500 acres, first enclosed as a hunting ground by Charles I in 1637. Bracken, oaks, spinneys and plantations in which herds of dappled deer live wild, squirrels drop half-chewed acorns on early morning joggers, grown-ups ride horses and children sail boats on the Pen Ponds, which are well stocked with fish. The Isabella Plantation, in the heart of the park, is a magic garden of high trees, tiny waterfalls and miniature rustic bridges. Lovely views of the Thames Valley; also golf, polo and football. *Open 07.00–½ hour before dusk. Free.*
⊖ Richmond (then bus 65, 71)
🚌 65, 71, 72, 85
🚊 Richmond

### Riverside Studios
Crisp Rd W6. 01-748 3354. Ex-BBC studios neatly converted to provide two studio theatres, and a 200-seat cinema. There are also dance classes and workshops, a bookshop and art gallery. Drinks, snacks and light meals are available in the self-service restaurant which is part of the huge foyer with its plentiful chairs and tables. *Open 12.00–23.00 Mon–Sun; closed Nat Hols.* Bookshop and gallery *closed Mon.*
⊖ Hammersmith
🚌 9, 10, 11, 27, 33, 72, 91, 220, 266, 267, 283, 290, 295

### Ritz Hotel 3N3
Piccadilly W1. 01-493 8181. Edwardian baroque grandeur and elegance in a period hotel which has always been a rendezvous for visiting celebrities. Stylish international restaurant, exuberant cocktail bar, essential to dress correctly. Be sure to book if you want to take afternoon tea in the Palm Court.
⊖ Green Park
🚌 9, 14, 19, 22, 25, 38

### The Rock Garden 3M5
6–7 The Piazza, Covent Garden WC2. 01-240 3961. Restaurant upstairs and on street level, with tables outside, offering hamburgers, spare ribs and house specialities. Live bands downstairs in the evenings play anything from rock and roll through R&B to new wave. *Open 12.00–01.00 Mon–Sun.* Music venue *open 21.30–03.00 Mon–Sat; 21.30–24.30 Sun.*

⊖ Covent Garden
🚌 14, 19, 22, 22B, 24, 29, 38, 176

**Ronnie Scott's** **3M4**
47 Frith St W1. 01-439 0747. This is the most famous and respected jazz club in London where you can be sure to see all the top jazz bands, mainly from the USA. The lighting is subtle, the atmosphere is crowded and mellow, but it is advisable to book. On the menu – chicken, steaks, pasta and salads. *Open 20.30–03.00 Mon–Sat. Closed Sun.* Charge.
⊖ Leicester Square, Piccadilly Circus, Tottenham Court Road
🚌 14, 19, 22, 22B, 24, 29, 38, 176

**Rotten Row** **2G6**
Hyde Park W2. Originally 'Route en Roi', the King's route to Kensington Palace; now a wide sandy ride where those who have access to horses exercise them daily.
⊖ Knightsbridge
🚌 9, 10, 14, 19, 22, 30, 52, 52A, 74, 137, 503, C1

**Rotunda Museum**
Woolwich Common SE18. 01-854 2242. Pavilion by Nash 1814. Renowned museum displaying a highly impressive array of artillery starting with the 1346 Crècy bombard. *Open Apr–Oct 12.00–17.00 Mon–Fri, 13.00–17.00 Sat & Sun; Nov–Mar 12.00–16.00 Mon–Fri, 13.00–16.00 Sat & Sun.* Free.
🚌 53, 54, 75
⭆ Woolwich Arsenal

**Royal Academy of Arts** **3N3**
Burlington House, Piccadilly W1. 01-734 9052. Much dignified research and study is conducted in private rooms here by the Academy itself and by the Society of Antiquaries, the Royal Society of Chemistry, the Geological Society, the Royal Astronomical Society and the Linnean Society. The public galleries present a series of important loan exhibitions throughout the year, containing work by major artists. The Summer Exhibition from May to August displays the work of new and aspiring, living artists. *Open 10.00–18.00 Mon–Sun.* Charge.
⊖ Piccadilly Circus
🚌 9, 14, 19, 22, 38

**Royal Albert Hall** **2H4**
Kensington Gore SW7. 01-589 8212. Oval, Victorian domed hall, perhaps best known for the summer 'Prom' concerts. Throughout the year, stages orchestral, choral and pop concerts, sporting events and even large meetings. One of London's premier all-purpose auditoria. There's also a newly introduced guided tour which includes views of the amphitheatre from a private box and the Queen's box regally dressed for a gala concert. Gift shop, refreshments and annual theme exhibitions.
⊖ Knightsbridge (then bus 9, 10, 52, 52A), South Kensington (then bus 49, C1 or walk)
🚌 9, 10, 33, 52, 52A, C1

**Royal College of Arms** **4T4**
Queen Victoria St EC4. Discreet brick building of 1671, wherein the three Kings of Arms, six Heralds and four Pursuivants arrange matters ceremonial and heraldic and store the official records of English and Welsh genealogy. *Not open to the general public, except for bona fide research.*
⊖ Blackfriars, Mansion House
🚌 6, 9, 11, 15, 15B, 17, 76, 95, 149, 513

### Royal College of Music   2H5

Prince Consort Rd SW7. 01-589 3643. Holds a wide range of recitals – solo, symphonic, full operas – all by students. No refreshments (no space). The Museum of Instruments, which has a clavicytherium and Handel's spinet, is *open term time 11.00–14.30 Mon & Wed only*. Charge. The small Department of Portraits, high in one of the towers, is *open 10.00–17.00 Mon–Fri by appointment only*. Free.
Θ Knightsbridge (then bus 9, 10, 52, 52A), South Kensington (then walk)
🚌 9, 10, 33, 52, 52A, C1

### Royal College of   3M5
### Surgeons

Lincoln's Inn Fields WC2. 01-405 3474. The collection on anatomy, physiology and pathology assembled by the 18thC surgeon John Hunter is on display here – though not to children under 14. *Open by appointment only*. Free.
Θ Chancery Lane (not Sun)
🚌 4, 6, 8, 9, 11, 15, 15B, 22, 22B, 25, 68, 77, 77A, 168, 171, 171A, 188, 501, 502, 509, 513

### Royal Court Theatre   5W3

Sloane Sq SW1. 01-730 1745. This is where John Osborne's 'Look Back in Anger' launched a new wave of drama in the 50s, and experimental work is still staged here. The studio Theatre Upstairs, 01-730 2554, also puts on new plays and rehearsed play readings. Two bars, snack bar and bookstall.
Θ Sloane Square
🚌 11, 19, 22, 137, C1

### The Royal Docks

E16. When they were built in the mid-19thC the Royals – made up of the Victoria, Royal Albert and King George V Docks – were the largest inland docks in the world, enclosing a total of 245 acres of water. They flourished until the early 70s – with a spell as a Naval base and food port during World War II. Containerisation and the re-siting of the docks at Tilbury finished them off and they are now being redeveloped.

At first glance they seem to be no more than a monumental building site but watersports are already well-established, London City Airport is connecting the City with the Continent, British Telecom Teleport conducts a different kind of communication, North Woolwich Station Museum appeals to railway buffs and the Thames Barrier, in addition to protecting London from flooding, has become a splendid tourist attraction.
🚌 69, 101, 262, 276
🚉 Custom House, North Woolwich

### Royal Exchange   4S5

Threadneedle St and Cornhill EC3. 01-606 2433. The premises of LIFFE (London International Financial Futures Exchange). Originally planned in 1564, as a meeting place for merchants, by Sir Thomas Gresham whose family emblem of a golden grasshopper crouches on top of this third building on the site.
Θ Bank
🚌 6, 8, 9, 11, 15B, 21, 22, 25, 43, 76, 133, 149, 501

### Royal Festival Hall   4U1

South Bank SE1. 01-928 3191. Built for the Festival of Britain in 1951 and now a part of the South Bank Arts complex. Orchestral and choral concerts are staged in the 3,000-seat concert hall, and the large foyers offer exhibitions, bars, a wine and salad bar, a licensed restaurant, a book and score shop and music on occasional lunchtimes. *Open all day.*
Θ Waterloo
🚌 1, 4, 68, 76, 149, 168, 171, 171A, 176, 188, 501, 502, 505, 507, 513, C1, P11

**Royal Free Hospital**
Pond St NW3. 01-794 0500. Large general hospital founded in a small way in 1828 as The London General Institution for the Gratuitous Care of Malignant Diseases. George IV was its first Royal Patron, Queen Victoria was responsible for the change of title. Not only London's first free hospital, but the first to admit female medical students and to introduce an obstetrics and gynaecology unit – suitably enough since it was the death of an impoverished woman, refused admission at all London hospitals, which persuaded the surgeon William Marsden to found it in the first place. Has been on its present site since 1978. *24-hr casualty.*
⊖ Belsize Park
🚌 24, 46, 168, 268, C11

**Royal Garden Hotel** *2H3*
Kensington High St W8. 01-937 8000. Modern, imposing and smart hotel with good food in both restaurants – one of which, The Roof Restaurant, has lovely views over Kensington Gardens and a dance floor. Morning coffee and full afternoon tea, as well as snacks, are served in The Garden Room. *Open LD Mon–Sun.*
⊖ High Street Kensington
🚌 9, 10, 27, 28, 31, 33, 49, 52, 52A, C1

**Royal Horticultural** *5W5*
**Society Halls**
Vincent Sq SW1. 01-834 4333. Sixty exhibitions of flowers and plants are held here annually, clustered in spring, summer and autumn. The Society was founded in 1805 to promote the knowledge of horticulture and botany and has an extensive library *(by appointment only). Open daily when shows are on.*
⊖ St James's Park
🚌 76, 507, 510

**Royal Mews** *5W4*
Buckingham Palace Rd SW1. 01-930 4832. The home of the royal horses, the stage coaches, including the elaborate golden coronation coach and the fairytale glass coach, and of the royal cars. *Open 14.00–16.00 Wed & Thur. Closed during Ascot week.* Charge.
⊖ Victoria

🚌 2, 2A, 2B, 11, 16, 24, 25, 29, 36, 36A, 36B, 38, 39, 52, 73, 76, 82, 185, 506, 507, 510, C1

**Royal Naval College**
Greenwich SE10. Box office: 01-317 8687. There is a season of classical concerts in the beautiful Wren Chapel from October to April and again during the Greenwich Festival in June. Although it is traditional to view the Painted Hall – structure by Wren, painted by Thornhill – in the interval the rest of the college is out of bounds.
⊖ Surrey Docks (then bus 1, 88) Docklands Light Railway: Island Gardens (then by foot tunnel)
🚌 1, 177, 180, 188, 286
🚄 Maze Hill

**Royal Opera Arcade** *3N4*
Between Pall Mall and Charles II St SW1. London's first arcade, designed in 1816 by John Nash. Pure Regency, with its bow-fronted shops, glass-domed vaults and elegant lamps.
⊖ Piccadilly Circus
🚌 3, 6, 9, 12, 13, 14, 15, 15B, 19, 22, 22B, 38, 53, 88, 159, 509

**Royal Opera House** *3M5*
Floral St WC2. 01-240 1066. 24-hour recorded information on: 01-240 1911. England's foremost opera house, a splendid construction by Barry, is often referred to simply as 'Covent Garden'. It is

home to the Royal Opera Company and the Royal Ballet Company and provides a suitably lavish setting for the great names who perform here. Cold buffet and drinks are served in all the bars. Champagne in the Crush Bar is *de rigueur*.

ӨCovent Garden

1, 6, 9, 11, 13, 15, 15B, 77, 77A, 170, 176, 509 to the Strand

**Rules**   *3N5*
35 Maiden La WC2. 01-836 5314. Famous Edwardian restaurant. Edward VII dined Lily Langtry in an upstairs room and Thackeray and Dickens ate here in their day. Electric chandeliers now, but authentic panelling, pictures and playbills. Roast beef or jugged hare are recommended. Booking essential. *Open LD Mon–Sat. Closed Sun.*

ӨCharing Cross

1, 6, 9, 11, 13, 15, 15B, 77, 77A, 170, 176, 509 to the Strand

**Rumours Cocktail Bar**   *3M5*
33 Wellington St WC2. 01-836 0038. Once a flower market, now a large pillared and mirrored room in which to try an imaginative range of new and classic cocktails in the lively and rather fashionable setting of Covent Garden. Very much a venue for the now-people with sturdy eardrums! *Open Mon–Sat & Sun eve only.*

ӨCovent Garden

1, 4, 6, 9, 11, 13, 15, 15B, 68, 77, 77A, 168, 170, 171, 171A, 176, 188, 502, 505, 509, 513

**Russian Orthodox Church**   *2H5*
Ennismore Gdns SW7. The Patriarchal Church of the Dormition and All Saints was designed in the 1840s by Vulliamy in Early Christian style. The rich interior has sgraffito work by Heywood Sumner, one of the leaders of the Arts and Crafts movement.

ӨKnightsbridge (then bus 9, 10, 52, 52A)

9, 10, 52, 52A to Prince of Wales Gate

---

**London Transport 24-hour information service**
For any information on travel in Greater London – routes, fares, times – telephone 01-222 1234 at any time of the day or night.

**Sadler's Wells Theatre** *4Q2*
Rosebery Av EC1. 01-278 8916.
This venerable theatre, home of
Sadler's Wells Royal Ballet, en-
gages visiting international companies to present seasons of opera,
dance and mime. The name comes
from a well discovered by a Mr
Thomas Sadler – it still exists, under
a trap-door at the back of the stalls.
⊖ Angel
🚌 19, 38, 171, 171A, 279

**St Andrew's Church** *4S2*
Holborn Circus EC1. Wren's largest
parish church, built in 1686 but restored after bombing in World War II
with a cool, simple, modern interior. The pulpit, font, organ, and
tomb of Thomas Coram come from
the chapel of his 18thC Foundling
Hospital.
⊖ Chancery Lane (not Sun),
Farringdon
🚌 8, 17, 22, 22B, 25, 45, 46,
171A, 221, 243, 259, 501

**St Andrew Undershaft** *4S5*
**Church**
St Mary Axe EC3. 01-283 7382.
Early 16thC East Anglian Gothic –
once overshadowed by a maypole.
The monument by John Stow,
London's first historian, is annually
furnished with a fresh quill pen by
the Lord Mayor.
⊖ Aldgate, Bank
🚌 15B, Mon–Fri 25

**St Anne's Church**
Commercial Rd E14. 01-987 1502.
One of Docklands grandest
churches, designed by Nicholas
Hawksmoor and built between
1712 and 1730. The imposing
tower was once a landmark for
shipping. The churchyard has a
mysterious stone pyramid – the
carvings still faintly visible on its
south side are believed to be Masonic symbols. *Open during services
and by appointment.*
Docklands Light Railway:
Limehouse, Shadwell
🚌 5, 15, 15B, 40

**St Bartholomew the Great** *4S3*
**Church**
West Smithfield EC1. 01-606 5171.
Great indeed, and the oldest church
in London (apart from the chapel in
the Tower). It is the Norman choir of
the Augustinian Priory founded in
1123, together with St Bartholomew's Hospital, by Rahere, a
courtier of Henry I.
⊖ St Paul's
🚌 4, 8, 22, 22B, 25, 141, 279A,
501, 502, 509

**St Bartholomew's** *4S3*
**Hospital**
West Smithfield EC1. 01-600 9000.
A famous teaching hospital and one
of London's oldest. St Thomas's
was probably founded earlier, but
Barts has remained on the same
site since 1123. It was originally
connected to a Priory of which St
Bartholomew the Great Church is
all that remains. Large general hospital incorporating many specialist
departments. Regular guided tours,
*Sun at 14.00*, include the church.
(Donation welcome). *24-hr casualty.*
⊖ Barbican
🚌 4, 8, 22, 22B, 25, 141, 279A,
501, 502, 509

**St Bride's Church** *4T2*
Fleet St EC4. 01-353 1301. Known
as the printers' church, its crypt
museum (itself part Roman part
Saxon) is warmed by the heat of
Reuters press agency next door.
This is the Wren church whose
tiered spire has been the model for
countless wedding cakes. Restored after war damage; Christ almost dances in the stained glass
window in the Wren-style altar-
piece. *Museum open 09.00–17.00
Mon–Sun.* Donation appreciated.
⊖ Blackfriars
🚌 4, 6, 9, 11, 15, 15B, 17, 45, 59,
63, 76, 141, 502, 509, 513

**St Bride's Printing** *4T2*
**Library**
St Bride's Institute, Bride La EC4.
01-353 4660. A public reference library of books on graphic design,

papermaking, printing, binding and everything to do with the production of books. Occasional special exhibitions. *Open 09.30–17.30 Mon–Fri.*
⊖ Blackfriars
🚌 4, 6, 9, 11, 15, 15B, 17, 45, 59, 63, 76, 141, 502, 509, 513

### St Christopher's Place   3M2
W1. Attractive little enclave of fashion shops and boutiques, mainly for the young and modern who want to be ahead of the trend.
⊖ Bond Street
🚌 6, 7, 8, 10, 12, 13, 15, 16A, 25, 73, 88, 113, 135, 137, 159, 503

### St Clement Danes Church   4T2
Strand WC2. 01-242 8282. The church of the nursery rhyme whose carillon includes 'Oranges and Lemons' in its repertoire. Built for the Danes in the 9thC, rebuilt by Wren, destroyed in 1941, rebuilt again in the 50s and now the central church of the RAF.
⊖ Temple (not Sun), Charing Cross (then any bus along the Strand), Holborn (then bus 68, 77, 77A, 501 to Aldwych)
🚌 4, 6, 9, 11, 15, 15B, 171A, 502, 509, 513

### St Dunstan in the West Church   4S2
Fleet St EC4. 01-242 6027. Rebuilt in 1832 as a copy of All Saints

Church in York. The clock with its two striking jacks is 17thC and the statue of Queen Elizabeth I is the only known, contemporary three-dimensional likeness of her.
⊖ Temple (not Sun), Charing Cross (then bus 6, 9, 11)
🚌 4, 6, 9, 11, 15, 15B, 171A, 502, 509, 513

### St George's Cathedral   3P6
Lambeth Rd SE1. 01-928 5256. This Roman Catholic cathedral, barrack-like from without but gracious within, was designed by Pugin in the 1840s and never completed. Destroyed by bombing in 1941 and rebuilt by Romily Croze, who adapted the original plans.
⊖ Lambeth North
🚌 1, 12, 44, 45, 53, 63, 68, 141, 171, 176, 184, 188, 510

### St George-in-the-East Church
Cannon St Rd E1. 01-709 9074. Imaginatively designed church-within-a-church. Nicholas Hawksmoor's massive, elegant structure of 1714–26 was gutted by a World War II incendiary bomb. In the early 1960s Arthur Bailey created a modern church within the outer walls, using an extensive glass wall to reflect the original tower. *Open for services and in the afternoon of the first Sat each month.*
⊖ Shadwell
🚌 100

### St George's Hotel   3L3
Langham Pl W1. 01-580 0111. Modern hotel on the top floors of a tall structure next to Broadcasting House. 85 rooms, efficient service, and an attractive restaurant, serving English food, which is open to non-residents – and patronised by broadcasting types, among others.
⊖ Oxford Circus
🚌 3, 6, 7, 8, 10, 12, 13, 15, 15B, 16A, 25, 53, 73, 88, 113, 135, 137, 159, 176, 503, 509, C2

### St Giles Cripplegate Church   4S4
Fore St EC2. 01-606 3630. The massive Barbican surrounds this church where Cromwell was married and Milton is buried. Its interior was almost wholly rebuilt after bombing. Behind it stands a corner bastion of the Roman city wall. 'Cripplegate' comes from 'crepel', Anglo-Saxon for a kind of pedes-

trian underpass used for entry after curfew.

⊖ Barbican, St Paul's

🚌 4, 141, 279A, 502, 509

### St James's Church 3N3

Piccadilly W1. 01-734 4511. A Wren church restored in 1954 after bomb damage. The reredos and font garlanding are by Grinling Gibbons. A place of tremendous activity with craft markets in the courtyard, music, lectures, exhibitions, events. Well-attended church services, too. Very pleasant little café.

⊖ Piccadilly Circus

🚌 9, 14, 19, 22, 38

### St James's Palace 3N4

Pall Mall SW1. In warm red brick with blue diapering, its Tudor gatehouse gives on to courtyards and buildings planned for Henry VIII, but with important additions by Wren and others. Still officially a royal residence – foreign ambassadors and commissioners are 'accredited to the Court of St James'.

⊖ Green Park, St James's Park

🚌 9, 14, 19, 22, 38

### St James's Park 3O3

SW1. 01-930 1793. The oldest of the royal parks and one of the most attractive with its long lake, delicate bridge and weeping willows. Especially rich in bird life, including 20 species of ducks and geese and, on Duck Island, some magnificent pelicans who have occasionally been known to snack on pigeons. The present design is mainly by Nash, and Buckingham Palace, Carlton House Terrace, the domes and spires of Whitehall, and Westminster Abbey overlook it with apparent approval. *Open 05.00– 24.00.* Free.

⊖ St James's Park

🚌 11, 24, 29, 76, 507, 510, C1 (to Victoria Street)

### St John's Church 4R3
Clerkenwell

St John's Sq EC1. 01-253 6644. Mostly 18thC but the crypt is part of the original 12thC priory church of the Order of St John of Jerusalem. Used by the St John's Ambulance Brigade for ceremonies and services. Apply to curator for admission.

⊖ Farringdon

🚌 55, 243, 277, 279, 505

### St John's Church 3P4
Smith Square

SW1. 01-222 1061. 18thC church whose curious appearance has been likened to an upside-down footstool. Has regular lunchtime and evening concerts – solos, chamber, orchestral and choral works. The crypt has exhibitions of works by contemporary artists and a good licensed buffet and restaurant.

⊖ Westminster

🚌 3, 76, 77A, 88, 159 (not Sun), 507, 510

### St John's Gate Museum 4R3

St John's Sq EC1. 01-253 6644 extn 35. The old gatehouse of the Priory of St John of Jerusalem is now a small museum on all aspects of the Knights Hospitallers. The St John Ambulance was launched from the gatehouse in 1877 – and the museum is in the hands of the Order of St John. *Open 10.00–18.00 Tue, Fri & Sat. Closed Mon, Wed, Thur, Sun & Nat Hols.* Tours, at *11.30 & 14.30,* include the 12thC crypt of the Priory Church. Donation welcome.

⊖ Farringdon

🚌 55, 243, 277, 279, 505

**St Katharine Docks**     **4U6**

St Katharine's Way, Tower Bridge E1. One-time commercial docks importing ivory, ostrich feathers, carpets and cigars, which ceased trading in 1968. Now a yacht haven surrounded by the Tower Hotel, the World Trade Centre, the London Futures and Options Exchange, and an office development short-listed to house the EEC Trade Marks office. The only two original buildings are the Ivory House and the Dockmaster's House – though the old King's Brewery was only moved 100 yards or so before being refurbished as the popular Dickens Inn.

⊖ Tower Hill

Docklands Light Railway: Tower Gateway

🚌 15, 42, 78, 100, 510, Sat & Sun 25

**St Margaret Church**     **3O4**
**Westminster**

Parliament Sq SW1. 01-222 6382. Somewhat dwarfed by the massive bulk of Westminster Abbey is this parish church of the House of Commons, rebuilt in the 16thC, with a splendid east window and some wondrous modern stained glass by John Piper.

⊖ Westminster

🚌 3, 11, 12, 24, 29, 53, 77, 77A, 88, 109, 159, 170, 184, C1

**St Margaret Pattens**     **4T5**
**Church**

Rood La, Eastcheap EC3. 01-623 6630. The locally-made pattens, or shoes, are displayed in a cabinet in this Wren church of 1684–9, with its unusual canopied pews and punishment bench for naughty children.

⊖ Monument

🚌 15, 40, 510, Sat & Sun 25

**St Martin-in-the-Fields**     **3N4**
**Church**

Trafalgar Sq WC2. 01-930 1862. This is the parish church of Buckingham Palace (though not used as such) and above the congregation is a Royal Box complete with fireplace. There is now tremendous activity in the crypt with a licensed restaurant, Fields, *open 10.00–21.00 Mon–Sat; 12.00–18.00 Sun,* (snacks only, hot food served *12.00–15.15 & 17.30–20.30 Mon–Sat; 12.00–15.15 Sun),* a visitor

centre and a theological bookshop. Still puts on the regular lunchtime music recitals and Christmas choral concerts for which it has become famous.

⊖ Charing Cross

🚌 1, 3, 6, 9, 11, 12, 13, 15, 15B, 22B, 24, 29, 53, 77, 77A, 88, 109, 159, 170, 176, 184, 509

**St Martin's Theatre**     **3M4**

West St, Cambridge Circus WC2. 01-836 1443. Intimate playhouse with unusual polished teak doors. 'The Mousetrap' continues its record run here.

⊖ Leicester Square

🚌 14, 19, 22, 22B, 24, 29, 38, 176

**St Mary-le-Bow Church**     **4S4**

Cheapside EC2. 01-248 5139. Bow Bells still ring out from this Wren church, gutted in 1941 and rebuilt by Laurence King. The modern rood is a present from Germany. The 11thC crypt, with its quiet chapel, houses the Ecclesiastical Court of Arches, the Archbishop of Canterbury's appeal court.

⊖ Bank, Mansion House

🚌 8, 22, 22B, 25, 501

**St Mary le Strand Church**     **3M5**

Strand WC2. 01-836 3126. A per-

fect small baroque church, built 1714–17 by James Gibb, perched nervously on an island in the middle of the busy road.
θ Temple (not Sun), Holborn (then bus 68, 77, 77A, 188, 501 to the Aldwych), Charing Cross (then any bus along the Strand)
🚌 1, 4, 6, 9, 11, 13, 15, 15B, 68, 77, 77A, 168, 170, 171, 171A, 176, 188, 502, 505, 509, 513

### St Mary's Church, Rotherhithe
St Marychurch St SE16. 01-231 2465. An 18thC rebuild of an older church with strong maritime connections – the crew of the 'Mayflower' worshipped here, her captain is buried in the churchyard, the communion table and two bishop's chairs are carved of oak taken from the warship 'Fighting Temeraire' – whose voyage to the Rotherhithe breaker's yard is the subject of a famous Turner painting.
θ Rotherhithe
🚌 47, 188, 225, P11, P14

### St Michael Paternoster Church    4T4
College Hill EC4. Dick Whittington lies buried in this recently restored Wren church. The tower is used as an office by the Mission to Seamen.
θ Cannon Street (not evenings or weekends), Mansion House
🚌 6, 9, 11, 15, 15B, 17, 76, 95, 149, 513

### St Michael-upon-Cornhill Church    4T5
Cornhill EC3. 01-626 8841. First-

rate choir, also lunchtime organ recitals and choral evenings. Send s.a.e. for list of events. Magnificent peal of bells, too. A Wren church restored by Scott.
θ Bank
🚌 15B, Mon–Fri 25

### St Olave Church    4T5
8 Hart St EC3. 01-488 4318. A 15thC survivor of the Great Fire. The arch of skulls in the churchyard indicates that the dead from the Plague were buried here as were Samuel Pepys and, so says the parish register, Mother Goose.
θ Aldgate
🚌 15, 40, 510, Sat & Sun 25

### St Pancras Old Church    1B6
Pancras Rd NW1. 01-387 7301. On the third oldest Christian site in Europe stands this small country-style church with 4thC foundations and Saxon altar stone. Atmospheric churchyard. *Open for services Wed & Sun.*
θ King's Cross St Pancras
🚌 46, 214

### St Pancras Station    1C6
Euston Rd NW1. Information on 01-387 7070. Gothic extravaganza by Sir George Gilbert Scott. The vast pinnacled frontage was once a grand hotel but now houses offices. The 19thC train shed is an impressive feat of engineering, its glass and iron tunnel vault spanning 243 feet without supporting pillars. The trains from here go to the Midlands.
θ King's Cross St Pancras
🚌 10, 14, 14A, 17, 18, 30, 45, 46, 63, 73, 77A, 214, 221, 259, C11
≠ St Pancras

### St Paul's Cathedral    4S3
EC4. 01-248 4619/2705. Sir Christopher Wren's greatest work, built from 1675–1710. The superb dome and porches are dwarfed by modern building, but the interior has lost nothing with its magnificent stalls by Grinling Gibbons, ironwork by Tijou, paintings by Thornhill, mosaics by Salviati and Stephens. Rich in memorials to the great and famous – soldiers, artists, statesmen. The crypt, the largest in Europe, has a worthwhile museum. It is worth the heart-pounding climb to the Whispering Gallery not only

for the weird phenomenon but to get a different view of the whole. Holds occasional lunchtime organ recitals and the choir is exceptional.
θ St Paul's, Mansion House
⊒ 4, 6, 8, 9, 11, 15, 15B, 17, 22, 22B, 25, 76, 141, 501, 502, 509, 513

**St Paul's Church**                    **3M4**
**Covent Garden**
Covent Garden WC2. 01-836 5221. The actors' church. Built by Inigo Jones in the 1630s it contains memorials to Marie Lloyd, Boris Karloff, Sybil Thorndike, Lewis Casson and many more.
θ Covent Garden
⊒ 1, 6, 9, 11, 13, 15, 15B, 77, 77A, 170, 176, 509 to the Strand

**St Peter-upon-Cornhill**              **4S5**
**Church**
Bishopsgate Corner EC3. 01-626 9483. Built by Wren on the City's oldest church site. Holds regular performances of Elizabethan music and of medieval plays at Christmas.
θ Bank
⊒ 15B, 35, 47, 48, 505, Mon–Fri 25

**St Sophia's Cathedral**               **2F3**
Moscow Rd W2. Oldrid Scott, son of Sir George Gilbert Scott, designed this red brick Byzantine Cathedral of the Greek Orthodox Church inside in 1877. The lovely mosaic work inside is by Boris Anrep.
θ Bayswater, Queensway
⊒ 12, 88

**St Stephen's Church**                 **4T4**
Walbrook EC4. 01-283 3400. The parish church of the Lord Mayor of London and a centre for the Samaritans, 01-283 3400, formed to help the suicidally desperate. One of Wren's masterpieces, its beautifully restored dome was possibly a prototype for St Paul's.
θ Bank, Cannon Street (not evenings or weekends)
⊒ 6, 8, 9, 11, 15, 15B, 21, 22, 22B, 25, 43, 76, 133, 149, 501

**St Stephen's Tavern**                 **3O4**
10 Bridge St SW1. 01-930 3230. Parliament's local, with a division bell to summon drinking Members back across the road to vote. Three bars, with food available at lunchtime during the week. Good

place to spot famous faces and listen to the gossip of political journalists. *Open Mon–Sat & Sun morning. Closed Sun evening.*
θ Westminster
⊒ 3, 11, 12, 24, 29, 53, 77, 77A, 88, 109, 159, 170, 184, C1

**St Thomas's Hospital**                **3O5**
Lambeth Palace Rd SE1. 01-928 9292. The enormous general hospital has been resited, rebuilt and extended since its foundation in the 12thC when it may have been connected to the Priory of St Mary Overie at Southwark. Originally named after St Thomas the Martyr, its allegiance was changed to St Thomas the Apostle after the Dissolution of the Monasteries. Florence Nightingale established her famous Nursing School here and nurses at Tommy's are still known as Nightingales. *24-hr casualty.*
θ Waterloo
⊒ 76, 77, 170, 507

**Samuel Pepys**                        **4T3**
Brooks Wharf, 48 Upper Thames St EC4. 01-248 3048. A warehouse converted into a rambling pub with a two-tiered, river-view terrace bar and a spacious cellar bar with a well-stocked food counter. The light airy restaurant has good river views, and transcriptions of Pepys' diaries and an original letter are on display among the old lamps and

prints. *Pub open normal licensing hours Mon–Sun. Restaurant open LD Mon–Fri & D Sat; closed L Sat and all Sun.*
⊖ Mansion House
🚍 6, 9, 11, 15, 15B, 17, 76, 95, 149, 513

### Savill Gardens
Windsor Great Park, Windsor, Berks. 0784 35544. The 35 acres of woodland garden were created by Sir Eric Savill in the 1930s. Beautiful throughout the spring and summer with azaleas, roses, herbaceous borders, alpine plants and a lake. *Open 10.00–18.00 Mon–Sun. Closed Oct–Mar. Free.*
Green Line 700, 701, 718, 726
⭜ Windsor and Eton Riverside, Windsor and Eton Central (then walk)

### Savoy Hotel 3N5
Strand WC2. 01-836 4343. World-famous hotel with stylish decor, lovely river views and famous clients. Outstanding cuisine in Grill Room or River Restaurant, champagne and seafood 'upstairs'; classy cocktails in the American Bar.
⊖ Charing Cross (then any bus along the Strand), Temple (not Sun)
🚍 1, 6, 9, 11, 13, 15, 15B, 77, 77A, 170, 176, 509

### Savoy Theatre 3N5
Strand WC2. 01-836 8888. Built by Richard D'Oyly Carte as a home for the comic operas of Gilbert and Sullivan – now presenting a wide vari-

ety of plays and musicals. Attached to the Savoy Hotel.
⊖ Charing Cross (then any bus along the Strand), Temple (not Sun)
🚍 1, 6, 9, 11, 13, 15, 15B, 77, 77A, 170, 176, 509

### Science Museum 2H5
Exhibition Rd SW7. 01-589 3456. Vast national collection on science and its applications to industry. Most of the items on display are real, not models, and large numbers still function and are demonstrated daily. Transport and exploration, meteorology and time measurement, telecommunications and computing, space exploration and the Apollo 10 capsule, and, on the top floor, The Wellcome Museum of the History of Medicine are all here. Lectures, films, school holiday events, a shop and a cafeteria round off the experience. *Open 10.00–18.00 Mon–Sat; 14.30–18.00 Sun. Closed Nat Hols in winter & spring. Free.*
⊖ South Kensington
🚍 14, 30, 45, 49, 74, 219, 503, C1

### Scotch House 2H6
2 Brompton Rd SW3. 01-581 2151. Those who are entitled to wear the tartan will find the appropriate one here. Also Fair Isle, Shetland and Pringle knitwear and top quality Scottish tweeds for men, women and children. Other branches. *Open 09.00–18.00 (to 19.00 Wed) Mon–Sat. Closed Sun.*
⊖ Knightsbridge
🚍 9, 10, 14, 19, 22, 30, 52, 52A, 74, 137, 503, C1

### See Woo Supermarket 3N4
18–20 Lisle St WC2. 01-439 8325. Enormous Chinese supermarket stocking most of the requisites of Chinese cooking, including fish that is not so much fresh as actually alive. *Open 10.00–21.00 Mon–Sun.*
⊖ Leicester Square, Piccadilly Circus
🚍 3, 6, 9, 12, 13, 14, 15, 15B, 19, 22, 22B, 38, 53, 88, 159, 509

### Selfridges 3M1
400 Oxford St W1. 01-629 1234. Established since 1909, this is one of the most comprehensive of the

large department stores with lavish food halls and glamorous displays of clothes, toys, furniture, household goods, books and a large and fragrant perfumery. Refreshments range from a fully licensed silver service à la carte restaurant to a coffee shop. *Open 09.00–18.00 (to 19.30 Thur) Mon–Sat. Closed Sun.*
Ѳ Bond Street, Marble Arch
🚌 2A, 2B, 6, 7, 8, 10, 12, 13, 15, 16A, 30, 73, 74, 82, 88, 113, 135, 137, 159, 503

### Serpentine  2G6
Hyde Park W2. A fine artificial lake, created with the Long Water to the west by damming the old Westbourne River. There are boats to hire from the north bank, restaurants at either end, fishing, ornamental ducks, and promenades and deckchairs all around. *Park open 05.00–24.00 Mon–Sun.* Small charge for boat hire.
Ѳ Knightsbridge, Lancaster Gate
🚌 9, 10, 12, 52, 52A, 88, C1

### Serpentine Gallery  2G5
Kensington Gardens W8. 01-402 6075. The old Kensington Gardens tea house is a lovely setting for a variety of exhibitions of contemporary art which change monthly. The Serpentine restaurant, buffet and bars are only a duck's waddle away. *Open 10.00–18.00 Mon–Sun. Closed dusk in winter and between exhibitions.* Free.
Ѳ Knightsbridge (then walk)
🚌 9, 10, 52, 52A, C1

### Serpentine Restaurants  2G5
Hyde Park W2. 01-723 8784. The elaborate 'modern' structure which has lovely views over the water and the park is shortly to be demolished. The Government-commissioned replacement will also house a restaurant complex but will not be open until 1993. A temporary restaurant will operate from a marquee by the Lido.
Ѳ Knightsbridge (then bus 9, 10, 52, 52A), South Kensington (then walk)
🚌 9, 10, 52, 52A, C1

### Shaftesbury Theatre  3M4
Shaftesbury Av WC2. 01-836 6596. Was acquired in the spring of 1983 by a company of some of the best of British comedy actors, and is the permanent base of the Theatre of Comedy.
Ѳ Tottenham Court Road, Holborn
🚌 7, 8, 19, 22, 22B, 25, 38, 55, 503

### Shakespeare Globe Museum  4T4
Bear Gardens SE1. 01-620 0202. Elizabethan Bankside was a riotous assemblage of theatres, bear-baiting gardens, inns and brothels, and the intriguing exhibitions in this small museum offer a convincing evocation of this lively, if murky, past. About 45 seconds walk from the museum, Shakespeare's Globe Theatre is rising again, built by traditional methods, its design as exact a reconstruction as possible of the original. A model of the project can be seen in the museum. Work began in April 1988 and should be completed in 1992 – visitors are encouraged to watch from the safe vantage points provided. *Museum open 10.00–17.00 Mon–Sat; 14.00–17.30 Sun.* Charge.
Ѳ London Bridge, Cannon Street
🚌 17, 44, 95, 149, P11

### Shaw Theatre  1C6
100 Euston Rd NW1. 01-388 1394. The permanent home of the New Shaw Theatre Company, which presents a varied programme of plays, musicals, concerts and children's events, punctuated by a lavish Christmas pantomime and a summer season by the National Youth Theatre. Regular lunchtime concerts in the bar.
Ѳ Euston
🚌 10, 14, 14A, 18, 30, 68, 73, 77, 77A, 168, 188

## Shepherd Market 3N2
W1. Mayfair's village centre – a picturesque little 18thC quarter of tiny streets and alleys and a diminutive piazza, with market stalls, antique shops, pubs and eating houses.
⊖ Green Park
🚌 9, 14, 19, 22, 25, 38

## Shepherd's Bush Market
Uxbridge Rd W12. Scruffy, busy and long-established, with exotic foods, books, records and general household necessities. *Open 09.00–17.00 (to 13.00 Thur) Mon–Sat.*
⊖ Shepherd's Bush
🚌 11, 12, 49, 72, 88, 105, 207, 220, 237, 260, 283, 295

## Sheraton Park Tower 2H6
101 Knightsbridge SW1. 01-235 8050. Modern hotel with interesting circular design by Richard Seifert, attractive shrubbery on the forecourt, and an 'English country house' decor. In the Restaurant Chef Jacobmeyer presents an interesting menu with a British slant, relying on local produce. There is also a Champagne Bar, Lobby Bar, the Rotunda for tea and coffee, and a well-equipped Business Centre.
⊖ Knightsbridge
🚌 9, 10, 14, 19, 22, 30, 52, 52A, 74, 137, 503, C1

## Sherlock Holmes 3N4
10 Northumberland St WC2. 01-930 2644. Upstairs, next to the restaurant, is a perfect reconstruction of Holmes's study, and down in the bar are all manner of relevant cuttings and curios, including the footprints of the legendary 'Hound of the Baskervilles'. *Restaurant open LD Mon–Fri & D Sat; closed L Sat & all Sun. Pub open normal licensing hours Mon–Sun.*
⊖ Charing Cross, Embankment
🚌 1, 3, 6, 9, 11, 12, 13, 15, 15B, 22B, 24, 29, 53, 77, 77A, 88, 109, 159, 170, 176, 184, 509

## Shooter's Hill
SE18. 01-856 3610. Hundreds of acres of woodland and open parkland which encompass Oxleas Woods, Jackwood and Eltham Parks. Castlewood has a folly erected in 1784 to commemorate the Indian exploits of Sir William James. *Open 24 hrs. Free.*
🚌 89, 178
⇌ Lewisham (then bus 89, 178)

## Simpsons of Piccadilly 3N3
203 Piccadilly W1. 01-734 2002. A department store specialising in top quality men's and women's clothes especially knitwear and sportswear. *The* place to get country casuals. Also good quality luggage and handbags. *Open 09.00–17.30 Mon–Wed, Fri & Sat; 09.00–19.00 Thur. Closed Sun.*
⊖ Piccadilly Circus
🚌 9, 14, 19, 22, 38

## Simpson's in the Strand 3N5
100 Strand WC2. 01-836 9112. Very English restaurant in the grand style – booking and correct dress are essential. The roast beef and mutton are unfailingly splendid – remember to tip the carver – and may be followed by treacle roll or a savoury. The Stilton is always creamy and there is vintage port by the glass to accompany it. *Open LD Mon–Sat. Closed Sun.*
⊖ Charing Cross (then any bus along the Strand), Temple (not Sun)
🚌 1, 6, 9, 11, 13, 15, 15B, 77, 77A, 170, 176, 509

## The Singing Tree
69 New King's Rd SW6. 01-736 1527. Not just for children, this amazing shop stocks new and antique dolls' houses and everything

imaginable to go in them. Collectors' items in miniature. Mail-order service. *Open 10.00– 17.30 Mon– Sat.*

⊖ Fulham Broadway, Parsons Green

🚍 22

**Sir John Soane's Museum** *4S1*
13 Lincoln's Inn Fields WC2. 01-405 2107. The eccentric and inventive Neo-Classical architect (1753–1837) designed here his own house to accommodate his uniquely obsessive collection of antiquities and architectural models; among them the 1370BC sarcophagus of Seti 1 and 12 Hogarth pictures. *Open 10.00–17.00 Tue– Sat. Closed Sun, Mon & Nat Hols. Free.*

⊖ Holborn

🚍 7, 8, 19, 22, 22B, 25, 38, 55, 68, 77, 77A, 168, 171, 188, 501, 505

**Sir Winston Churchill** *3O4*
Parliament Sq SW1. Ivor Roberts-Jones, 1973. Large bronze statue of one of Britain's greatest statesmen, half-facing the House of Commons.

⊖ Westminster

🚍 3, 11, 12, 24, 29, 53, 77, 77A, 88, 109, 159, 170, 184, C1

**W. H. Smith, Sloane Square** *5W2*
36 Sloane Sq SW1. 01-730 0351. One of a nation-wide, high street chain of booksellers, with a large stock of popular titles and paperbacks. Also sells stationery, magazines, toys, records and cassettes. *Open 09.00–18.30 Mon, Thur & Fri; 09.30–18.30 Tue; 09.00–19.00 Wed; 09.00–18.00 Sat. Closed Sun.*

⊖ Sloane Square

🚍 11, 19, 22, 137, C1

**Smithfield Market** *4S3*
EC1. The world's largest wholesale meat market on a site originally called Smooth Field. The 19thC Italianate-style buildings are interesting, but for most people this is 10 acres of sheer horror. *Open 05.00–12.00 Mon–Fri. Closed Sat & Sun.*

⊖ Barbican (not Sun), Farringdon

🚍 8, 22, 22B, 25, 63, 221, 243, 259, 277, 279

**Society of Genealogists** *2J4*
37 Harrington Gdns SW7. 01-373 7054. The library contains a huge collection of copies of parish registers, which those researching their ancestry may consult for a fee. Or, for a larger fee, the Society will undertake the research itself. *Open 10.00–17.00 Mon–Fri. Charge.*

⊖ Gloucester Road

🚍 49

**Soho** *3M3*
W1. London's oldest foreign quarter is gradually changing. Still a curious mixture of charm and corruption, the area is beginning to acquire a cleaner-cut image as Westminster Council implements its plans to smarten up its patch. The tide of erotica is gradually going out, though sex in its most indelicate and expensive forms lingers on in porno movies, sex shops, live shows and 'young models' of all ages.

The good foreign restaurants remain; the delicatessens and patisseries, though sadly fewer in number, continue to be excellent; Berwick Street Market still sells the cheapest fruit and veg in the West End; and the partial refurbishment of Chinatown, with its new pagoda, has not diminished its distinctive character.

Soho was once a hunting ground and 'So-ho' was the rallying cry of the huntsmen.

Θ Leicester Square, Piccadilly Circus, Oxford Circus, Tottenham Court Road

🚍 7, 8, 10, 14, 19, 22, 22B, 24, 29, 38, 55, 73, 176

**Soho Brasserie** 3M4
23–25 Old Compton St W1. 01-439 9301. Pub converted into an arty French-style brasserie – coffee and drinks at the front, meals at the back, doors which fold back so that one or two tables are half in the street in true Continental style. *Open 11.00–23.00 Mon–Sat. Closed Sun.*
Θ Piccadilly Circus
🚍 14, 19, 22, 22B, 38

**Somerset House** 3N4
Strand WC2. 01-438 6622. Designed by Sir W. Chambers, Somerset House is built on the site of an unfinished 16thC palace. It used to house the register of births, marriages and deaths in England and Wales, but now holds the registry of divorce, wills and probate and the Inland Revenue.
Θ Aldwych (Mon–Fri peak hours only)
🚍 1, 4, 6, 9, 11, 13, 15, 15B, 68, 77, 77A, 168, 170, 171, 171A, 176, 188, 502, 505, 509, 513

**Sotheby's** 3M2
34–35 New Bond St W1. 01-493 8080. Auctioneers who began as rare book specialists, but now dispose of anything that comes under the heading of antiques or works of art – with a turnover that runs into millions of pounds. *Open 09.00–16.30 Mon–Fri. Closed Sat. Viewing some Suns.*
Θ Bond Street
🚍 25

**South Bank Arts Centre** 4U1
South Bank SE1. The massive concrete group contains the National Theatre, the Royal Festival Hall and Queen Elizabeth Hall, the Purcell Room, the National Film Theatre, the Museum of the Moving Image, the Hayward Gallery (each with their separate entries in this guide), together with bookstalls, bars, snack bars, restaurants, a riverside terrace and live entertainment in the theatre foyers. *Open 09.00–23.30 Mon–Sun.*
Θ Waterloo

🚍 1, 4, 68, 76, 149, 168, 171, 171A, 176, 188, 501, 502, 505, 507, 513, C1, P11

**South London Art Gallery**
Peckham Rd SE5. 01-703 6120. Temporary exhibitions, sometimes of new work, sometimes made up from its own collection of the work of British artists from 1700, which includes many pictures of local relevance. *Open 10.00–18.00 Tue–Sat; 15.00–18.00 Sun. Closed Mon & between exhibitions.* Free.
Θ Elephant and Castle (then bus 12, 171), Oval (then bus 36, 36A, 36B)
🚍 12, 36, 36A, 36B, 171

**South Molton Street** 3M2
W1. Traffic-free shopping street with tables set temptingly outside the restaurants in warm weather. Some very expensive dress shops are here and also slightly more moderately priced young fashions. Pleasant, civilised ambience.
Θ Bond Street
🚍 6, 7, 8, 10, 12, 13, 15, 16A, 25, 73, 88, 113, 135, 137, 159, 503

**Southwark Cathedral** 4U4
Borough High St SE1. 01-497 2939. Officially the Cathedral and Collegiate Church of St Saviour and St Mary Overie (the last word meaning 'over the water') which has had cathedral status only since 1905. Founded in the 12thC, and restored and partially rebuilt over the years, it contains the tomb of the 15thC English poet John Gower and a chapel commemorating John Har-

vard, founder of the University. Frequent concerts and organ recitals are held here and there is regular choral evensong.

θ London Bridge

🚌 17, 21, 35, 40, 43, 44, 47, 48, 133, 501, 505, 510, 513, P3, P11

### Spaniards Inn

Hampstead La NW3. 01-455 3276. Renowned 16thC inn, once the residence of the Spanish Ambassador to the court of James I. Dick Turpin stayed here and is said still to ride past on certain nights, and other regular customers included Shelley, Keats, Byron and, of course, Charles Dickens. Lovely rose garden and good food both at lunchtime and in the evening. *Open LD Mon–Sun.*

θ Archway (then bus 210), Golders Green (then bus 210)

🚌 210

### Speaker's Corner          2F6

Hyde Park W2. At the Marble Arch corner of the park. Every Sunday, in celebration of the British right of free speech, unknown orators express strong and often strange views on life, death and politics. At least half the wit and insight comes from the hecklers. *Every Sun.*

θ Marble Arch

🚌 2A, 2B, 6, 7, 8, 10, 12, 15, 16, 16A, 30, 36, 73, 74, 82, 88, 135, 137, 503, 506

### Spitalfields          4R6

Commercial St E1. Five acres of wholesale fruit, vegetable and flower market, undercover and with extensive underground chambers. Large quantities of bananas are ripened here, and have travelled green from their native countries. *Open from 04.30 Mon–Sat. Closed Sun.*

θ Liverpool Street

🚌 5, 6, 8, 22, 22A, 22B, 35, 47, 48, 67, 78, 149, 505

### Steam Museum

Green Dragon La, Brentford, Middx. 01-568 4757. Five gigantic beam engines are under steam every weekend in this huge Victorian pumping house. There is a working forge here, too, and a collection of old traction engines, not to mention a tea room for those who prefer their steam rising from a cup. *Open 11.00–17.00 Mon–Sun.* Charge.

θ Gunnersbury (then bus 237, 267)

🚌 27, 65, 237, 267, Sun only 7

🚈 Kew Bridge

### Steinway Pianos          3M2

Steinway Hall, 44 Marylebone La W1. 01-487 3391. Manufacturers and purveyors of pianos since 1853 – by appointment to HM the Queen. A modest but impressive selection of grands and uprights are on display – pianos can also be custom-built. *Open 09.30–17.30 Mon–Fri; 09.30–16.30 Sat. Closed Sun.*

θ Bond Street

🚌 6, 7, 8, 10, 12, 13, 15, 16A, 25, 73, 88, 113, 135, 137, 159, 503

### Stepping Stones Farm

Stepney Way E1. 01-790 8204. Community-run city farm with cows, sheep, pigs, goats, ducks, geese, rabbits and a donkey. Children in particular are encouraged to handle and work with the animals and though you can simply drop by, a pre-booked visit will include a guided tour. Holds special events throughout the summer. *Open 09.30–13.00 & 14.00–18.00 Tue–Sun. Closed Mon (except Nat Hols).* Donation welcome.

θ Whitechapel

🚌 5, 15, 15B, 25, 40, 253

### Stock Exchange          4S5

Old Broad St EC2. 01-588 2355. Capitalism in action and computerised! The dealers in negotiable securities began their transactions in

a coffee house, but moved here into formal premises in 1901. There is a visitors' gallery and a daily film show which explains all. *Open 09.30–17.00 Mon–Fri. Closed Sat & Sun.* Free.
⊖ Bank
🚌 6, 8, 9, 11, 22B, 149

**Strand** ***3N5***
WC2. Once truly a strand, a riverside walk, before the river was embanked and pushed southwards. With Fleet Street as its continuation, it links the City with Westminster. In Tudor times great mansions stood along it, their gardens reaching to the Thames. One of these was York House and when George Villiers, Duke of Buckingham, had to sell it to pay his debts, he asked to be remembered in the streets on the site. This accounts for George Court, Villiers Street, Duke Street, York Place (formerly Of Alley) and Buckingham Street. The Strand now is a major commercial thoroughfare.
⊖ Temple (not Sun), Charing Cross
🚌 1, 4, 6, 9, 11, 13, 15, 15B, 68, 77, 77A, 168, 170, 171, 171A, 176, 188, 502, 505, 509, 513

**Strand Palace Hotel** ***3N5***
Strand WC2. 01-836 8080. Large, practical and accommodating hotel, rebuilt in the 1920s, with integral shops, two bars and three restaurants – The Carvery, the Italian Connection and the Café at the Strand.
⊖ Charing Cross
🚌 1, 6, 9, 11, 13, 15, 15B, 77, 77A, 176, 509

**Strand Theatre** ***3M5***
Aldwych WC2. 01-836 2661. Large theatre staging a mixture of major comedies, straight plays and musicals.
⊖ Temple (not Sun), Charing Cross
🚌 1, 4, 6, 9, 11, 13, 15, 15B, 68, 77, 77A, 168, 170, 171, 171A, 176, 188, 502, 505, 509, 513

**Stringfellows** ***3M4***
16–19 Upper St Martin's La WC2. 01-240 5534. Celebrity spot. Art deco motifs in restaurant. Mirrored walls create endless reflections of pulsating coloured lights in disco below. *Open to 03.00 Mon–Sat.*
⊖ Leicester Square
🚌 24, 29, 176

**Sun Inn**
7 Church Rd, Barnes SW13. 01-876 5893. Famous, crowded pub, popular with the young. Rebuilt in 1750 on an old pub site, opposite Barnes Pond with its lush rushes, ducks and surrounding trees. Country inn atmosphere within easy reach of London. Doesn't go in for meals but has good sandwiches. *Open Mon–Sun.*
⊖ Hammersmith (then bus 9)
🚌 9
⇌ Barnes Bridge

**Sun Inn** ***4R1***
63 Lamb's Conduit St WC1. 01-405 8278. A specialist in real ale with old vaulted cellars spreading under the streets which make it possible to store up to 70, and to make 20 available at any one time, including little known but excellent guest bitters. *Open LD Mon–Sun.*
⊖ Russell Square
🚌 17, 18, 19, 38, 45, 46, 55, 171, 171A, 243, 259, 505

**Surrey Docks**
SE1. On early maps the somewhat remote peninsular of Rotherhithe and Bermondsey gives the impression of being more water than land. Since the closure of the Commercial Docks in 1970, most have been filled in, and redevelopment is under way, much of it residential and retail though luxury office accommodation is apparent too. There is a strong sense of community here, which may survive the improvements. The main points of interest for visitors are probably the watersports on the surviving docks; the hill, the ecological park and mixed woodland in the centre; the engaging urban farm; the beautiful St Mary's Church in Rotherhithe Village (with its busy craft workshops); the archaeological site dating from the 14thC; the curious mixed architecture of Southwark Cathedral; and the glamour of London Bridge City and Hay's Galleria.
⊖ Surrey Docks
🚌 1, 47, 108B, 188, 225, P11, P13, P14

**Surrey Docks Farm**
Rotherhithe St SE16. 01-231 1010. Run by a Provident Society and funded by the LDDC, Southwark

Council and others, this small urban farm has pigs, goats, donkeys, ducks, quail, geese and hens, a small orchard and a vegetable garden. Local schoolchildren are closely involved with the work – visitors can buy goats' milk, yoghurt, soft cheese and eggs. *Open 10.00–13.00 & 14.00–17.00 Tue–Sun. Closed Mon & Fri in school hols. Free.*
⊖ Rotherhithe
🚌 225, P11, P14

### Swaine, Adeney, Briggs & Sons          3N3
185 Piccadilly W1. 01-734 4277. World famous for hand-made Briggs umbrellas (by appointment to the Queen Mother), and luxury goods. Whip and glove makers by appointment to HM the Queen. *Open 09.00–17.30 Mon–Fri; 09.00–17.00 Sat. Closed Sun.*
⊖ Green Park, Piccadilly Circus
🚌 9, 14, 19, 22, 38

### The Swiss Centre          3N4
1 New Coventry St W1. 01-734 1291. Don't be perturbed by the chiming of bells or the midday crowing of a cock as you enter this complex. Outside the Swiss Tourist Centre is a glockenspiel and clock with 25 bells surrounded by moving wooden figures. As well as the time, the clock shows the signs of the zodiac and the phases of the moon. Inside the centre is a selection of shops and restaurants specialising in Swiss delicacies: on the ground level there is Gourmet Corner, selling Swiss meats, cheeses and chocolates along with truffles, bread and patisserie made on the premises. *Open 09.30–21.00 Mon–Sat; 11.00–18.00 Sun.*

Downstairs is a spacious basement holding four restaurants. The Chesa is the most up-market with a Swiss and international menu; the Tavern, very popular, serves raclette, meat and fish dishes; the Rendez-vous emphasises fondues, be it cheese or chocolate; and finally the Locanda where you can be sure of fast service, fresh salads and good business lunches. *Restaurants open 12.00–24.00 Mon–Sat, 12.00–23.00 Sun.*

Around the corner on Wardour Street the Swiss Imbiss serves breakfast, pastries and savoury snacks. *Open 08.30–23.30 Mon–Sat; 12.00–21.00 Sun. Centre closed Xmas day.*
⊖ Leicester Square, Piccadilly Circus
🚌 3, 6, 9, 12, 13, 14, 15, 15B, 19, 22, 22B, 24, 29, 38, 53, 88, 159, 176, 509

### Syon House and Park
London Rd, Brentford, Middx. 01-560 0884. Tudor house, set in 55 acres of parkland which is owned by the Percys, dukes of Northumberland. The present Duke still lives here for part of the year. The interior design is by Robert Adam, and the garden is by Capability Brown. Paintings by Huysmans, Lely and Van Dyck, and views stretching across the river to Kew Gardens. Within the grounds is the London Butterfly House, in which exotic specimens fly free and land on visitors. There is also an excellent garden centre and the Heritage Collection of historic British cars. *House open Easter–Sep 12.00–17.00 Sun–Thur; Oct 12.00–17.00 Sun only; Butterfly House open Mar–Oct 10.00–17.00 Mon–Sun; Grounds open all year 10.00–18.00 or dusk Mon–Sun. Charge.*
⊖ Gunnersbury (then bus 237, 267)
🚌 117, 203, 237, 267, E2
🚉 Syon Lane

*T*

### Tate Gallery 5X6
Millbank SW1. 01-821 1313. This classical 19thC building by Sidney R. J. Smith has been enlarged six times to provide adequate housing for the national collections of British painting from the 16thC to the present day, and of 20thC painting and sculpture. There is also an extensive collection of modern prints. The Gallery and its original collection of contemporary British painting was given to the nation by Henry Tate, founder of the sugar manufacturers Tate and Lyle. It opened to the public in 1897. There are special concentrations of works by Hogarth, Blake, Constable, the pre-Raphaelites, Picasso, Giacometti, Francis Bacon, Naum Gabo, Mark Rothko, Henry Moore and Barbara Hepworth.

The adjoining Clore Gallery, designed by James Stirling, exhibits the Turner Bequest of 300 oils and over 20,000 drawings and water colours.

Wander at will or enjoy film shows, lectures and guided tours. In the basement there is a licensed coffee shop and also the Tate Gallery Restaurant, decorated with murals by Rex Whistler, with historical English dishes among those on the menu. *Open 10.00–17.50 Mon–Sat; 14.00–17.50 Sun.* Free (charge for loan exhibitions).
⊖ Pimlico
▄▄▄ 77A, 88, or 2, 2A, 2B, 36, 36A, 36B, 185 (to Bessborough Gardens)

### Telecom Technology Showcase 4T3
135 Queen Victoria St EC4. 01-248 7444. Lively museum of the history of telecommunications, with working examples of modern chip-operated technology, archaic set-ups of early telephone exchanges, and glimpses of the bright future of fibre optics. *Open 10.00–17.00 Mon–Fri. Closed Sat, Sun & Nat Hols.* Free.
⊖ Blackfriars
▄▄▄ 45, 59, 63, 76, 141

### The Temple 4T2
Inner Temple, Crown Office Row EC4. 01-353 8462; Middle Temple, Middle Temple La EC4. 01-353 4355. You may wander around the courtyards, alleys and manicured gardens of these ancient inns of court by privilege, not by right, Visit on a winter afternoon to see London's last lamplighter igniting the 19thC gas lamps. *Open 10.30–16.00 Mon–Fri. Closed weekends, Nat Hols & legal vacations.* Free.
⊖ Temple (not Sun), Blackfriars
▄▄▄ 4, 6, 9, 11, 15, 15B, 171A, 502, 509, 513

### The Temple Church 4T2
Inner Temple La EC4. This 12th–13thC early Gothic round church, built by the Knights Templar, has a chillingly romantic air with its stone effigies of knights lying in stately wait below grey marble pillars.
⊖ Temple (not Sun), Blackfriars
▄▄▄ 4, 6, 9, 11, 15, 15B, 171A, 502, 509, 513

### Temple of Mithras 4T4
Queen Victoria St EC4. Mithraic temples were always underground.

This one was raised to its present site from 18 feet below Walbrook and has lost something in the translation. The finds from the site are in the Museum of London.
⊖ Mansion House, Bank
🚌 6, 9, 11, 15, 15B, 17, 76, 95, 149, 513

## Thames Barrier

Unity Way, Eastmoor St SE18. This impressive piece of modern engineering was set up as a bulwark against dangerously high tides which were causing floods as far up river as Richmond. The Thames Barrier Visitor Centre on the south bank of the river houses an exhibition and an audio-visual presentation, explaining the technology involved. There is also a souvenir shop and cafeteria. *Open 10.30–17.00 Mon–Sun.* Charge.
⊖ New Cross, New Cross Gate, Elephant & Castle (then bus 177)
🚌 177, 180 to Eastmoor Street
🚆 Charlton

## Theatre Museum          3M5

Russell St WC2. 01-836 7891. Covent Garden's old Flower Market has been transformed into the Theatre Museum, an outpost of the V & A, covering major developments, events and personalities from all the performing arts. There is a permanent exhibition on the lower floor, temporary exhibitions drawing on loan material and on the museum's own rich collection in the Sir John Gielgud and Sir Henry Irving Galleries; a museum, shop and a pleasant licensed café. Admission tickets are sold from the old Duke of York Theatre's box office; a separate Ticketmaster office sells seats for all London shows. *Open   11.00–19.00   Tue–Sun*; shop, café & ticketmaster *open 11.00–20.00   Tue–Sat.   Closed Mon.* Charge (free to Friends of the V & A).
⊖ Covent Garden
🚌 1, 4, 6, 9, 11, 13, 15, 15B, 68, 77, 77A, 168, 170, 171, 171A, 176, 188, 502, 505, 509, 513

## Theatre Royal, Stratford East

Gerry Raffles Sq E15. 01-534 0310. Joan Littlewood's brainchild which first rose to fame in the 50s; is flourishing still with new drama, traditional   panto   and   well-known names on its billboards. Watch out for their infamous Variety Nights, once a month on *Sun.*
⊖ Stratford
Docklands Light Railway: Stratford
🚌 25, 69, 86, 108, 147, 158, 173, 238, 241, 257, 262, 262A, 276, 278, 299, S1, S2

## Tobacco Dock

Pennington St E1. The huge 19thC warehouse at Tobacco Dock is known as the Skin Floor because, though designed to hold tobacco, it was used to store furs. The extensive wine vaults below and the vast above-ground structure have been developed into a 'shopping village' with bars, restaurants, shops, craft and gift shops.
Docklands Light Railway: Shadwell
🚌 100

## Top Shop               3M3

214–21 Oxford St W1. 01-636 7700. A huge and colourful venue, with its own resident DJ, in which to buy bright inexpensive clothes and accessories for men and women. Popular styles for every whim or occasion. Other branches dotted around the West End. *Open 10.00–18.30   Mon–Wed & Fri;   10.00–20.00   Thur;   09.00–18.00   Sat. Closed Sun.*
⊖ Oxford Circus
🚌 3, 6, 7, 8, 10, 12,13, 15, 15B, 16A, 25, 53, 73, 88, 113, 135, 137, 159, 176, 503, 509, C2

## Tottenham Court Road      3L3

W1. These days the road is best known   for   electronics.   Hi-fis, videos and all their hi-tech relations can be priced, compared and cross-checked within the confines of one road. There are also furniture and household shops here, including the 50,000 square feet of Maples, and several camera shops.
⊖ Tottenham Court Road (south end), Goodge Street (centre), Warren Street (north end)
🚌 10, 14, 14A, 24, 29, 73, 134, 253

## Tower Bridge            4U6

EC3.   Splendid   Victorian   Gothic structure with hydraulically operated drawbridge by Jones and Wolfe Barry, 1894. The lattice-work footbridges   with   their   wonderful river views are open to the public. *Open Apr–Oct 10.00–18.30 Mon–Sun; Nov–Mar 10.00–16.45 Mon–Sun.* Charge.

⊖ Tower Hill

Docklands Light Railway: Tower Gateway

▦ 15, 42, 78, 100, 510, Sat & Sun 25 (north side), 42, 47, 78, 188, P11 (south side)

## Tower Thistle Hotel 4T6

St Katharine's Way E1. 01-481 2575. Large and luxuriously appointed modern hotel – much prettier inside than out. The Thames Bar and the three restaurants – The Carvery, The Picnic Basket, which is a coffee shop, and the lavishly refurbished Princes Room Restaurant – all have impressive river views. All are *open daily* (The Princes Room is *closed on Sun*, wise to book on other days).

⊖ Tower Hill

Docklands Light Railway: Tower Gateway

▦ 15, 42, 78, 100, 510, Sat & Sun 25

## Tower of London 4T6

Tower Hill EC3. 01-709 0765. Famous fortress. Red-clad Yeomen warders, or Beefeaters, and black ravens guard the Bloody Tower, the Traitor's Gate, the armoury, the executioner's block and axe, the instruments of torture, the tragic graffiti and, of course, the Crown Jewels. The massively plain Norman chapel of St John is the oldest church in London. It is now possible to walk almost all the way around the curtain wall of the inner ward,

visiting most of the outer towers. To watch the ancient ritual of the Ceremony of the Keys, when the Tower is locked for the night, apply in writing with a s.a.e. to the Yeoman Clerk, H.M. Tower of London EC3. *Open Mar–Oct 09.30–17.00 Mon–Sat, 14.00–17.00 Sun; Nov–Feb 09.30–16.00 Mon–Sat, closed Sun.* Charge.

⊖ Tower Hill

Docklands Light Railway: Tower Gateway

▦ 15, 42, 78, 100, 510, Sat & Sun 25

## Tower Records 3N3

1 Piccadilly Circus W1. 01-439 2500. Billed as the 'greatest record store in the world', this prime site record shop on four floors offers the full spectrum of sounds from golden oldies to opera, trad jazz to hard rock. Huge selection of compact discs, videos and US imports too. Amazing opening hours should ensure high volume popularity. Also in Kensington High Street. *Open all year (inc Nat Hols) 09.00–24.00 Mon–Sat.*

⊖ Piccadilly Circus

▦ 3, 6, 9, 12, 13, 14, 15, 15B, 19, 22, 22B, 38, 53, 88, 159, 509

## Town of Ramsgate Pub

62 Wapping High St E1. 01-488 2685. 17thC tavern with a glamorous, grisly past. Captain Blood was captured alongside and Judge Jeffreys within; petty criminals were hanged in what is now the riverside garden; pirates were tied to a post in the river to be drowned by the incoming tide and secret tunnels are said to lead to the Tower of London. Bar snacks are available at most sessions. *Open Mon–Sun.*

⊖ Wapping

▦ 100

## Trafalgar Square 3N4

WC2. The whole square commemorates Admiral Lord Nelson's famous naval victory. His statue tops a 185-foot column in the centre. The pigeons and Landseer's lions are famous and provide a year-round attraction for visitors. Less well known are the Imperial Standards on the north wall and the minute police station inside a stone lamp on the east side. At Christmas, the annual gift from Nor-

way of a giant spruce draws the crowds.
θ Charing Cross
▆1, 3, 6, 9, 11, 12, 13, 15, 15B, 22B, 24, 29, 53, 77, 77A, 88, 109, 159, 170, 176, 184, 509

**Trafalgar Tavern**
Park Row SE10. 01-858 2437. Pictures of Nelson and some early navigational instruments are on display in this large Thames-side tavern near Wren's imposing naval college. Snacks are served in the bars, with their large windows overlooking the river, and there are full lunches and dinners in the restaurant, for which it is wise to book. *Bars open normal licensing hours Mon–Sun. Restaurant open LD Tue–Sat, L only Sun & Mon (closed D Sun & Mon).*
θ New Cross, New Cross Gate, Elephant & Castle (then bus 177) Docklands Light Railway: Island Gardens (then by foot tunnel)
▆1, 177, 180, 188, 286
≠ Greenwich

**Travis & Emery**          *3N4*
17 Cecil Ct WC2. 01-240 2129.

Cloud of musical and theatrical ephemera with a rich core of new and second-hand books on music and second-hand and antiquarian printed music. *Open 10.00–18.00 Mon–Fri; 10.00–13.00 Sat.*
θ Leicester Square
▆24, 29, 176

**Trocadero**          *3N3*
Piccadilly Circus W1. A large modern complex, with entrances on Shaftesbury Avenue and Coventry Street. Shops, cafés, restaurants and wine bars are grouped on two floors around a huge central foyer with trees and a fountain. A moving stairway leads up a floor to The Guinness Book of World Records Exhibition and The London Experience. *Open 09.00–24.00 (shops and exhibitions close 17.30).* Charge for exhibitions.
θ Piccadilly Circus
▆3, 6, 9, 12, 13, 14, 14A, 15, 15B, 19, 22, 22B, 38, 53, 88, 159, 509

**Tuttons**          *3M5*
11–12 Russell St WC2. 01-836 1167. Spanish Tapas Bar downstairs and a pleasant, airy restaurant at street level, with tables outside for clement weather, offering breakfasts, imaginative snacks, lunches and dinners. *Open 09.30–23.30 Sun–Thur; 09.30–24.00 Fri & Sat.*
θ Covent Garden
▆1, 4, 6, 9, 11, 13, 15, 15B, 68, 77, 77A, 168, 170, 171, 171A, 176, 188, 502, 505, 509, 513

**Twickenham Rugby Football Ground**
Whitton Rd, Twickenham, Middx. 01-892 8161. Known as HQ – the headquarters of The Rugby Football Union, and the setting for international championship games. Tours of the ground and the small museum can be arranged by writing to The Secretary at the above address. Tours usually at *10.30 & 14.15 Mon–Fri.* Charge. See press for details of matches.
θ Hounslow East (then bus 281 from Hounslow Bus Station)
▆281
≠ Twickenham

### Unicorn Theatre          3M4
Gt Newport St WC2. 01-836 3334.
Presents an extensive programme
of new and classic plays suited to
children within the 4–12 age group.
During term time there are performances for school parties every
afternoon from Tuesday to Friday;
and public matinees are held at
weekends. Café Bar in the basement.
⊖ Leicester Square
🚌 24, 29, 176

### United States Embassy          3N1
Grosvenor Sq W1. 01-499 9000.
The entire west side of London's
largest square is taken up by Eero
Saarinen's monumental building,
topped by a somewhat threatening
bald eagle with a 35-foot wing span.
In the six-acre square itself stands
W. Reid Dick's lifelike statue of
Franklin D. Roosevelt.
⊖ Bond Street
🚌 2A, 2B, 10, 16, 30, 36, 73, 74,
82, 137, 503, 506 (to Park Lane),
2A, 6, 7, 8, 10, 12, 13, 15, 16A,
73, 88, 113, 135, 159, 503 (to
Oxford Street)

### University Boat Race
Putney to Mortlake. This annual
contest between the universities of
Oxford (dark blue) and Cambridge
(light blue) can be viewed from the
banks of the Thames. *Sat afternoon
in Mar or Apr.*
Start of race:
⊖ Putney Bridge
🚌 14, 22, 39, 74, 220, C4
Finish of race:
🚌 9 (to Mortlake)
⇌ Barnes Bridge

### University College          1D5
### Department of Egyptology
### Museum
Gower St WC1. 01-387 7050. Includes the collections of Amelia
Edwards, Sir Flinders Petrie and
part of Sir Henry Wellcome's collection. *Open 10.00–12.00 & 13.15–
17.00 Mon–Fri during university
terms only. Closed Nat Hols & university hols.* Charge.

⊖ Euston Square
🚌 10, 14, 14A, 18, 24, 27, 29, 30,
73, 134, 135, 253

### University College          3L3
### Hospital
Gower St WC1. 01-387 9300. Built
in 1834 and greatly enlarged since,
this large general hospital and medical school has a distinguished history – Europe's first amputation
under ether was conducted in
1846; Joseph Lister trained here
and past consultants have included
the neurologist Sir William Gowers,
the neurosurgeon Sir Victor
Horsley, and Sir Thomas Lewis,
one of the first to use electrocar-
diography. *24-hr casualty.*
⊖ Euston Square, Warren Street
🚌 10, 14, 14A, 24, 29, 73, 134,
253

### University of London          1D6
Malet St WC1. Centred around the
Bloomsbury area, the University
was founded in 1826 by supporters
of religious liberty to provide higher
education in literature, science and
art. It received its charter in 1836
and in 1878 became the first university in the UK to allow women to sit
for degrees. Now incorporates
many colleges and institutes of
specialist studies spread all over
the capital. The monolithic Senate
House building (completed 1936)
was rumoured to have been consid-
ered by Hitler as a potential HQ in
the event of a British defeat in
World War II. The Princess Royal is
Chancellor of the University.
⊖ Goodge Street, Russell Square
🚌 10, 14, 14A, 24, 29, 68, 73, 77,
77A, 134, 168, 188, 253, 503

### Up All Night          2K4
325 Fulham Rd SW10. 01-352
1996. An informal restaurant that
really stands by its name, serving
hamburgers, steaks and spaghetti
*until 06.00* in the morning. *Open LD
Mon–Sun.*
⊖ Fulham Broadway (then bus 14)
🚌 14, N14

## Vanbrugh Castle
3 Westcombe Pk Rd, Maze Hill SE3. Sir John Vanbrugh's own house, built 1717–26. It is now private flats, so there is no admission, but it may be admired from the outside. The best view is from the east side of Greenwich Park.
⊖ New Cross, New Cross Gate (then bus 53)
🚌 53, 54, 75, 108, 286
🚆 Maze Hill

## Vanbrugh Theatre     1D5
Malet St WC1. 01-580 7982. A theatre club in which students of the Royal Academy of Dramatic Art present a complete range of classic and contemporary drama. Members bar. Membership details from RADA, 62 Gower St WC1.
⊖ Goodge Street, Russell Square
🚌 10, 14, 14A, 24, 29, 73, 77, 77A, 134, 168, 188, 253, 503

## Vaudeville Theatre     3N5
Strand WC2. 01-836 9987. A listed building which originally ran farce and burlesque – vaudeville, in short – and then went 'straight', which for the most part it still is.
⊖ Charing Cross
🚌 1, 6, 9, 11, 13, 15, 15B, 77, 77A, 170, 176, 509

## The Veeraswamy     3N3
99–101 Regent St (entrance in Swallow St) W1. 01-734 1401. This is one of the oldest Indian restaurants in London. Imposing uniformed doorman, glamorous interior, authentic, mainly northern-Indian food. *Open LD Mon–Sun.*
⊖ Piccadilly Circus
🚌 3, 6, 9, 12, 13, 14, 15, 15B, 19, 22, 22B, 38, 53, 88, 159, 509

## Victoria and Albert Museum     2J5
Cromwell Rd SW7. 01-589 6371. One of the most extravagant pieces of Victorian architecture in London and a wonderfully rich museum of decorative art, officially known as the National Museum of Art and Design. Vast collections from all categories, countries and ages are displayed in more than 10 acres of museum, set around the newly designed Italianate Pirelli garden. There are extensive and choice collections of paintings, sculpture, graphics and typography, armour and weapons, carpets, ceramics, clocks, costume, fabrics, furniture, jewellery, metalwork, musical instruments, prints and drawings. There are regular free lectures and exhibitions and a nice café where a soloist often plays classical music at lunchtime. *Open 10.00–17.50 Mon–Sat; 14.30–17.50 Sun. Closed some Nat Hols.* Voluntary contribution.
⊖ South Kensington
🚌 14, 30, 45, 49, 74, 219, 503, C1

## Victoria Embankment Gardens     3N5
WC2. The joy of lunchtime office workers on a fine day. Banked flowers, a band, shady trees, deckchairs and an open-air café.
⊖ Embankment
🚌 1, 3, 6, 9, 11, 12, 13, 15, 15B, 22B, 24, 29, 53, 77, 77A, 88, 109, 159, 170, 176, 184, 509 (to Trafalgar Square)

## Victoria Memorial     3O3
In front of Buckingham Palace SW1. An impressive memorial to Queen Victoria designed in 1911 which includes a fine dignified figure of the Queen, the best of many statues of her.

⊖ St James's Park

🚌 2, 2A, 2B, 11, 16, 24, 25, 29, 36, 36A, 36B, 38, 39, 52, 52A, 73, 76, 82, 185, 506, 507, 510, C1

### Victoria Palace 3P3

Victoria St SW1. 01-834 1317. Huge theatre, intended for music hall, where the 'Black and White Minstrel Show' once ran and ran. Popular musicals and variety shows are still what to expect.

⊖ Victoria

🚌 2, 2A, 2B, 11, 16, 24, 25, 29, 36, 36A, 36B, 38, 39, 52, 52A, 73, 76, 82, 185, 506, 507, 510, C1

### Victoria Park

E9. 01-985 1957. With 217 acres and a 4-mile perimeter, this park, established in 1845, was known as 'the lung of the East End'. Several listed buildings survive; of note are two alcoves from the original London Bridge which were placed at the east end of the park in 1861, a splendid drinking fountain erected for Burdett Coutts, and two gate pillars at Bonner Bridge. Of natural interest are planes, oaks, birches, hawthorns, cherries, honey locusts, gladitsia, a kentucky coffee tree and a bitter orange. A wide variety of sports. Also fallow deer, guinea pigs, rabbits and various fowl. Old time dancing in *Aug*; children's shows in the *summer hols*; funfairs in *Apr, May & Aug (not Nat Hols)*. Open 06.00–½ hour after sunset.

⊖ Mile End (then bus 277)

🚌 277

⮞ Cambridge Heath

### Victoria Station 3P2

Terminus Pl, Victoria St SW1. Information on 01-928 5100. The Brighton side of the station was built in 1860 and the Dover side in 1862. The concourse and platforms are currently being modernised but trains still depart for the south and south-east London suburbs, Kent, Sussex, East Surrey, Brighton, Gatwick Airport and the Continent.

⊖ Victoria

🚌 2, 2A, 2B, 11, 16, 24, 25, 29, 36, 36A, 36B, 38, 39, 52, 52A, 73, 76, 82, 185, 506, 507, 510 C1

⮞ Victoria

### Victoria Coach Station 5W3

164 Buckingham Palace Rd SW1. 01-730 0202. The main provincial coach companies operate from here, sending coaches all over Britain and the Continent. Booking is necessary.

⊖ Victoria

🚌 11, 39, C1

⮞ Victoria

### Virgin Games Centre 3M3

100 Oxford St W1. 01-637 7911. Renowned for its incredible fantasy games. Whole department devoted to war games. Also full Trivial Pursuit range and computer games. *Open 09.00–19.00 (to 20.00 Thur) Mon–Sat.*

⊖ Tottenham Court Road

🚌 7, 8, 10, 25, 73, 176, 503

### The Virgin Megastore 3M4

14–16 Oxford St W1. 01-631 1234. A vast entertainment store selling records, videos, hi-fis, compact discs and players, music books and tapes. Also resident DJs, live entertainment, and a large licensed upstairs café. A total experience! *Store open 10.00–21.00 Mon–Sat. Café open 09.30–21.00 Mon–Sat. Closed Sun.*

⊖ Tottenham Court Road

🚌 7, 8, 10, 14, 14A, 19, 22, 22B, 24, 25, 29, 38, 55, 73, 134, 176, 503

## Waldorf Hotel                4T1
Aldwych WC2. 01-836 2400. Take tea in this classic hotel in the opulent Pancock tea lounge. Revel in Edwardian elegance, comfort and good service. Thé dansant to the band and full set tea *Fri–Sun 15.30–18.30*.
θ Aldwych
🚌 1, 4, 6, 9, 11, 13, 15, 15B, 68, 77, 77A, 168, 170, 171, 171A, 176, 188, 502, 505, 509, 513

## Wallace Collection           1E3
Hertford House, Manchester Sq W1. 01-935 0687. This dignified town house, with its small landscaped garden, contains an outstanding private collection of art treasures amassed by two marquesses of Hertford and Sir Richard Wallace and bequeathed to the nation by Lady Wallace in 1897. The French 17thC and 18thC are especially well represented. There are also Rembrandts, Titians, Rubens, Canalettos, Bonnington oil and water colours and Sèvres porcelain. *Open 10.00–17.00 Mon–Sat; 14.00–17.00 Sun. Closed Nat Hols.* Free.

θ Bond Street
🚌 2A, 2B, 6, 7, 8, 10, 12, 13, 15, 16A, 30, 73, 74, 82, 88, 113, 135, 137, 159, 503

## Wapping
This is the site of the old London Docks – now almost entirely filled in with only Limehouse and Shadwell Basins still holding water. Narrow Wapping High Street – a wall of 19thC warehouses between it and the river – has been familiar to visitors to the historic Town of Ramsgate pub and also the Wapping Wine Warehouse, whose predecessor was the first of the cash-and-carry wine merchants. Most of the warehouses are now transformed into luxury apartments and studios, and other pubs are beginning to pack them in, too.
θ Wapping
🚌 100

## Wapping Police Station
98 Wapping High St E1. 01-488 5212. The HQ of the world's oldest uniformed police force, founded in the 1790s as the Marine Police, to protect cargoes, and incorporated into the younger Metropolitan Police in 1839 as the Thames Division. They are now 'the motorway police' of the river. The station is a listed building of Grade II and it has its own small museum. Apply in writing for permission to visit, ideally a month in advance. (No visitors under 12.) Free.
θ Wapping
🚌 100

## Warner West End Cinema      3N4
Leicester Sq WC2. 01-439 0791. Five cinemas showing new Warner general releases.
θ Leicester Square
🚌 24, 29, 176

## The Water Rats              4Q1
328 Gray's Inn Rd WC1. 01-837 7269. This 17thC refurbished inn is now the home of the Abadaba Music Hall which uses professional

actors to present lively, sometimes bawdy, modern music hall, panto and sing-songs. The rear bar has a small stage and is licensed to 24.00. Enjoy a traditional English meal before the show; drinking and singing during the performance. Booking essential on 01-722 5395. *Open Mon–Sun. Music Hall Thur–Sat.*

⊖ King's Cross St Pancras

🚌 10, 14, 14A, 17, 18, 30, 45, 46, 63, 73, 77A, 214, 221, 259, C11

## Waterloo Bridge 3N5
Designed by Sir Giles Gilbert Scott and built in 1940–5 of concrete. Connects Waterloo Station and the South Bank Arts complex with the Strand and Aldwych.

⊖ Temple (not Sun, north side), Waterloo (south side)

🚌 1, 4, 68, 168, 171, 171A, 176, 188, 501, 502, 505, 513

➤ Waterloo

## Waterloo Station 4U2
York Rd SE1. Information on 01-928 5100. Originally built in 1848, it was modernised in the 1920s and again in the 1980s but still retains its grand Edwardian entrance in Mepham Street with sweeping steps and guardian statues. Trains go to the south-west London suburbs, west Surrey, Hampshire, Dorset with fast trains to Portsmouth, Southampton and Bournemouth. The adjoining Waterloo East station sends trains to the south-east London suburbs and Kent.

⊖ Waterloo

🚌 1, 4, 68, 76, 149, 168, 171, 171A, 176, 188, 501, 502, 505, 507, 513, C1, P11

➤ Waterloo

## Watermen's Hall 4T5
18 St Mary at Hill EC3. The guildhall of the Thames ferrymen, a beautiful building with an Adam-style frontage surviving from 1780. Visits arranged in summer through City Information Centre, St Paul's Churchyard EC4. 01-606 3030 extn 2456.

⊖ Tower Hill

🚌 15, 510, Sat & Sun 25

## Waterstone's Bookshop 3M4
121 Charing Cross Rd WC2. 01-434 4291. Enterprising general booksellers. Will undertake a free search for second-hand books for account customers. This branch is particularly strong on second-hand books. Other branches are at High Street Kensington (where it all started) which is strong on art and antiquarian books, Old Brompton Road, Hampstead High Street, Richmond and a relatively new one in Kingston upon Thames. This branch *open 09.30–19.30 Mon–Fri; 11.00–19.30 Sat. Closed Sun.* (Some branches open longer hours, inc. *Sun.*)

⊖ Tottenham Court Road

🚌 14, 19, 22, 22B, 24, 29, 38, 176

## Wellington Arch 3O1
Hyde Park Corner W2. By Decimus Burton who also designed the nearby screen opening on to Hyde Park. It has a tiny police station concealed in one massive leg. The surmounting bronze of peace, her quadriga drawn by vigorously lifelike horses, is by Adrian Jones, a cavalry officer and vet who entertained seven friends within the structure before it was erected.

⊖ Hyde Park Corner

🚌 2A, 2B, 9, 10, 14, 16, 19, 22, 25, 30, 36, 38, 52, 52A, 73, 74, 82, 137, 503, 506

## Wembley Stadium Complex
Wembley, Middx. 01-902 1234. The complex incorporates the Stadium, which holds 100,000 people under cover, the Arena, the Conference Centre and the International Squash Centre (the courts are open to the public, book on 01-902 9230). Perhaps most famous as the venue for the FA Cup Final, but the Horse of the Year Show happens here, too, and also ice shows, pop concerts and a variety of important sporting events.

⊖ Wembley Park

🚌 18, 83, 92, 182, 297

➤ Wembley Stadium, Wembley Central

## Wesley's House and 4R5
## Chapel
47 City Rd EC1. 01-253 2262. The chapel, built in 1777, has a statue of John Wesley in front of it, his pulpit inside it and his grave behind it. In the crypt below the chapel, there is a well-presented museum about Methodism, and some fascinating

items of Wesleyan memorabilia. The house has simple relics – his bed, his umbrella, some letters, the electrical machine he used in the treatment of melancholia. Opposite the house is the Nonconformist Burial Ground, Bunhill Fields, where Daniel Defoe and William Blake lie. *Open 10.00– 16.00 Mon–Sat; 12.00 (after service) Sun. Charge (free on Sun).*
⊖ Old Street
🚌 5, 43, 55, 76, 141, 214, 243, 263A, 271, 505

### West End

The capital's biggest shopping area consisting of three main streets. Oxford St is over a mile long and has nearly all the major department stores including Selfridges, London's biggest Marks & Spencer and an overwhelming assortment of individual fashion shops. It gets very crowded here, especially on Saturday and at lunchtime. Regent St is less hectic and offers luxurious items at Liberty's plus several china, glass and clothing stores. (Carnaby St – just off Regent St – is still worth a visit and is undergoing a face-lift some years after its decline as a 60s hotspot). For real luxury try New Bond St, particularly for shoes, jewellery, pictures, prints and designer clothes. Two pedestrian-style streets just off Oxford St are well worth exploring – St Christopher's Place and South Molton St. Both are packed with stylish small shops and attractive eating places.

⊖ Oxford Circus, Bond Street, Piccadilly Circus
🚌 3, 6, 7, 8, 9, 10, 12, 13, 14, 15, 15B, 16A, 19, 22, 22B, 25, 38, 53, 73, 88, 113, 135, 137, 159, 176, 503, 509, C2

### Westminster Abbey  3P4

(The Collegiate Church of St Peter in Westminster), Broad Sanctuary SW1. 01-222 5152. Magnificent repository of much of the royal history of Britain and also a living place of worship with services at *08.00, 12.30 & 17.00 Mon–Fri; 09.20 & 15.00 Sat; 10.30, 11.40 & 15.00 Sun.* The original church by Edward the Confessor, 1065, was rebuilt by Henry III, completed in 1376–1506, with the towers finished by Hawksmoor in 1734. In fine Perpendicular style with a mighty and soaring Gothic nave, lavish and beautiful side chapels, elaborate tombs and prestigious monuments. The Abbey has been the scene for the coronation of England's sovereigns since the time of William the Conqueror. In July 1986, Prince Andrew and Sarah Ferguson, Duke and Duchess of York, were married here with full pomp and pageantry. *Open 09.00– 16.00 Mon–Fri; 09.00–14.00 & 15.45–17.00 Sat; services only Sun.* Free. (Small entry charge for Royal Chapels and Museum of Plates and Effigies.)
⊖ Westminster
🚌 3, 11, 12, 24, 29, 53, 77, 77A, 88, 109, 159, 170, 184, C1

### Westminster Bridge  3O5

SW1. Here, in September 1803, Wordsworth observed of the view, in his sonnet 'Upon Westminster Bridge', "Earth has not anything to show more fair" . . . The view is still fair, though both it and the bridge have changed considerably since his day. The present flat stone structure, by Thomas Page, was erected in 1862.
⊖ Westminster
🚌 3, 11, 12, 24, 29, 53, 77, 77A, 88, 109, 159, 170, 184, C1

### Westminster Cathedral  3P3

Ashley Pl SW1. 01-834 7452. This most important of England's Roman Catholic churches has a striking exterior of red brick with pale stone stripes and a tall slim campanile with magnificent views (a lift

operates daily, for a small charge).
The unfinished interior, its exquisite
marble facings and darkly gleaming
mosaics fading into the plain dark
brick of the domed ceiling, has a
true atmosphere of sanctity.
Amidst the Byzantine beauty, by
John Francis Bentley, 1895–1903,
don't miss Eric Gill's stone reliefs of
the Stations of the Cross. *Open
06.45–20.00 Mon–Sun; to 18.00
Nat Hols; to 16.00 Xmas day.*
Masses at *07.00, 08.00, 08.30,
09.00, 10.30, 13.00, 13.30 & High
Mass at 17.30 Mon–Fri; at 07.00,
08.00, 08.30, 09.00, 10.30, 12.30 &
18.00 Sat; 07.00, 08.00, 09.00
(High Mass 10.30), 12.00, 17.30 &
19.00 Sun.*
⊖ Victoria
🚌 11, 24, 29, 76, 507, 510, C1

### Westminster Hospital          5W6
Dean Ryle St, Horsferry Rd SW1.
01-828 9811. Large general teaching hospital where Dr John Snow –
best known for his efficient control
of an outbreak of cholera in 1854 –
was trained. The Westminster Children's Hospital is in Vincent
Square. *24-hr casualty.*
⊖ Westminster
🚌 76, 88, 507, 510

### Westminster Pier          3O5
Victoria Embankment SW1. 01-839
2349/01-930 4097. The main starting point for boat trips along the
Thames. Some go east through the
City and docks calling at The Tower
of London and Greenwich; others
go west to the exotic greenery of
Kew Gardens and the Palace at
Hampton Court. The River Boat Information Service (01-730 4812)
has full details.
⊖ Westminster
🚌 3, 11, 12, 24, 29, 53, 77, 77A,
88, 109, 159, 170, 184, C1

### Westminster Theatre          3P3
Palace St SW1. 01-834 0238. Puts
on straight plays and musicals and
children's productions – with occasional school workshops to accompany the latter. Snack bar opens on
performance nights.
⊖ Victoria
🚌 2, 2A, 2B, 11, 16, 24, 25, 29,
36, 36A, 36B, 38, 39, 52, 52A, 73,
76, 82, 185, 506, 507, 510, C1

### Whitbread Shires Stables          4R4
Garrett St EC1. 01-606 4455. A visit
to these working stables includes a
chance to meet the magnificent
shire horses which pull the Lord
Mayor's coach on special occasions, and the brewery's drays
around the City throughout the
year. *Open 11.00–12.30, 13.30–
15.00 Mon–Fri.* Free (charge for
over 16s).
⊖ Old Street
🚌 55, 243, 505

### Whitechapel Art Gallery          4S6
80 Whitechapel High St E1. 01-377
0107. This gallery has blossomed
since its renovation. Behind the attractive Art Nouveau frontage are
two floors of flexible exhibition
space. There is also an audio-visual
room, a 100-seat lecture theatre
and an Education Room offering
films, talks, seminars and workshops, a bookshop, foyer information desk and a large café serving
wholesome snacks and sticky
cakes. *Open 11.00–17.00 Tue &
Thur–Sun; 11.00–20.00 Wed.
Closed Mon & Nat Hols.* Free, except for a few exhibitions.
⊖ Aldgate East
🚌 5, 15, 15B, 25, 40, 67, 253

### Whitechapel Market　　　　4S6

Whitechapel E1. Famous East End high street market with an immense array of stalls selling fruit, veg, foodstuffs, household goods, gifts and knick-knacks. *Open 08.00–17.00 Mon–Sat. Closed Sun.*
θ Whitechapel
🚌 25, 253

### Whitehall　　　　3N4

SW1. Impressive, governmental and sometimes imperialist architecture fronts on to this wide processional way leading to the Houses of Parliament. The principal buildings are:
The Old Admiralty by T. Ripley, 1725–8, with a fine Adam columnar screen of 1760. The new Admiralty of 1887 lies behind.
The Horse Guards by William Kent, 1750–60. The Horse Guards Parade behind is the scene of the ceremony of Trooping the Colour *every Jun.*
The Old War Office by William Young, 1898–1907.
The Ministry of Defence, designed by Vincent Harris in 1913 and finished in 1959, incorporating Henry VIII's wine cellar.
The Banqueting House by Inigo Jones.
Dover House (The Scottish Office) by Paine in 1755–8, the entrance

screen and rotunda by Henry Holland in 1787.
The Treasury by Sir Charles Barry, 1846.
The Foreign Office and The Home Office, mostly by Gilbert Scott in mid-Victorian palazzo style.
The New Government Offices, late Victorian, by J. M. Brydon.
The Cabinet War Rooms, Churchill's secret wartime HQ, now a museum.
In the centre stands The Cenotaph, memorial to the dead of two world wars, and the most notable side road is Downing Street.
θ Charing Cross (north end), Westminster (south end)
🚌 3, 11, 12, 24, 29, 53, 77, 77A, 88, 109, 159, 170, 184, C1

### Whitehall Theatre　　　　3N4

14 Whitehall SW1. 01-930 7765. 1930s theatre whose name was at one time synonymous with farce. Refurbished in 1986 – its interior restored to its original Art Deco splendour – it is now one of the Wyndham Theatres Group staging varied productions.
θ Charing Cross
🚌 1, 3, 6, 9, 11, 12, 13, 15, 15B, 22B, 24, 29, 53, 77, 77A, 88, 109, 159, 170, 176, 184, 509

### Whittington Stone

Highgate Hill N6, near junction with Dartmouth Park Hill. In theory this is the stone on which Dick Whittington rested on his way home from London, and where he heard Bow Bells apparently ringing out 'Turn again Whittington, thrice Lord Mayor of London'. In fact this is about the third replacement stone, set up in 1821, with the famous cat added in 1964. The stone may not be genuine, but man and cat were, and the former was Lord Mayor of London four times.
θ Archway
🚌 4, 17, 27, 41, 43, 134, 135, 143, 210, 263, 263A, 271, C11

### Widow Applebaum's　　　　3M2

46 South Molton St W1. 01-629 4649. American-Jewish deli offering 101 dishes. Mirrors and photos of New York in the jazz age. Wooden bench seating, with tables outside in summer too. Matzo balls, hot salt beef and pastrami, apfelstrudel and ice-cream sodas.

*Open to 21.00. Closed Sat evening
& Sun.* No credit cards.

⊖ Bond Street

🚌 6, 7, 8, 10, 12, 13, 15, 16A, 25,
73, 88, 113, 135, 137, 159, 503

### Wigmore Hall 3M2

36 Wigmore St W1. 01-935 2141.
An intimate atmosphere in which to
hear chamber music, orchestral recitals, solo singers and instrumen-
talists. By tradition, international
musicians make their London
debut here. Also welcomes the
lesser known and more unusual –
medieval music and poetry readings for example.

⊖ Bond Street

🚌 6, 7, 8, 10, 12, 13, 15, 16A, 25,
73, 88, 113, 135, 137, 159, 503

### William Morris Gallery

Lloyd Park, Forest Rd E17. 01-527
5544 extn 4390. William Morris,
designer, socialist, poet, craftsman
and towering figure in the 19thC
Arts and Crafts Movement lived
here from 1848, when he was 14,
until 1856. An excellent exhibition
of his life and work and that of a few
of his contemporaries. There is also
a gallery of pre-Raphaelite paintings
and sketches. *Open 10.00–13.00 &
14.00–17.00 Tue–Sat; 10.00–
12.00 & 14.00–17.00 on first Sun of
each month. Closed Sun, Mon &
Nat Hols.* Free.

⊖ Blackhorse Road (then bus 123)

🚌 34, 34A, 97, 97A, 123, 215,
257, 275

### Williamson's Tavern 4T4

1–3 Grovelands Ct, Bow La EC4.
01-248 6280. Reputedly the oldest
tavern in the City and said to mark
its exact centre. The wine bar in the
basement serves food at lunchtimes but, in common with most
City pubs, there is no food in the
evening and the doors close early
when the City workers wend their
way home. *Open Mon–Fri. Closes
21.00 & all Sat & Sun.*

⊖ Mansion House

🚌 6, 8, 9, 11, 15, 15B, 17, 22,
22B, 25, 76, 95, 149, 501, 513

### Wimbledon Common

SW19. 01-788 7655. 1,100 acres of
wild woodland, open heath and
ponds protected by an Act of 1871
as a 'wild area' for perpetuity. There
are Bronze Age remains here,
abundant bird life and the wild-
flowers include some rare specimens. There are also 16 miles of
horse rides, a famous old 19thC
windmill, a golf course, playing
fields, commonside pubs and nude
bathing in Queensmere (traditional
since Victorian times – it's historic
so it must be OK). *Open 24 hours.*
Cars not admitted after dusk.

⊖ Putney Bridge (then bus 93)

🚌 93

🚉 Wimbledon then bus 93

### Wimbledon Windmill

Wimbledon Common SW19. A hol-
low post mill, built in 1817, now
housing a museum with models
and photographs which explain
how windmills work. *Open Apr–
Oct 14.00–17.00 Sat, Sun & Nat
Hols.* Charge.

⊖ Putney Bridge (then bus 93)

🚌 93

🚉 Wimbledon then bus 93

### Wimbledon Lawn Tennis Association Museum

Church Rd SW19. 01-946 6131.
The history of lawn tennis from its
origins to the latest championships
– including dioramas, audio-visual
shows and a popular quiz entitled
'So You Think You Know About
Wimbledon'. Excellent shop. *Open
11.00–17.00 Tue–Sat; 14.00–
17.00 Sun. Closed Mon. Opening
times vary during Championships,
enquire.* Charge.

⊖ Southfields (then walk), Putney
Bridge (then bus 93)

🚌 39 (to Southfields then walk),
93 (to Wimbledon High Street
then walk via Church Rd)

### Winkworth Arboretum

Hascombe Rd, Godalming, Surrey.
048 632 477. 95 acres of steep
hillside planted with trees and
flowering shrubs, many rare species and many modern introduc-
tions. There are two lakes, plentiful
wild birds, a small National Trust
shop and tea-room and fine views
of the North Downs from many of
the footpaths. *Grounds open dawn
to dusk all year Mon–Sun. Shop &
tearoom open Apr–Oct 14.00–
18.00 Tue–Thur, Sat & Sun, & Nat
Hols; Mar & Nov Sat & Sun only.*

🚉 Godalming

### Windsor Castle

Windsor, Berks. 0753 868286. An

imposing medieval fortress. The Round Tower is 12thC, built by Henry II, and St George's Chapel is fine 16thC Perpendicular. Very much a royal residence, with magnificent State Apartments which are still used for royal functions. Within the castle complex there are countless treasures to be seen: Gobelin tapestries; paintings and drawings by Van Dyck, Canaletto, Rubens, Reynolds, Leonardo da Vinci and Holbein; superb furniture, glass and porcelain; coaches and carriages; and Queen Mary's dolls' house, designed by Lutyens, is not to be missed. *Castle precinct open Jan–end Mar & end Oct–end Dec 10.00–6.15 Mon–Sun; May–end Aug 10.00–19.15 Mon–Sun; Apr, Sep & Oct 10.00–17.15 Mon–Sun. State Apartments open Jan–end Mar & end Oct–end Dec 10.30–15.00 Mon–Sat; Apr–end Oct 10.30–17.00 Mon–Sat; open Sun 13.30–17.00 May–Oct only. State Apartments closed when Queen in official residence – usually 6 weeks at Easter, 3 weeks in Jun and 3 weeks at Xmas*. Charge.
Green Line 700, 701, 702, 718, 726
≈ Windsor & Eton Riverside, Windsor & Eton Central

### Windsor Safari Park
Winkfield Rd, Windsor, Berks. 0753 869841. Lions, tigers, llamas, zebras, camels, deer, giraffes, and monkeys are all here and there is much excitement to be had from driving round those areas of the park where the animals roam free. Bear in mind that windows must be fully wound up at all times and also that there may be long queues. The Dolphinarium features killer-whale, dolphin and sea-lion shows; there's a chimpanzee enclosure, a bear reserve and a children's zoo. Other attractions include walks through the tropical plants and butterfly house, and the adventure play centre. *Open 10.00–two hours before dusk Mon–Sun all year. Closed Xmas Day*. Charge.
Green Line 700
≈ Windsor & Eton Riverside, Windsor & Eton Central (then local bus)

### Wisley Horticultural Gardens
Wisley, Woking, Surrey. 0483 224234. A 250-acre horticultural garden, acquired by the Royal Horticultural Society in 1904, now used for trials and improvements of new varieties. There are greenhouses and a pinetum, magnificent collections of roses, camellias, heathers and rock garden plants, and a series of small exhibition gardens – a perfumed garden for those who cannot see, a raised garden for people with physical disabilities, and so on. The rhododendrons and azaleas, on their hillside, suffered badly in the storms of October 1987 and it will be some time before they return to their full glory. *Open 10.00–19.00 Mon–Sat in summer; 10.00–dusk Mon–Sat in winter*. Members only on *Sun*. Charge.
Green Line 715, 740

### Woolwich Arsenal
Woolwich SE18. A fine example of early 18thC ordnance architecture by Sir John Vanbrugh. Open by appointment only.
🚍 51, 53, 54, 75, 96, 99, 122, 161, 177, 178, 180, 244, 272, 291
≈ Woolwich Arsenal

### Wyndham's Theatre     *3N4*
Charing Cross Rd WC2. 01-836 3028. Small, pretty and successful theatre founded by Sir Charles Wyndham, the famous actor-manager. Straight plays, comedies and musicals are presented here.
⊖ Leicester Square
🚍 24, 29, 176

# Y

## YMCA & Y Hotel & Hostel  1E5

112 Gt Russell St WC1. 01-637 1333. Large, modern building (opened in 1976) incorporating a hotel and extensive sporting and leisure facilities. It has a heated swimming pool, gymnasium, sauna and squash courts. Wide range of activities – weight training, aerobics, dance, sub-aqua, badminton, chess, bridge, photography, trampoline, basketball, keep fit, pottery, drama. Cafeteria and bar. Apply for membership by 1st Thur in month. *Open 08.00–22.00 Mon–Fri; 10.00–21.30 Sat & Sun.* Charge.
⊖ Tottenham Court Road
🚍 7, 8, 10, 14, 14A, 19, 22, 22B, 24, 25, 29, 38, 55, 73, 134, 176, 503

## York Watergate  3N5

Watergate Walk, off Villiers St WC2. When it was built in 1626, the gate stood on the bank of the Thames at the river entrance to the Duke of Buckingham's York House. It hasn't moved – the Embankment Gardens have been reclaimed from the river. The sadly eroded lions support the Villiers' family arms.
⊖ Embankment, Charing Cross
🚍 1, 6, 9, 11, 13, 15, 15B, 77, 77A, 170, 176, 509

## Young Friends Chinese Restaurant

11 Pennyfields, Poplar E1. 01-987 4276. One of the popular and reliable 'Friends' group of licensed restaurants, serving Pekingese and Cantonese dishes. Try Aromatic Duck, Prawns Cantonese Style or Crispy Fried Shredded Beef. *Open 12.00–24.00 Mon–Sun.*
Docklands Light Railway: Westferry
🚍 5, 15, 15B, 40, 86, 106, 277, 278, D4, D5, D6, D7, P14

## Young Vic  3O6

66 The Cut SE1. 01-928 6363. Established as a young people's repertory theatre with the emphasis on the classics and established modern plays. When the Young Vic Company is touring the Royal Shakespeare Company and the Ballet Rambert visit. Licensed vegetarian cafeteria.
⊖ Waterloo
🚍 1, 4, 68, 76, 149, 168, 171, 171A, 176, 188, 501, 502, 505, 507, 513, C1, P11

# Z

**Zamana Gallery**                    *2J5*
1 Cromwell Gdns SW7. 01-584
6612. A new gallery, in the basement of the architecturally interesting Ismaili Centre, but administered
separately from it. The gallery is
dedicated to the display of the art,
crafts and architecture of the Third
World in a series of changing exhibitions. Interesting bookstall. *Open
10.00–17.30 Tue–Sat; 12.00–
17.30 Sun. Closed Mon.* Charge
sometimes.
⊖ South Kensington
▭ 14, 30, 45, 49, 74, 219, 503,
C1

**Zandra Rhodes**                    *3NZ*
14A Grafton St W1. 01-499 6695.
The retail outlet for the luscious,
dramatic and ultra-feminine cre-
ations of this highly individual designer. *Not* cheap, though the day-
wear range is financially more accessible. *Open 09.30–18.00 Mon–
Fri; 09.30–17.00 Sat.*
⊖ Green Park
▭ 9, 14, 19, 22, 25, 38

**Zen**                    *2J6*
Chelsea Cloisters, Sloane Av SW3.
01-589 1781. Smart Chinese restaurant with a designery decor,
using water and glass, and elegant
food – try minced quail, egg fried
fresh asparagus, dim sum lunches.
On the expensive side. *Open LD
Mon–Sun.*
⊖ Sloane Square, South
Kensington
▭ 11, 14, 19, 22, 45, 49, 219

**The Zoo**                    *1B2*
Regent's Park NW1. 01-722 3333.
Variously known as London Zoo,

Regent's Park Zoo or, more properly, The Zoological Gardens. First
laid out by Decimus Burton in 1827,
with imaginative new animal
houses, by famous architects,
added in recent years, of which the
most famous is probably still the
pointed structure of Lord Snow-
don's aviary. One of the largest collections of creatures in the world
saunters in the enclosures, swims
or shambles in the Marine and Tropical Aquarium or obligingly reverses
its nocturnal habits in the eerie light
of the Moonlight Hall. Worthy of a
very full day out and with a good
restaurant-cum-cafeteria to make
this possible. To assist funding you
can Adopt-An-Animal for one year
(from cheapish ant to pricey elephant) and see your name inscribed
on its enclosure. *Open 09.00–
18.00 Mon–Sat; 09.00–19.00 Sun
& Nat Hols. Closed Xmas day.*
Charge.
⊖ Camden Town (then bus 74)
▭ 74 (also Z1, summer service),
C2

# *Ten Days Out in London*

Here are suggestions for ten days of sightseeing in London, using London Transport. For further details on all the places mentioned, check the A–Z gazetteer section of this guide.

The specific times of departure and arrival are offered as a guide only – keep to them and it will be possible to fit in all the recommended ports of call, but if the pace of any one day seems too much, simply spend longer in one place, miss out the next, and use the guide to check transport information.

In almost every case, buses have been recommended rather than the Underground, because the bus traveller has the added pleasure of sightseeing en route. However, it is always quicker by tube, so if running late check with the guide and take a quick Underground trip.

---

The diagrams on the following pages have been designed only to give an overall impression of the routes recommended. To pinpoint the exact geographical location of individual places on the suggested itineraries, it is essential to use a Nicholson *London Streetfinder* or a detailed street map.

---

The following symbols have been used in this section:

<table>
<tr><td>🚌 Bus journey</td><td>🍺 Pub</td></tr>
<tr><td>⊖ Nearest Underground station</td><td>♀ Wine bar</td></tr>
<tr><td>⇌ Nearest British Rail station</td><td>● Parks and green spaces</td></tr>
<tr><td>✕ Restaurant meal</td><td>▮ Shops</td></tr>
<tr><td>⛝ Tea/coffee/snacks</td><td></td></tr>
</table>

A day out in the oldest part of London, its business centre, a place of medieval alleys, huge modern office blocks, Wren churches and ancient taverns is exciting on any weekday. At weekends the quiet streets make sightseeing easier, but everywhere, apart from the churches and the Barbican Arts Centre, is closed.

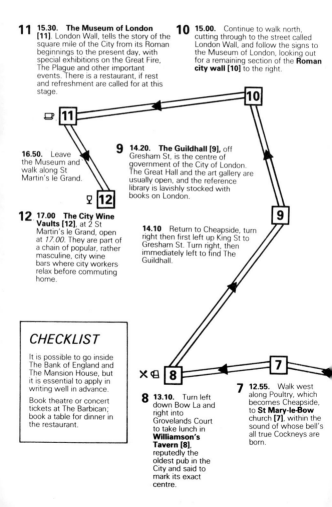

**11 15.30. The Museum of London [11]**. London Wall, tells the story of the square mile of the City from its Roman beginnings to the present day, with special exhibitions on the Great Fire, The Plague and other important events. There is a restaurant, if rest and refreshment are called for at this stage.

**10 15.00.** Continue to walk north, cutting through to the street called London Wall, and follow the signs to the Museum of London, looking out for a remaining section of the **Roman city wall [10]** to the right.

**16.50.** Leave the Museum and walk along St Martin's le Grand.

**9 14.20. The Guildhall [9]**, off Gresham St, is the centre of government of the City of London. The Great Hall and the art gallery are usually open, and the reference library is lavishly stocked with books on London.

**12 17.00 The City Wine Vaults [12]**, at 2 St Martin's le Grand, open at *17.00*. They are part of a chain of popular, rather masculine, city wine bars where city workers relax before commuting home.

**14.10** Return to Cheapside, turn right then first left up King St to Gresham St. Turn right, then immediately left to find The Guildhall.

## CHECKLIST

It is possible to go inside The Bank of England and The Mansion House, but it is essential to apply in writing well in advance.

Book theatre or concert tickets at The Barbican; book a table for dinner in the restaurant.

**8 13.10.** Turn left down Bow La and right into Grovelands Court to take lunch in **Williamson's Tavern [8]**, reputedly the oldest pub in the City and said to mark its exact centre.

**7 12.55.** Walk west along Poultry, which becomes Cheapside, to **St Mary-le-Bow** church **[7]**, within the sound of whose bell's all true Cockneys are born.

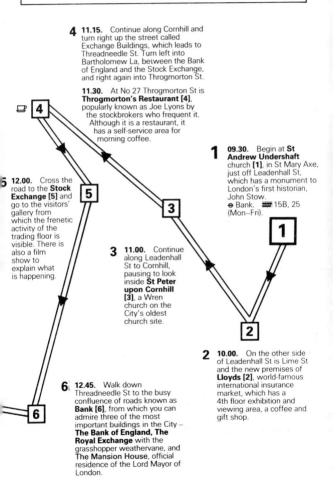

## THE EVENING

Try a night out at the **Barbican Arts Centre** (the country's largest arts centre) which has bars, a restaurant, a main theatre housing the Royal Shakespeare Company, a small fringe theatre, three cinemas (two of which are usually open to the public and the other used for conferences), and a concert hall where the London Symphony Orchestra plays.

**4** **11.15.** Continue along Cornhill and turn right up the street called Exchange Buildings, which leads to Threadneedle St. Turn left into Bartholomew La, between the Bank of England and the Stock Exchange, and right again into Throgmorton St.

**11.30.** At No 27 Throgmorton St is **Throgmorton's Restaurant [4]**, popularly known as Joe Lyons by the stockbrokers who frequent it. Although it is a restaurant, it has a self-service area for morning coffee.

**1** **09.30.** Begin at **St Andrew Undershaft** church **[1]**, in St Mary Axe, just off Leadenhall St, which has a monument to London's first historian, John Stow.
⊖ Bank. ▦ 15B, 25 (Mon–Fri).

**5** **12.00.** Cross the road to the **Stock Exchange [5]** and go to the visitors' gallery from which the frenetic activity of the trading floor is visible. There is also a film show to explain what is happening.

**3** **11.00.** Continue along Leadenhall St to Cornhill, pausing to look inside **St Peter upon Cornhill [3]**, a Wren church on the City's oldest church site.

**2** **10.00.** On the other side of Leadenhall St is Lime St and the new premises of **Lloyds [2]**, world-famous international insurance market, which has a 4th floor exhibition and viewing area, a coffee and gift shop.

**6** **12.45.** Walk down Threadneedle St to the busy confluence of roads known as **Bank [6]**, from which you can admire three of the most important buildings in the City – **The Bank of England, The Royal Exchange** with the grasshopper weathervane, and **The Mansion House**, official residence of the Lord Mayor of London.

London abounds in royal landmarks from the Queen's residence at Buckingham Palace to the Tower of London, where royals lived from the time of William the Conqueror to King James I and where some died on the executioner's block. For centuries and to this day, London has been the scene of royal parades, processions and weddings – here is a suggested itinerary designed to give the visitor a glimpse of London's royal associations both past and present.

(Note: you can also do this day on a Thursday; but on Sunday & Monday the Queen's Gallery is closed; on Monday, Tuesday & Friday to Sunday the Royal Mews is closed; on Sunday the Horse Guards change at *10.00*.)

**11  15.15.** Walk up Broad Walk to **Kensington Palace [11]**, Kensington Gardens W8. Here is where Queen Victoria was born and received the news of her accession, and where the Prince and Princess of Wales, Princess Margaret, Prince Michael of Kent and the Duke and Duchess of Gloucester still have apartments.

**14.45.** Catch a No 52 or 52A bus to Palace Gate.

**12  16.45.** Having viewed the public rooms which close at *17.00*, walk along Palace Avenue to the **Royal Garden Hotel [12]**, Kensington High St W8, and have afternoon tea in The Garden Room. Bear in mind that tea is 'off' by *17.30*.

## ALTERNATIVE AFTERNOON

You may decide that an afternoon at **The Tower of London** to gaze at the Crown Jewels and other, more gruesome, sights is preferable to the suggested itinerary. If so, after lunch at The Albert, walk down Palmer St (alongside the pub) to St James's Park Station and take the District or Circle Line direct to Tower Hill. For full details on The Tower and travel information, refer to the gazetteer entry on p.123.

**10  14.30.** Walk along Buckingham Palace Rd to **Victoria Bus Station [10]** to arrive by *14.45*. *Or* spend longer in the pub and walk right along Victoria St to Victoria Bus Station to arrive by *14.45*.

**9  13.50.** A choice. *Either* take Minibus C1 or walk along Victoria St, past the Army & Navy Store, turn right up Palace St, turn left into Buckingham Palace Rd and cross the road to **The Royal Mews [9]**, Buckingham Palace Rd SW1, which opens at *14.00*, where you can admire the Queen's horses and carriages.

**8  12.50.** Walk through Buckingham Gate to Victoria St and on the corner find **The Albert [8]**, 52 Victoria St SW1. Only the name has royal connections (Prince Albert was married to Queen Victoria), but this is an excellent Victorian pub with good bar snacks and an upstairs restaurant serving English roast beef. (You would be wise to reserve a table in the restaurant, telephone 01-222 5577.)

**7  12.00.** Return to Buckingham Palace and slip round the side to the **Queen's Gallery [7]**, Buckingham Palace Rd SW1, to view the selection of paintings from the Royal Collection currently on show. Admission charge.

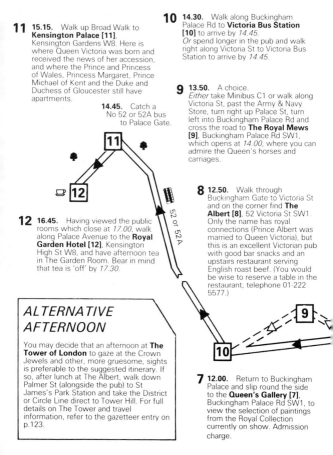

## THE EVENING

There are two 'royal' options for the evening.
*Either* return to base, put the children (if any) to bed, change and go to **The Royal Opera House**, Bow St WC2, 01-240 1066, where the Royal Ballet and Royal Opera Companies perform. (Advance booking is essential.)
*Or* return to base, change, and take the children (if any) to **The Theatre Royal**, Drury La, Catherine St WC2, 01-836 8108. The Royal Box has accommodated every monarch since Charles II and the theatre is justly famous for its lavish musical productions. (Advance booking is essential.)

## CHECKLIST

Book a table for lunch in the restaurant at The Albert (no need to book for a bar snack).
Book tickets for The Royal Opera House or The Theatre Royal, Drury Lane.

**2**
**3** **10.30.** Walk along Storey's Gate to **Horse Guards Parade [2]**, Whitehall SW1. Here you watch the **Changing of the Queen's Life Guard** on their magnificent black mounts, at *11.00*, come rain or shine. Virtually opposite Horse Guards Parade in Whitehall is the **Banqueting House [3]** where King Charles I went to the scaffold on 30 January 1649. There is a fine bronze statue of the King seated on his mount at the top of Whitehall, south side of Trafalgar Square.

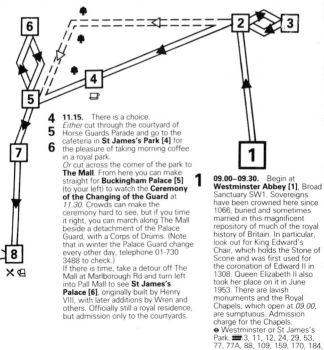

**4**
**5**
**6** **11.15.** There is a choice.
*Either* cut through the courtyard of Horse Guards Parade and go to the cafeteria in **St James's Park [4]** for the pleasure of taking morning coffee in a royal park.
*Or* cut across the corner of the park to **The Mall**. From here you can make straight for **Buckingham Palace [5]** (to your left) to watch the **Ceremony of the Changing of the Guard** at *11.30*. Crowds can make the ceremony hard to see, but if you time it right, you can march along The Mall beside a detachment of the Palace Guard, with a Corps of Drums. (Note that in winter the Palace Guard change every other day, telephone 01-730 3488 to check.)
If there is time, take a detour off The Mall at Marlborough Rd and turn left into Pall Mall to see **St James's Palace [6]**, originally built by Henry VIII, with later additions by Wren and others. Officially still a royal residence, but admission only to the courtyards.

**1** **09.00–09.30.** Begin at **Westminster Abbey [1]**, Broad Sanctuary SW1. Sovereigns have been crowned here since 1066, buried and sometimes married in this magnificent repository of much of the royal history of Britain. In particular, look out for King Edward's Chair, which holds the Stone of Scone and was first used for the coronation of Edward II in 1308. Queen Elizabeth II also took her place on it in June 1953. There are lavish monuments and the Royal Chapels, which open at *09.00*, are sumptuous. Admission charge for the Chapels.
⊖ Westminster or St James's Park. ▥ 3, 11, 12, 24, 29, 53, 77, 77A, 88, 109, 159, 170, 184, C1.

London's principal shopping areas are: Oxford St for mass-market purchases; Regent St for quality clothes, department stores, toys, china and glassware; Bond St for designer clothes, smart shoes, jewellery and Persian rugs; Covent Garden and the King's Road for fashionable and trendy clothes and paraphernalia; Tottenham Court Rd for electronics, cameras, stereos and furniture; Knightsbridge for all-purpose luxury shopping. In fact, the quantity and variety of shops in London is huge. This suggested shopping trip takes in just a few of the most famous and popular. It can be enjoyed on any day of the week except Sunday – although on a Saturday in high season the shops and all facilities will be very crowded.

**1** **09.30.** Begin at the Marble Arch branch of **Marks & Spencer [1], Oxford St** W1. This is one of the largest shops in the internationally-famous high street chain which sells men's, women's and children's clothes, lingerie, food, home furnishings, books and gifts.
⊖ Marble Arch, 🚌 2A, 2B, 6, 7, 8, 10, 12, 15, 16A, 30, 73, 74, 82, 88, 135, 137, 500, 503, 506.

**2** **10.30.** Walk east along Oxford St, crossing Orchard St, to **Selfridges [2]** department store (about 2 mins). In the course of exploring the store's many departments you will encounter a ground floor coffee shop and a first floor cafeteria, both of which serve coffee and rolls or cakes.

## CHECKLIST

There is no need to book anything in advance.

**14.45.** Catch a 9, 14, 19, or 22 to **Harrods [8]**, in Brompton Rd SW1.

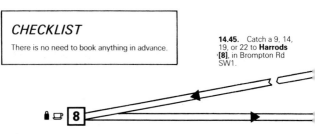

## 8 Harrods [8]

**15.00.** Allow at least an hour to explore this most famous of all department stores and be sure not to miss the magnificent, marbled Edwardian food halls.

**16.00.** Shopping is tiring and by now the idea of sitting down will probably be very attractive – try full afternoon tea in Harrods Restaurant or something lesser in one of the snack bars.

## THE EVENING

Spend it enjoying the pubs, cafés and restaurants of Covent Garden – or, for a really suitable conclusion to a shopping day, browse in **Covent Garden General Store**, Long Acre WC2, open until *24.00 Mon–Sat* , which has a popular salad bar, open until *23.00*.

**4**   **12.00.** *Either* turn right in to Charing Cross Rd and walk down until you find, on
**5**   your right, two bookshops – **Waterstones [4]**, very enthusiastic general booksellers, and **Foyles [4]**, London's largest bookshop which aims to stock every British title currently in print. *Or*, walk back a short distance along Oxford St to **The Virgin Megastore [5]**, 14–16 Oxford St W1, where you can browse or buy in a vast entertainment store selling records, tapes, videos, hi-fis, compact discs, music books and games. Also has a licensed café.

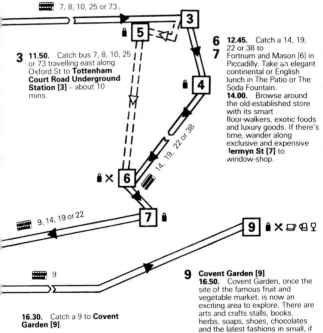

🚌 7, 8, 10, 25 or 73

**3**   **11.50.** Catch bus 7, 8, 10, 25 or 73 travelling east along Oxford St to **Tottenham Court Road Underground Station [3]** – about 10 mins.

🚌 9, 14, 19 or 22

🚌 9

**16.30.** Catch a 9 to **Covent Garden [9]**.

**6**   **12.45.** Catch a 14, 19,
**7**   22 or 38 to Fortnum and Mason [6] in Piccadilly. Take an elegant continental or English lunch in The Patio or The Soda Fountain.
**14.00.** Browse around the old-established store with its smart floor-walkers, exotic foods and luxury goods. If there's time, wander along exclusive and expensive **Jermyn St [7]** to window-shop.

**9**   **Covent Garden [9]**
**16.50.** Covent Garden, once the site of the famous fruit and vegetable market, is now an exciting area to explore. There are arts and crafts stalls, books, herbs, soaps, shoes, chocolates and the latest fashions in small, if pricey shops, many of which stay open until *18.00, 19.00* or even *20.00* in season. It is also an area rich in pubs, cafés, wine bars and restaurants so, rather than look further afield for the evening's entertainment, remain in the area to sample them at leisure.

The River Boat Information Service, see *Checklist*, has details of the great variety of river trips which run each day, weather and tides permitting. Here are suggestions for two outings, using other forms of transport as well.

These days out can be enjoyed on any day of the week, but services are limited between October and Easter and to Hampton Court cease altogether.

## HAMPTON COURT DAY

(Note: this river trip can only be done between Easter and the end of October.)

**2  14.30–17.30.** Allow two or three hours to explore the huge riverside palace of **Hampton Court [2]** in its beautiful formal gardens. Interior treasures include paintings by Titian and Tintoretto and ceiling paintings by Thornhill and Verrio. There is a café for afternoon tea between the palace and the famous maze.

**3  17.30–18.00.** Walk to the bridge and take an evening drink at **The Mitre [3]** with its large riverside garden.

**1  10.30.** Begin at **Westminster Pier [1]** and take a boat trip to Hampton Court (check times of departure). The journey takes from 4 to 5 hours, depending on tides, and passes right out of London through a delightful variety of scenery. There are always refreshments on board.

**4  18.30.** Cross the bridge to the station to catch a British Rail train back to **Waterloo [4]**. The trains run at half-hourly intervals and the journey takes 32 mins.

### THE EVENING

Supper cruises, which last 1½ hours, leave Westminster Pier at *21.00* from May–Oct, Mon–Fri & Sun. Disco Cruises, which last hours, leave the Pier at *19.00* or *20.00* throughout the year, Fri & Sat (the rest of the week according to demand). Booking essential.

## LANDMARKS EN ROUTE TO HAMPTON COURT

*North Bank:* Houses of Parliament, Westminster Abbey, Millbank Tower, Tate Gallery, Cheyne Walk, Hurlingham House, Strand on the Green pubs, Syon House, London Apprentice pub, Marble Hill Park, Strawberry Hill, Thames TV Studios, Hampton Court Park.
*South Bank:* Battersea Power Station, St Mary's Church Battersea, Harrods Depository, Kew Gardens, Richmond Hill, Ham House, Kingston upon Thames.
*Bridges (upriver):* Westminster Bridge, Lambeth Bridge, Vauxhall Bridge, Chelsea Bridge, Albert Bridge, Battersea Bridge, Wandsworth Bridge, Putney Bridge, Hammersmith Bridge, Chiswick Bridge, Kew Bridge, Richmond Bridge, Kingston Bridge.

## CHECKLIST

Times of river trips fluctuate according to the weather and the tides, so it is wise to telephone check before setting out. Useful numbers are: London Tourist Board & Convention Bureau River Boat Information Service, 01-730 4812; Charing Cross Pier 01-930 0971; Greenwich Pier 01-930 4097; Kew 01-930 2062; Putney Embankment 01-930 2062; Richmond 01-940 2244; Tower Pier 01-488 0344; Westminster Pier 01-839 2349/01-930 4097/01-930 4721.
Book supper or disco cruises on 01-839 2349.

## GREENWICH DAY

### LANDMARKS EN ROUTE FROM GREENWICH

*North Bank:* Isle of Dogs dockland development, Town of Ramsgate pub, St Katharine's Dock, Tower of London, Custom House, Fishmongers Hall, St Paul's Cathedral, The Temple, Somerset House, Savoy Hotel, Cleopatra's Needle.
*South Bank:* Old Royal Observatory, Royal Naval College, Cutty Sark, Mayflower pub, HMS Belfast, Southwark Cathedral, Bankside Power Station, South Bank Arts Centre, Royal Festival Hall, Shell Building.
*Bridges (upriver):* Tower Bridge, London Bridge, Southwark Bridge, Blackfriars Bridge, Waterloo Bridge.

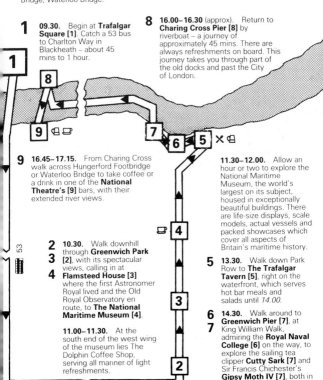

**1** **09.30.** Begin at **Trafalgar Square [1]**. Catch a 53 bus to Charlton Way in Blackheath – about 45 mins to 1 hour.

**8** **16.00–16.30** (approx). Return to **Charing Cross Pier [8]** by riverboat – a journey of approximately 45 mins. There are always refreshments on board. This journey takes you through part of the old docks and past the City of London.

**9** **16.45–17.15.** From Charing Cross walk across Hungerford Footbridge or Waterloo Bridge to take coffee or a drink in one of the **National Theatre's [9]** bars, with their extended river views.

**11.30–12.00.** Allow an hour or two to explore the National Maritime Museum, the world's largest on its subject, housed in exceptionally beautiful buildings. There are life-size displays, scale models, actual vessels and packed showcases which cover all aspects of Britain's maritime history.

**2** **10.30.** Walk downhill
**3** through **Greenwich Park [2]**, with its spectacular views, calling in at
**4** **Flamsteed House [3]** where the first Astronomer Royal lived and the Old Royal Observatory en route, to **The National Maritime Museum [4]**.

**11.00–11.30.** At the south end of the west wing of the museum lies The Dolphin Coffee Shop, serving all manner of light refreshments.

**5** **13.30.** Walk down Park Row to **The Trafalgar Tavern [5]**, right on the waterfront, which serves hot bar meals and salads until *14.00*.

**6** **14.30.** Walk around to
**7** **Greenwich Pier [7]**, at King William Walk, admiring the **Royal Naval College [6]** on the way, to explore the sailing tea clipper **Cutty Sark [7]** and Sir Francis Chichester's **Gipsy Moth IV [7]**, both in dry dock near the pier.

This day out can also be enjoyed on other days of the week, but not on Sunday when opening times are limited. For alternative places to take the children – see *FAMILY DAY OUT* on p.150.

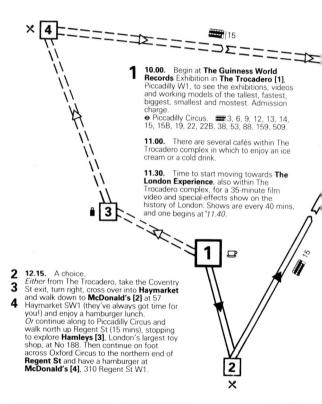

**1** **10.00.** Begin at **The Guinness World Records** Exhibition in **The Trocadero [1]**, Piccadilly W1, to see the exhibitions, videos and working models of the tallest, fastest, biggest, smallest and mostest. Admission charge.
⊖ Piccadilly Circus. 🚌 3, 6, 9, 12, 13, 14, 15, 15B, 19, 22, 22B, 38, 53, 88, 159, 509.

**11.00.** There are several cafés within The Trocadero complex in which to enjoy an ice cream or a cold drink.

**11.30.** Time to start moving towards **The London Experience**, also within The Trocadero complex, for a 35-minute film video and special-effects show on the history of London. Shows are every 40 mins, and one begins at *11.40*.

**2**
**3**
**4**
**12.15.** A choice.
*Either* from The Trocadero, take the Coventry St exit, turn right, cross over into **Haymarket** and walk down to **McDonald's [2]** at 57 Haymarket SW1 (they've always got time for you!) and enjoy a hamburger lunch.
*Or* continue along to Piccadilly Circus and walk north up Regent St (15 mins), stopping to explore **Hamleys [3]**, London's largest toy shop, at No 188. Then continue on foot across Oxford Circus to the northern end of **Regent St** and have a hamburger at **McDonald's [4]**, 310 Regent St W1.

## CHECKLIST

Apply well in advance, by post, for admission to The Ceremony of the Keys at The Tower of London. If tickets are not available for the appropriate night, look in 'Time Out', 'City Limits' or the 'London Standard' for a suitable film and, if necessary, book seats in the cinema.

**6   14.45.**   Walk up Fish St and turn right into **Eastcheap** to catch a No 15 bus for the short distance to The Tower of London. If you look up at the wall of the building on the corner of Philpot Lane – the first turning left off Eastcheap – you will see two tiny plaster mice [6], carved there by the builders who had shared their lunchtime sandwiches with the local mice.

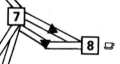

**7   15.00.   The Tower of London** [7] – fortress, arsenal, prison and palace – has ravens and Beefeaters, armour and instruments of torture, the executioner's block, London's oldest church and, of course, the Crown Jewels. Admission charge.

**5   13.30.**   From the Haymarket or from Oxford Circus, catch a No 15 bus to **The Monument [5]** (about 30 mins).

**14.00–14.15.**   The Monument, which marks the point at which London's Great Fire began in 1666, is a tall column with 311 steps going up inside it. Those who climb to the top get a breathtaking view of London – if they have any breath left to be taken.

**8   17.00.**   When The Tower closes walk round to **The Tower Hotel [8]** in St Katharine's Way. The hotel coffee shop, called **The Picnic Basket**, has a special children's menu of snacks, high teas and ice creams in summer.
(The adults in the party may be glad to know it is licensed.)

## THE EVENING

Attend **The Ceremony of the Keys** at The Tower of London, at *21.40*, one of the oldest military ceremonies in the world and much the most impressive and exciting, as the great fortress is formally locked for the night.

**9   18.30.**   Take a trip on the **Docklands Light Railway [9]** from Tower Gateway to see the re-vitalisation of London's Docklands. The journey takes approximately 45 mins there and back.

A Sunday in London does not have to be a lazy morning in bed, followed by the newspapers, a few pints down the pub, a late lunch and an evening in front of the television. Here are some suggestions which will give you a Sunday as activity-filled as the rest of the week.

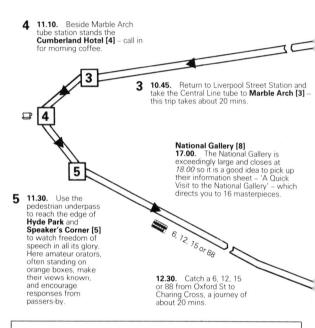

**4  11.10.** Beside Marble Arch tube station stands the **Cumberland Hotel [4]** – call in for morning coffee.

**3  10.45.** Return to Liverpool Street Station and take the Central Line tube to **Marble Arch [3]** – this trip takes about 20 mins.

**National Gallery [8]**
**17.00.** The National Gallery is exceedingly large and closes at *18.00* so it is a good idea to pick up their information sheet – 'A Quick Visit to the National Gallery' – which directs you to 16 masterpieces.

**5  11.30.** Use the pedestrian underpass to reach the edge of **Hyde Park** and **Speaker's Corner [5]** to watch freedom of speech in all its glory. Here amateur orators, often standing on orange boxes, make their views known, and encourage responses from passers-by.

6, 12, 15 or 88

**12.30.** Catch a 6, 12, 15 or 88 from Oxford St to Charing Cross, a journey of about 20 mins.

## CHECKLIST

It is wise to book a table for lunch at The Carvery at the Charing Cross Hotel, and also to book tickets for the evening concert.

## THE EVENING

London is one of the world's most exciting music centres. Perhaps the most suitable venue for a Sunday concert is **St John's, Smith Square**, but if there is no concert scheduled for any given Sunday, there is certain to be something on at **The Royal Festival Hall**. Both places have their own restaurants to supply sustenance before the performance.

**1** **08.00–09.00.** Start the day with a full English breakfast in **City Gates Bar and Restaurant** in **The Great Eastern Hotel [1]**.
⊖ Liverpool Street. 🚌 5, 6, 8, 9, 11, 22, 22A, 22B, 35, 47, 48, 78, 100, 133, 149, 243A, 263A, 279A, 502, 505, 509.

**2** **09.30.** Walk around to the front of Liverpool Street Station and cross Bishopsgate to Middlesex St. Here you will find **Petticoat Lane Market [2]**, one of the liveliest and most famous of London's Sunday markets, stocked with pretty well something for everyone at bargain prices.

**8** **16.15–16.30.** After Evensong, which lasts for about an hour, catch a 6, 9, 11, 15 or 15B back to Trafalgar Square and the **National Gallery [8]**. If you arrive before *17.00* there will be time for a cup of tea in the restaurant beneath the gallery.

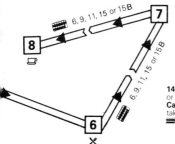

**7** **St Paul's Cathedral [7]**
**15.00.** Arrive at St Paul's in good time for Evensong at *15.15*. (Note that sightseeing is not permitted in the Cathedral on a Sunday, but visitors are welcome to attend the service.)

**14.40.** Catch a 6, 9, 11, 15 or 15B bus to **St Paul's Cathedral [7]**. The journey takes about 10 mins.
🚌 6, 9, 11, 15 or 15B

**6** **13.00.** Eat a traditional British Sunday lunch in **The Carvery** at the **Charing Cross Hotel [6]**. If lunch in The Carvery is fully booked, a hot meal is readily available in **Lyons Corner House [6]**, opposite, but it will not be a traditional Sunday roast.

This day out can be enjoyed from Monday to Saturday; but on Sunday the shops are shut, the museums don't open until *14.00*, and the Zoo doesn't open until *10.00*, although it remains open until *19.00*.

**4** **14.50.** Those who have followed Morning A and Morning B should all arrive at about the same time at **The Planetarium [4] and Madame Tussaud's [4]** in Marylebone Rd. Buy a Royal Ticket which gives admission to both places.

**15.00.** There are 30-minute shows in The Planetarium on the hour and the half-hour. If there is a queue, which usually is in high season, and you miss the *15.00* show, try for the *15.30*.

**15.35–16.05.** To Madame Tussaud's next door. There is a cafeteria for those who need refreshment, but there is a lot to see – tableaux of waxworks (royalty, pop stars, sporting champions, statesmen and film stars), the Chamber of Horrors, a reconstruction of The Battle of Trafalgar – and the exhibition closes at *17.30* so it might be wise to keep going.

**2** **12.00.** **The Science Museum [2]** is one of the most exciting in London with real locomotives and aircraft, a space capsule and numerous working models. It would be easy to spend the rest of the day here, but those who hope to include the other ports of call should leave by *13.30*.

**5** **17.30.** Madame Tussaud's closes. Stroll down Baker St to **Flanagan's Fish Parlour [5]**, which opens at *18.00* for fish and chips, tripe and onions etc. For those still in place at *20.00*, a pianist plays cockney songs.

**14.30.** For the sake of speed, catch the tube from South Kensington to Baker Street (change at Green Park, 20 mins). Alternatively, if there is time to spare take bus 30 direct to Baker Street Underground Station.

**3** **13.30.** Cross over to Pelham St, at the side of South Kensington tube station, and take lunch in **Dino's [3]** – large, friendly, serving Italian food, licensed and welcoming to children.

A choice.

□ ✕

## 1A

### Morning A
**09.30.** Begin at **London Zoo [1A]**, Regent's Park W1, which has one of the largest and best-displayed collections of animals in the world. There is also a cafeteria for refreshments and lunch. Allow until about *14.00* to enjoy it all and then stroll south through Regent's Park (or take bus 74 or Z1) to **The Planetarium [5]** and **Madame Tussaud's [5]** in Marylebone Rd.
⊖ Baker Street, Marylebone or Camden Town, then bus 74. ▦ 74, Z1.

## 1B

### Morning B
**10.00.** Begin at the **British Museum [1B]**, Gt Russell St WC1, which has something for everyone in its vast halls – don't miss the Egyptian mummies and the Rosetta stone.
⊖ Tottenham Court Road, Russell Square. ▦ 7, 8, 10, 14, 14A,
19, 22, 22B, 24, 25, 29, 38, 55, 68, 73, 77, 77A, 134, 168, 171, 176, 188, 501, 503, 505.

**11.00.** For those who can tear themselves away from the exhibits, there is a large cafeteria in the British Museum for morning coffee.

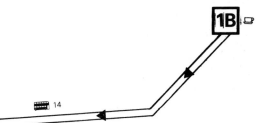

▦ 14

Catch a 14 bus in Bloomsbury St to the Victoria & Albert Museum (20 mins) and walk up Exhibition Rd at the side of the V&A to the Science Museum.

## CHECKLIST

Essential to book tickets for the London Palladium. Wise to book a table at Flanagan's Fish Parlour.

## THE EVENING

Choose between an early 'cockney' evening meal at Flanagan's Fish Parlour, 100 Baker St W1. Or return to base to change and rest and take in a show at the **London Palladium**, which specialises in family entertainment.

This day out can also be enjoyed on a Wednesday, Thursday or Friday but not on Monday, when the Imperial War Museum is closed, or on Saturday and Sunday when the Law Courts are closed.
(Note: The Law Morning is unsuitable for children because no-one below the age of 16 is admitted to the Law Courts, and at the Old Bailey, the minimum age for admission is 14 although an adult must accompany anyone under the age of 16. After lunch at The Magpie and Stump, the afternoon is accessible to the whole family.)

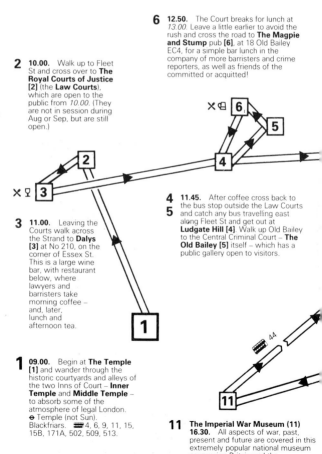

**6** **12.50.** The Court breaks for lunch at *13.00.* Leave a little earlier to avoid the rush and cross the road to **The Magpie and Stump** pub **[6]**, at 18 Old Bailey EC4, for a simple bar lunch in the company of more barristers and crime reporters, as well as friends of the committed or acquitted!

**2** **10.00.** Walk up to Fleet St and cross over to **The Royal Courts of Justice [2]** (the **Law Courts**), which are open to the public from *10.00.* (They are not in session during Aug or Sep, but are still open.)

**3** **11.00.** Leaving the Courts walk across the Strand to **Dalys [3]** at No 210, on the corner of Essex St. This is a large wine bar, with restaurant below, where lawyers and barristers take morning coffee – and, later, lunch and afternoon tea.

**4** **11.45.** After coffee cross back to the bus stop outside the Law Courts and catch any bus travelling east along Fleet St and get out at **5** **Ludgate Hill [4]**. Walk up Old Bailey to the Central Criminal Court – **The Old Bailey [5]** itself – which has a public gallery open to visitors.

**1** **09.00.** Begin at **The Temple [1]** and wander through the historic courtyards and alleys of the two Inns of Court – **Inner Temple** and **Middle Temple** – to absorb some of the atmosphere of legal London. ⊖ Temple (not Sun). 🚌 4, 6, 9, 11, 15, 15B, 171A, 502, 509, 513.

**11** **The Imperial War Museum (11)** **16.30.** All aspects of war, past, present and future are covered in this extremely popular national museum concerning Britain and the Commonwealth since 1914.

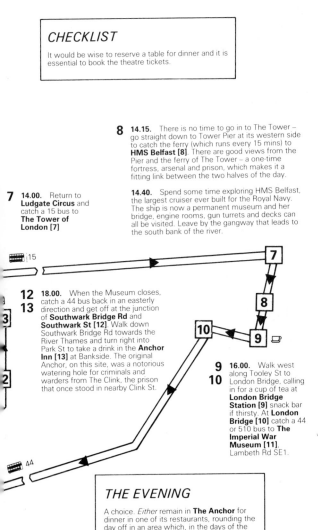

**8**  **14.15.** There is no time to go in to The Tower – go straight down to Tower Pier at its western side to catch the ferry (which runs every 15 mins) to **HMS Belfast [8]**. There are good views from the Pier and the ferry of The Tower – a one-time fortress, arsenal and prison, which makes it a fitting link between the two halves of the day.

**7**  **14.00.** Return to **Ludgate Circus** and catch a 15 bus to **The Tower of London [7]**

**14.40.** Spend some time exploring HMS Belfast, the largest cruiser ever built for the Royal Navy. The ship is now a permanent museum and her bridge, engine rooms, gun turrets and decks can all be visited. Leave by the gangway that leads to the south bank of the river.

**12**  **13**  **18.00.** When the Museum closes, catch a 44 bus back in an easterly direction and get off at the junction of **Southwark Bridge Rd** and **Southwark St [12]**. Walk down Southwark Bridge Rd towards the River Thames and turn right into Park St to take a drink in the **Anchor Inn [13]** at Bankside. The original Anchor, on this site, was a notorious watering hole for criminals and warders from The Clink, the prison that once stood in nearby Clink St.

**9**  **10**  **16.00.** Walk west along Tooley St to London Bridge, calling in for a cup of tea at **London Bridge Station [9]** snack bar if thirsty. At **London Bridge [10]** catch a 44 or 510 bus to **The Imperial War Museum [11]**, Lambeth Rd SE1.

## THE EVENING

A choice. *Either* remain in **The Anchor** for dinner in one of its restaurants, rounding the day off in an area which, in the days of the first Elizabeth, was definitely on the wrong side of the law. *Or* go to the **St Martin's Theatre** to see 'The Mousetrap', a detective thriller and London's longest-running play.

## THE DAY

Planning a day out of doors in London is rather like a game of chance because the weather, even at the height of summer, is so unpredictable. But on a fine, dry day all of London's parks repay exploration. Hyde Park and Kensington Gardens are the most central and cover, between them, the largest area. This day out may be enjoyed on any weekday, but park facilities are very limited between October and May.

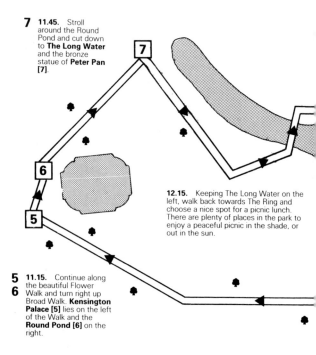

**7** **11.45.** Stroll around the Round Pond and cut down to **The Long Water** and the bronze statue of **Peter Pan [7]**.

**12.15.** Keeping The Long Water on the left, walk back towards The Ring and choose a nice spot for a picnic lunch. There are plenty of places in the park to enjoy a peaceful picnic in the shade, or out in the sun.

**5** **11.15.** Continue along
**6** the beautiful Flower Walk and turn right up Broad Walk. **Kensington Palace [5]** lies on the left of the Walk and the **Round Pond [6]** on the right.

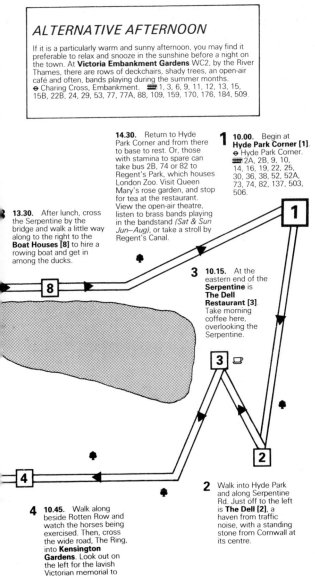

## ALTERNATIVE AFTERNOON

If it is a particularly warm and sunny afternoon, you may find it preferable to relax and snooze in the sunshine before a night on the town. At **Victoria Embankment Gardens** WC2, by the River Thames, there are rows of deckchairs, shady trees, an open-air café and often, bands playing during the summer months.
⊖ Charing Cross, Embankment. 🚌 1, 3, 6, 9, 11, 12, 13, 15, 15B, 22B, 24, 29, 53, 77, 77A, 88, 109, 159, 170, 176, 184, 509.

**1 10.00.** Begin at **Hyde Park Corner [1]**.
⊖ Hyde Park Corner. 🚌 2A, 2B, 9, 10, 14, 16, 19, 22, 25, 30, 36, 38, 52, 52A, 73, 74, 82, 137, 503, 506.

**14.30.** Return to Hyde Park Corner and from there to base to rest. Or, those with stamina to spare can take bus 2B, 74 or 82 to Regent's Park, which houses London Zoo. Visit Queen Mary's rose garden, and stop for tea at the restaurant. View the open-air theatre, listen to brass bands playing in the bandstand *(Sat & Sun Jun–Aug)*, or take a stroll by Regent's Canal.

**13.30.** After lunch, cross the Serpentine by the bridge and walk a little way along to the right to the **Boat Houses [8]** to hire a rowing boat and get in among the ducks.

**3 10.15.** At the eastern end of the **Serpentine** is **The Dell Restaurant [3]**. Take morning coffee here, overlooking the Serpentine.

**4 10.45.** Walk along beside Rotten Row and watch the horses being exercised. Then, cross the wide road, The Ring, into **Kensington Gardens**. Look out on the left for the lavish Victorian memorial to **Prince Albert [4]**.

**2** Walk into Hyde Park and along Serpentine Rd. Just off to the left is **The Dell [2]**, a haven from traffic noise, with a standing stone from Cornwall at its centre.

## *THE EVENING*

London Transport's night buses link key points in London. They take over from daytime transport between *23.00* and *24.00* and run through the night.

Like all big cities, London should be treated with caution and respect at night. It's not sin city, but late-night revellers using public transport should try to keep their eyes open and their valuables out of sight. (Note: this evening out can be enjoyed on other nights of the week, but London's theatres are closed on Sunday evenings and neither Spitalfields market nor the nearby pub are open on a Sunday morning.)

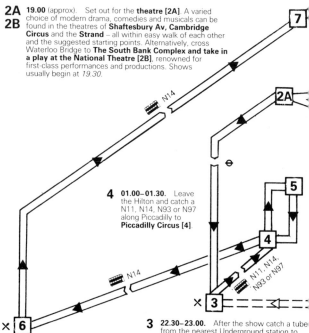

**2A**
**2B** **19.00** (approx). Set out for the **theatre [2A]**. A varied choice of modern drama, comedies and musicals can be found in the theatres of **Shaftesbury Av, Cambridge Circus** and the **Strand** – all within easy walk of each other and the suggested starting points. Alternatively, cross Waterloo Bridge to **The South Bank Complex and take in a play at the National Theatre [2B]**, renowned for first-class performances and productions. Shows usually begin at *19.30*.

**4** **01.00–01.30.** Leave the Hilton and catch a N11, N14, N93 or N97 along Piccadilly to **Piccadilly Circus [4]**.

**3** **22.30–23.00.** After the show catch a tube from the nearest Underground station to Hyde Park Corner, walk up Park Lane to the **Hilton Hotel [3]** and ascend to the **Roof Restaurant**. By now the special 'after theatre' menu will be on, and there is dancing to a live band.

**6** **03.00.** The Hippodrome closes. Walk back to Piccadilly Circus and catch the N14 direct to the **Fulham Rd** and an informal restaurant called **Up All Night [6]** at No 225 for a plateful of spaghetti and a cup of coffee to restore energy.

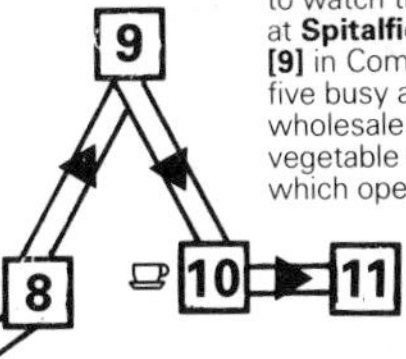

**9** **05.00.** Walk through to watch the day begin at **Spitalfields Market [9]** in Commercial St – five busy acres of wholesale fruit and vegetable market which opens at 05.00.

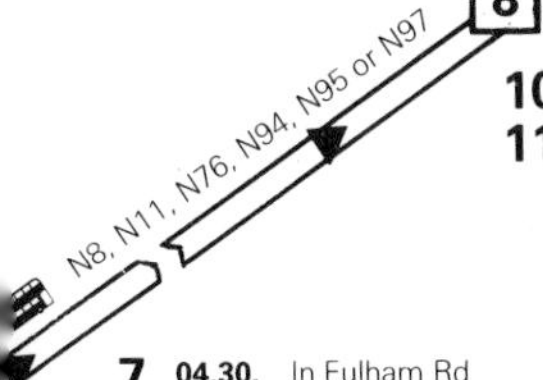

**10** **06.00.** Call in at **The Gun [10]** public house
**11** at 54 Brushfield St E1, which has a special licence allowing it to open between 06.00 and 09.00 to serve the market traders. Try a coffee with a dash of brandy and maybe a round of toast. Then cross the road to **Dino's Restaurant [11]** to start the new day with a full breakfast.

N8, N11, N76, N94, N95 or N97

**7** **04.30.** In Fulham Rd
**8** catch an N14 back to **Trafalgar Square [7]** and then an N8, N11, N76, N94, N95 or N97 to **Liverpool Street Station [8]** (about 30 minutes).

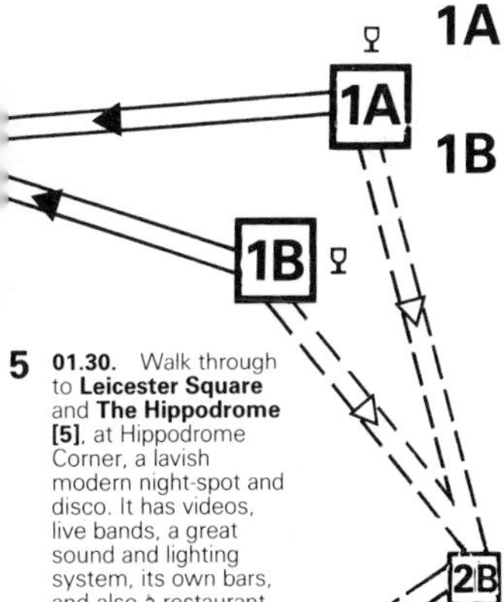

**1A** **18.00.** *Either* begin the evening with a drink at **Rumour's [1A]**, 33 Wellington St WC2, a large mirrored cocktail bar in Covent Garden. It's noisy, lively and has a predominantly young clientele.

**1B** *Or* begin in the **American Bar** at the **Savoy Hotel [1B]**, Strand WC2, where classic cocktails are served in peaceful elegance to the accompaniment of an unobtrusive piano.
⊖ Covent Garden, Temple (not Sun). ▅ 1, 6, 9, 11, 13, 15, 15B, 77, 77A, 170, 176, 509

**5** **01.30.** Walk through to **Leicester Square** and **The Hippodrome [5]**, at Hippodrome Corner, a lavish modern night-spot and disco. It has videos, live bands, a great sound and lighting system, its own bars, and also a restaurant – but you probably won't be ready to eat again yet.

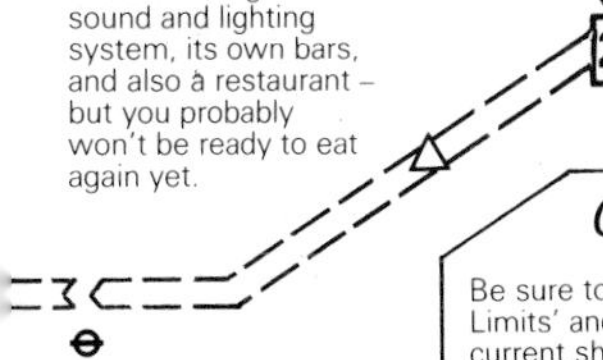

**2B**

## CHECKLIST

Be sure to book theatre tickets ('Time Out', 'City Limits' and the 'London Standard' have listings of current shows), and a table at the Roof Restaurant at the Hilton Hotel. Bear in mind that the full evening out will be very expensive. Currency and travellers cheques can be changed at the **Deak International Bureau**, 3–5 Coventry Street W1, throughout the night. Times of night buses are posted on bus stops – or you can ring 01-222 1234 for travel information at any time of the day or night.

(Note: You can also do this day on a Wednesday or Friday; but on Monday & Tuesday Carlyle's House is closed; on Saturday & Sunday Ye Olde Cheshire Cheese is closed; and on Sunday the houses are only open in the afternoon.)

## *CHECKLIST*

Book lunch at Ye Olde Cheshire Cheese (telephone 01-353 6170). Book tickets for the evening at the Canal Café Theatre (telephone 01-289 6054) or the King's Head (telephone 01-226 1916). At the Players Theatre Club (telephone 01-839 1134), temporary membership can be obtained on the spot at the door, but a full membership must be taken out in person 48 hours before the show. It is also wise to reserve a table for a proper supper in advance.

**10**  Sloane Square. Here is the tube (District and Circle Lines) or buses 11, 19, 22, 137, C1.

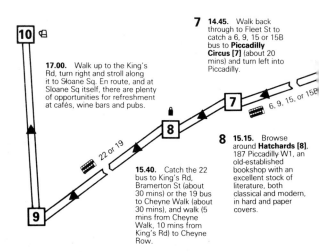

**7**  14.45.  Walk back through to Fleet St to catch a 6, 9, 15 or 15B bus to **Piccadilly Circus [7]** (about 20 mins) and turn left into Piccadilly.

**17.00.**  Walk up to the King's Rd, turn right and stroll along it to Sloane Sq. En route, and at Sloane Sq itself, there are plenty of opportunities for refreshment at cafés, wine bars and pubs.

6, 9, 15, or 15B

**8**  15.15.  Browse around **Hatchards [8]**, 187 Piccadilly W1, an old-established bookshop with an excellent stock of literature, both classical and modern, in hard and paper covers.

22 or 19

**15.40.**  Catch the 22 bus to King's Rd, Bramerton St (about 30 mins) or the 19 bus to Cheyne Walk (about 30 mins), and walk (5 mins from Cheyne Walk, 10 mins from King's Rd) to Cheyne Row.

**9**  16.15.  **Carlyle's House [9]**, 24 Cheyne Row SW3, remains much as it was when the author of 'The French Revolution' lived in it and worked in the sky-lit attic study. Note that the house closes at *17.00*.

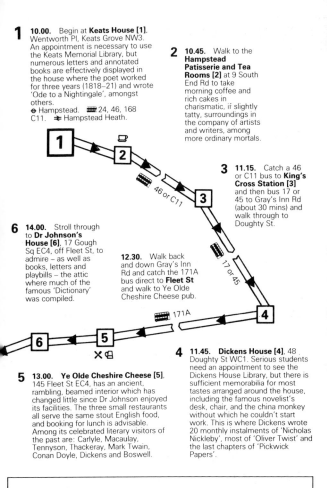

**1** **10.00.** Begin at **Keats House [1]**, Wentworth Pl, Keats Grove NW3. An appointment is necessary to use the Keats Memorial Library, but numerous letters and annotated books are effectively displayed in the house where the poet worked for three years (1818–21) and wrote 'Ode to a Nightingale', amongst others.

⊖ Hampstead. ▨▨▨ 24, 46, 168 C11. ⇌ Hampstead Heath.

**2** **10.45.** Walk to the **Hampstead Patisserie and Tea Rooms [2]** at 9 South End Rd to take morning coffee and rich cakes in charismatic, if slightly tatty, surroundings in the company of artists and writers, among more ordinary mortals.

**3** **11.15.** Catch a 46 or C11 bus to **King's Cross Station [3]** and then bus 17 or 45 to Gray's Inn Rd (about 30 mins) and walk through to Doughty St.

**6** **14.00.** Stroll through to **Dr Johnson's House [6]**, 17 Gough Sq EC4, off Fleet St, to admire – as well as books, letters and playbills – the attic where much of the famous 'Dictionary' was compiled.

**12.30.** Walk back and down Gray's Inn Rd and catch the 171A bus direct to **Fleet St** and walk to Ye Olde Cheshire Cheese pub.

**4** **11.45.** **Dickens House [4]**, 48 Doughty St WC1. Serious students need an appointment to see the Dickens House Library, but there is sufficient memorabilia for most tastes arranged around the house, including the famous novelist's desk, chair, and the china monkey without which he couldn't start work. This is where Dickens wrote 20 monthly instalments of 'Nicholas Nickleby', most of 'Oliver Twist', and the last chapters of 'Pickwick Papers'.

**5** **13.00.** **Ye Olde Cheshire Cheese [5]**, 145 Fleet St EC4, has an ancient, rambling, beamed interior which has changed little since Dr Johnson enjoyed its facilities. The three small restaurants all serve the same stout English food, and booking for lunch is advisable. Among its celebrated literary visitors of the past are: Carlyle, Macaulay, Tennyson, Thackeray, Mark Twain, Conan Doyle, Dickens and Boswell.

## THE EVENING

After all that high-minded literariness, try an evening of fringe theatre followed by late-night cabaret at the **Canal Café Theatre**, Delamere Terrace W2.
Home-cooked food is available and there's an all-inclusive price for both shows and dinner (or separate dinner, and either show). Alternatively, try dinner and a play at the **King's Head**, 115 Upper St, Islington N1, one of London's best-known theatre pubs, which again sells tickets for dinner-and-show, or just for the show. And for an evening of rollicking, frolicsome good fun, try the **Players Theatre Club**. Duchess Theatre, Catherine St WC2, where Queen Victoria and music-hall are alive and well. There are two bars, a supper room, and drinks and sandwiches are served during the performance.

# Index

# Central London Maps

## Key

| | |
|---|---|
| **16** | Regular Daily Service |
| **176** | Certain Days of the week only, or part-day only (Details shown at bus stops) |
| | Night Bus Services are shown on a separate map on page 175 of this book |
| ★ 31 | Terminus of Route |
| ☆ | Other Terminal Points |
| ⊖ | Underground Station |
| D.L.R. | Docklands Light Railway Station |
| ⇥ | British Rail Station |
| ⇥ | Main Line Terminal |
| ✈ | Air Terminal |
| ▭ | Coach Terminal |
| ▢ | Places of Interest |
| *i* | Information Centre - British Rail / London Regional Transport |
| *i* | Information Centre - London Tourist Board / City Information |

| | |
|---|---|
| SAVOY | Theatres and Cinemas |
| ••• | Main Shopping Street |
| M | Street Market |
| ⎀ | Monument or Statue |
| | Children's Playground |
| | Children's Zoo |
| | Refreshments |
| | Boating Lake |
| | River Trip |
| | Canal Trip |
| ▲ | Entrance to Towing Path Walk |
| ♫ | Open Air Music (Summer) |
| | University or College |
| | Hospital |
| △ | Embassy |
| ⊖ | Starting point for the Original London Transport Sightseeing Tour |

Scale 0 ···· ¼ ···· ½ ···· ¾ Mile

## Index

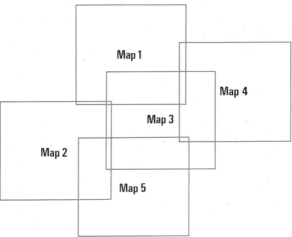

Map 1
Map 2
Map 3
Map 4
Map 5

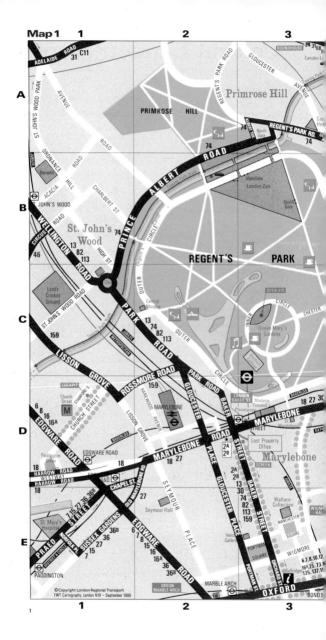

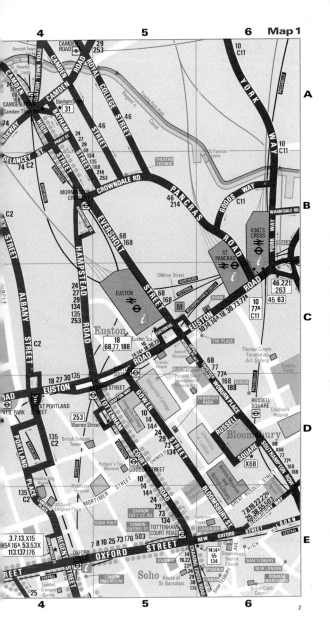

**Map 1**

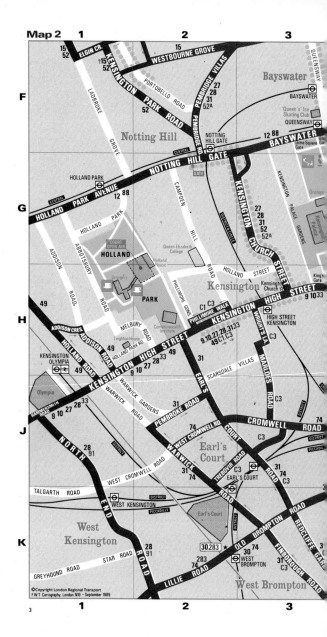

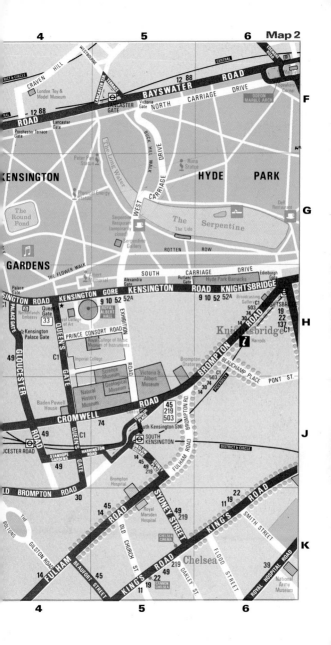

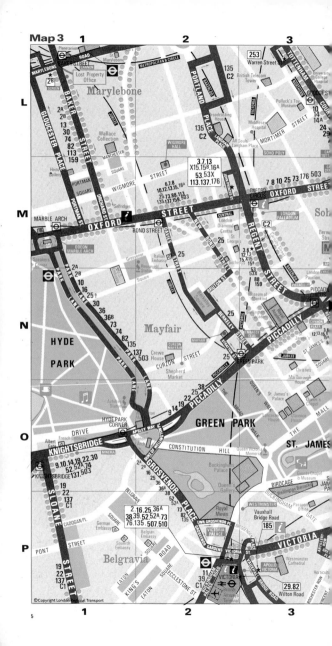

**Map 3**

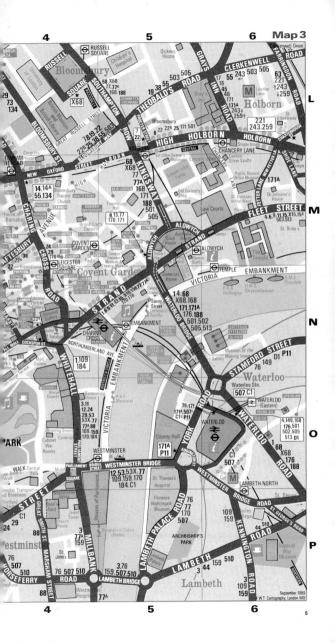

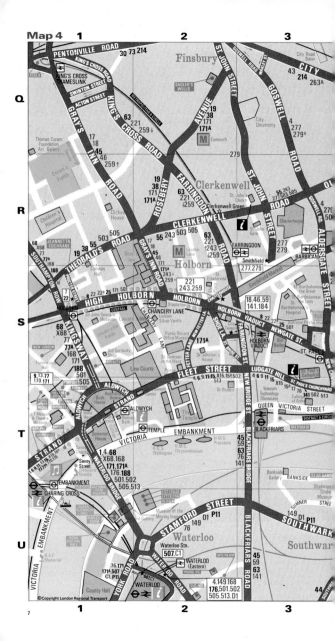

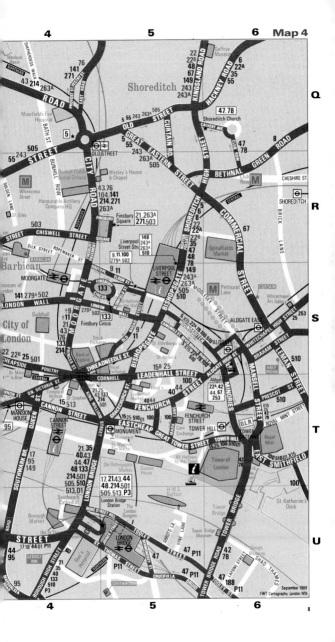

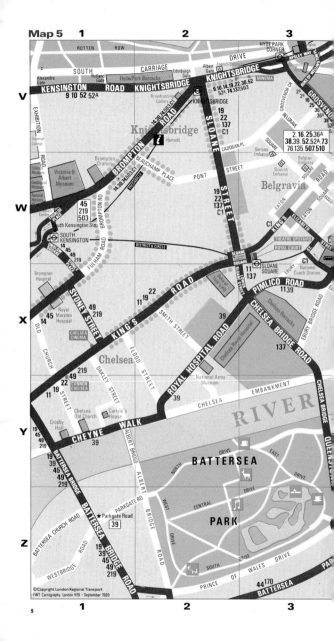

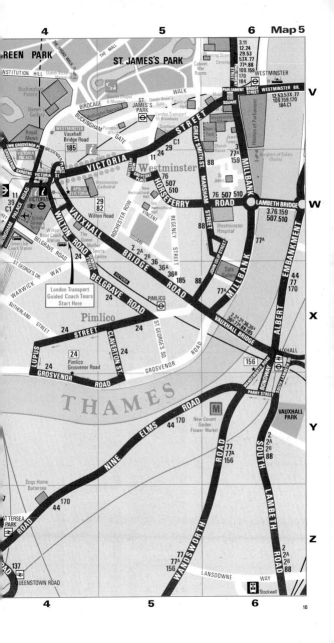

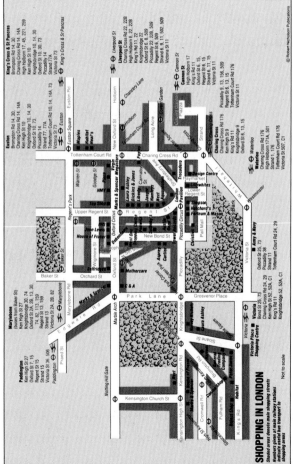

## SHOPS

Aquascutum 734 6090
Army & Navy 834 1234
Asprey 493 6767
Austin Reed 734 6789
BHS (Oxford St) 629 2011
C & A 629 7272
Cartier 493 6962
Christies 839 9060
Conran Shop 589 7401
Covent Garden Market 836 9137
Debenhams 580 3000
Design Centre 839 8000
Dickins & Jones 734 7070
Fenwick 629 9161
Fortnum & Mason 734 8040
Foyles 437 5660
General Trading Company 730 0411
Habitat (King's Rd) 351 1211
Habitat 17, 45, 021, 259
Habitat (Tott Ct Rd) 631 3880
Hamleys 734 3161
Harrods 730 1234
Harvey Nichols 235 5000
Hatchards 437 3924
Heal's 636 1666
HMV 631 3423
House of Fraser (Ken High St) 937 5432
House of Fraser (Oxford St) 629 8800
Jaeger 734 8211
John Lewis 629 7711
Laura Ashley (Regent St) 437 9760
Laura Ashley (Sloane St) 235 9728
Liberty 734 1234
Lillywhites 930 3181
London Pavilion 437 1838
Maples 387 7000
Marks & Spencer (Marble Arch) 935 7954
Marks & Spencer (Oxford St) 437 7722
Marks & Spencer (Ken High St) 938 3711
Mothercare 629 6621
Next (Ken High St) 937 0498
Next (Regent St) 434 2515
Peter Jones 730 3434
Plaza on Oxford St 436 4425
Regent St Shop 439 1250
Selfridges 629 1234
Simpson 734 2002
Sotheby's 493 8080
Top Shop 636 7700
Tower Records 439 2500
Trocadero 439 1791
Victoria Place Shopping Centre 931 8811
Virgin Megastore 631 1234

## SHOPPING IN LONDON

Shaded areas denote main shopping streets

Numbers given at main railway stations indicate useful bus transport to shopping areas

Not to scale

© Robert Nicholson Publications

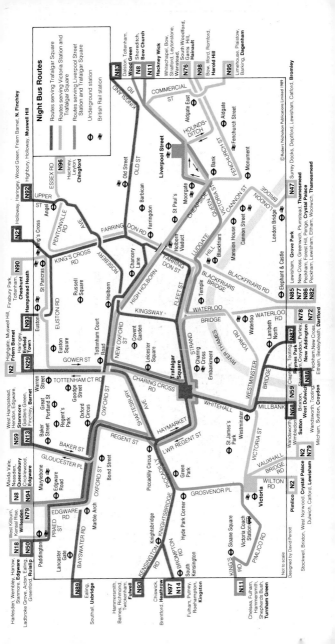

# Night Bus Routes

- Routes serving Trafalgar Square
- Routes serving Victoria Station and Trafalgar Square
- Routes serving Liverpool Street Station and Trafalgar Square
- ⊖ Underground station
- ⇌ British Rail station

© Robert Nicholson Publications Limited 1989

Designed by David Perrott

Not to scale

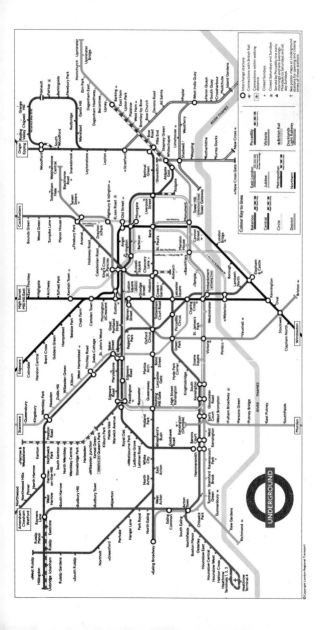

UNDERGROUND

© Copyright London Regional Transport